THE
REFERENCE
SHELF

REPRESENTATIVE

AMERICAN SPEECHES

1983-1984

edited by OWEN PETERSON
Professor, Department of Speech Communication
Louisiana State University

THE REFERENCE SHELF

Volume 56 Number 4

THE H. W. WILSON COMPANY

New York   1984

The books i   les, excerpts from books, and addı   nds in the United States and othei   ɔound numbers in each volume, all   the same calendar year. One numb   ɪch of the others is devoted to a sing   ɪnation and discussion from various points of view, concluding with a comprehensive bibliography. Books in the series may be purchased individually or on subscription.

International Standard Serial Number 0197-6928

Printed in the United States of America

CONTENTS

THE FUTURE OF SPORTS

PRESS FREEDOMS

FINDING MEANING IN LIFE AND DEATH

THE QUALITY OF LIFE IN AMERICA

LAW ENFORCEMENT PROBLEMS

PREFACE

Of the many issues addressed by speakers in 1983–1984, none seemed more enduring or more publicized than the quality of American education. Fueled by the publication of major studies by such reputable groups as the President's National Commission on Excellence in Education, the Twentieth Century Fund, the Task Force on Education for Economic Growth, and the Carnegie Foundation for the Advancement of Teaching, educators, politicians, and the general public expressed deep concern about the future of the American educational system. Polls indicated that the alleged "rising tide of mediocrity" in education could become a key issue in the presidential election. Public interest in this matter even prompted the United States Department of Education to sponsor a "summit" conference in December 1983, called the National Forum Conference on Excellence in Education. Four of the speeches on education reprinted in this volume reflect the concern about education during the year.

Since 1960 debates involving the major parties' nominees for the presidency have always commanded extensive media coverage, but a significant development in 1983–1984 was the attention given by the news media and the public to televised debates among Democrats seeking their party's nomination. Howell Raines observed:

Many political strategists and campaign officials have concluded that the televised debates now under way among the eight candidates for the Democratic nomination are emerging as the most important equalizing force in the race for the nomination. (*New York Times,* Ja. 27, '84, p 10)

In Raines's opinion, the debates among the Democratic contenders in New Hampshire would have more to do with how people voted than all the televised commercials broadcast before the election. Not everyone agreed with that assessment, but it was generally acknowledged among politicians that debates had come to occupy a pivotal place in the Democratic campaign. In an editorial, the *New York Times* approvingly observed that debates be-

tween presidential aspirants were no longer labeled "great," as
had been the case in the Kennedy–Nixon confrontations in 1960:

They were Great Debates. Not any more, and that's all to the good, for
candidates and for voters. As recently as last winter, presidential campaign debates tended to be tense, self-conscious affairs much concerned
with rules and red warning lights. And they provoked endless micro-
debates. Which format is better, formal or informal? Should reporters ask
questions or should candidates interview each other? Should the sponsor
be the League of Women Voters, news media or others?

The 1984 Democratic primary campaign, which has already produced a dozen televised debates, a variety of formats, and a variety of
sponsors have turned a stuffy, monumental device into a valuable staple
of American politics. (My. 6, '84, p 22)

In addition to our educational system and the role of debates
in political campaigns, other issues that commanded the attention
of speakers and the public included the United States's intervention in Central America, the invasion of Grenada, our Middle
East policy, unemployment, the economy, nuclear disarmament,
and relations with the Soviet Union.

Sponsored by such institutions as colleges, universities, professional bodies, trade associations, corporate groups, and civic and
philanthropic organizations, and delivered by speakers from government, business, the news media, the arts, and the professions,
public addresses continue to provide an important forum for the
discussion of ideas and issues.

I appreciate the assistance of the many persons who have sup-
plied me with information about the speeches, speakers, audiences, and occasions for the addresses in this year's collection. I
particularly want to thank Shirley Arden, Senator William Arm-
strong, Carol Barker, Nancy Bormann, C. David Cornell, Curtis
Deave, Patricia Del Pozzo, Senator Jeremiah Denton, Shirley M.
Green, Julia W. Hoye, Senator Carl Levin, Representative Bill
Lowery, Russell Mack, Leonard J. Moisan, Lance Morgan, Lan-
dis Neal, Rowena Olegario, Joy F. Phillips, Thomas Radeki,
Nancy S. Raley, Professor Robert Schmuhl, William Shabacker,
Nancy Cowger Slonim, Marsha Vick, and Gayle Yiotis.

As usual, my colleagues at Louisiana State University have
provided me with support and useful advice. I especially thank
Waldo W. Braden, Stephen L. Cooper, Gail Chabran, Randy

Duncan, Mary Frances HopKins, Jean Jackson, Harold Mixon, Eddie Myers, Mary Stewart, and Cynthia Willhite.

No one has been more helpful to me in the four years I have served as editor of *Representative American Speeches* than Beth Wheeler. I dedicate this volume to her, with thanks, appreciation, and best wishes for the future.

Owen Peterson

Baton Rouge, Louisiana
May 18, 1984

EDUCATION

SUGGESTED PRIORITIES AND GOALS FOR AMERICAN EDUCATION[1]

T. H. BELL[2]

In 1983–1984 America found itself caught up in an educational, and ultimately political, controversy the likes of which had not been seen since the Russian rocket Sputnik soared into the sky in 1957, causing many analysts to conclude that the United States had fallen behind in the space race because of an inadequate school system. Sparking the current controversy were reports by the President's National Commission on Excellence in Education, the Twentieth Century Fund, the Task Force on Education for Economic Growth, and the Carnegie Foundation for the Advancement of Teaching.

Evidence cited by these panels included a twenty-year decline in College Board scores; international comparisons showing American students consistently performing less well than pupils in other industrialized countries; a steady decline in high school enrollment for advanced academic subjects, and increases in enrollment for so-called frill courses. Among the recommendations for improving American education were higher performance standards for high school graduation and college admissions; greater emphasis on traditional academic subjects such as English, mathematics, history, science, and foreign languages; sterner discipline; and better—and better paid—teachers.

To focus attention on what one report called "the rising tide of mediocrity," the Reagan administration sponsored a three-day National Forum on Excellence in Education held in Indianapolis on December 6 to 8, 1983. Spearheading the organization of the meeting was Secretary of Education T. H. Bell, who twice addressed the group. The forum, which Bell called "a national town-hall meeting," capped a series of twelve regional conferences that had begun the previous May. Among the more than 2,300 attending were three governors and numerous college and university presidents, education specialists, state officials, teachers, school administrators, and parents.

Secretary Bell opened the forum with a keynote speech that was followed by addresses by Governor Bob Graham of Florida, Governor

---

[1]Delivered to the National Forum on Excellence in Education on the afternoon of December 8, 1983, in the Indianapolis Convention Center, Indianapolis, Indiana.

[2]For biographical note, see Appendix.

Thomas H. Kean of New Jersey, and University of Georgia President Fred C. Davidson. After the speeches, the assembly split into fifteen workshops to discuss strategies and teachers' pay and performance. On the final day, Secretary Bell, addressing the assembled group for a second time, presented a recommendation of three priorities and four performance goals for the next five years for American education. The conference ended after an address by President Ronald Reagan.

Reaction was mixed to the concluding speeches by Secretary Bell and President Reagan. Organized teacher groups criticized both for avoiding any mention of an increased federal role in the process of educational reform. Albert Shanker, president of the American Federation of Teachers, for example, issued a statement declaring that the administration was "doing nothing more than making speeches urging other people to do something about reforming schools." But others in the audience were enthusiastic about what they heard. (*New York Times*, D. 9, '83, p 9)

The address by T. H. Bell printed below was delivered just before President Reagan's concluding talk on the afternoon of December 8, 1983, to an audience of approximately 2,300 in the Indianapolis Convention Center.

Secretary Bell's speech: Following President's Reagan's address, this forum will be concluded. In my brief presentation before the president arrives, I want to discuss what I recommend as three priorities and four performance goals for the next five years for American education. These priorities and goals are suggested because, as I see it, schools have tried to do too much and, as a result, they have not been doing well that which is their prime responsibility. We must make a firm commitment to doing first things first even if that calls for a lower priority in use of time and resources to attain other desirable outcomes. I suggest that we cut out of the school curriculum whatever must be cut to reach three high-priority learning outcomes.

I suggest that the first priority, taking precedence over all else that we do, is to concentrate on the attainment by every student of the highest possible level of literacy so that each student will have reached the outer limits of his or her ability to read with comprehension, write and think systematically and logically, and to speak with clarity in a manner that is articulate, precise, and reflective of an intelligent, well-educated individual. This priority should be number one, and the schools of this nation must make a fully unambiguous commitment to its attainment.

Those responsible for setting the priorities and seeing that we accomplish our goals by keeping first things first should insist that all needful time and resources be devoted to this first priority regardless of any other worthy goal. We all know, of course, that our schools can and must accomplish much more than this, but we must insist that priority number one gets first choice on whatever it takes to attain this high level of literacy.

Students cannot fully attain other necessary proficiencies if they do not read and write the English language and if they do not attain a very high level of capability to express themselves clearly and to think logically. This capacity must be attained as the key to all other capabilities in mathematics, science, social studies, the arts, and the many varied vocational and professional skills.

I emphasize this because the schools have tried to do almost everything and to respond to many special concerns. I acknowledge that we need to enrich the lives of our students. They must attain certain coping skills. They need, for example, to learn to drive safely on our highways. Some will seek to learn athletic skills, dancing, and woodworking, and to pursue many interests. But the key to all of this and the key to the future of our great republic rests on highly literate, logically thinking, well-informed citizens. And this comes through mastery of the discipline of basic English.

Every measure available tells us that there has been a decline in the attainment of this, the number one priority and the first and foremost reason for the existence of our schools. Let us teach our students to write, to read, and to express themselves. In the process we will produce clear thinkers, critical readers, and a highly literate and intelligent society. Let us measure the results of our efforts. Let us promote and graduate students on the basis of their mastery of priority number one.

The second priority of our schools must draw upon the first for its attainment. We must teach all students to attain, within the limits of their ability, a high level of mastery of the basic elements of arithmetic and mathematics, and to observe intelligently and interpret the natural world that they inhabit. This means, of course, that our students must understand the basic structure or our natural world and its scientific laws. Mastery of basic mathematics is essential to this. From attainment of priority two, I believe we will have the basis for many other outcomes, such as how to care for our health and our environment. Students will also have the capacity for making intelligent decisions about how to preserve and how to use our natural resources.

As I see it, we cannot attain the aims of priority number two if we have in any way neglected number one. I am fully aware of the need to harness student interests, to motivate for learning, and to keep the nonacademically inclined from dropping out of school. But all of this is just another challenge to concentrate on priorities one and two in a manner that is self-satisfying because of new approaches to motivation.

Priority number three is essential to attaining what Benjamin Franklin meant when he announced after many meetings of the founders of our nation that we had a republic if we could keep it. Our schools must teach how we could keep our republic. To prepare our students for the responsibilities of the high office of private citizen must be priority number three. I place it behind numbers one and two because I firmly believe that students must attain the first two priorities to be fully proficient in the third. All students must study the story of mankind, our social, political, governmental, and economic history. We must understand our government and how it functions. To do this, we must understand the history and governments of other people. To vote intelligently today, one must have a grasp of the fundamentals of economics, taxation, and the great ideas of free enterprise.

It takes a sharp, clear thinking intellect that has been constantly fed through both stimulating and challenging reading and conversation on the issues of the day to make intelligent choices in the privacy of the voting booth. Our people must be participants and not spectators in the governing process. It takes years of study to do this, and priority number three should not yield to other demands for time and resources. We cannot neglect the in-depth study needed to prepare for the highest office in the land, that of holding citizenship responsibility in these great and magnificent United States of America.

As I stop with these three priorities for American education, I acknowledge that there must be room in the curriculum for the arts, the vocational and technical skills, for physical education and athletics, and for many other pursuits such as driver training, cheerleading, and all the rest. Our youth must prepare for the duties of a job and parenthood. Education must not ignore these.

I know that our schools must meet wide-ranging and varied interests. But in doing so, we reached a point where thirty-five of the fifty states in 1982 were saying to their school districts that one year of math and science and only one or two years of social studies were required to graduate from high school under statewide policies. Some states required only three years of English, and many were permitting almost any subject offered under the rubric of language arts to substitute for those requirements.

Even today, some states are considering a requirement of only two years of math and two years of science as a new minimum. I firmly believe that the National Commission on Excellence in Education was right when it emphasized in its report that all students should study English for four years, and math, science, and social studies for three.

It takes years of constant academic toil to reach a level of sophistication essential to function effectively in today's very complex world. For the student not bound for college, the study of English, math, science, and social studies is more critical than it is for the student who will have a further intellectually stimulating experience in college. Thus, I argue that priorities one, two, and three must be the prime purpose of American education and proficiency in these three areas must be required of all students except for those few who lack the mental capacity.

I will turn now from my discussion of the top three priorities for our nation's schools to a discussion of some measurable nationwide goals over the next five years.

As we look at the performance of the schools in the United States, we find vast differences across state lines and from one region to another throughout the nation. As you think of the discussion of priorities one, two, and three, what happens to the individuals and what happens to our nation as a whole when over 26 percent—one out of four—ninth graders drop out without graduating from high school? This is the source of our unemployment, adult illiteracy, and welfare dependency. This saps the strength and vitality of the nation and spells misery and disillusionment for the millions of young people who quit before they can fully reach their potential.

A look at the performance of our many statewide systems of education indicates that the dropout rate varies from 10.8 percent to a high of 42.4 percent. Moreover, from 1972 to 1983, only three states improved their dropout rates while the remaining forty-seven had declines. The difficult challenge for all the states is to reduce the dropout rate to less than 10 percent over the next five years. This should be done while you raise standards and make your academic programs much more rigorous.

Speaking of challenges, will we see a resurgence of college entrance examination scores with the high school class of 1984? I expect to see a big difference in 1985, but the recently increased standards will not have been in place long enough to make a difference in 1984.

I would like to see each state accept a challenge to attain at least four major goals over the next five years.

By 1989, all high school graduates in all fifty states will be required to study English (emphasis on priority one) for four years, and math, science, and social studies for three years (emphasis on outcomes of priorities two and three). All students will be required to pass examinations in these areas. Only those not intellectually competent will be excused. The percentage of students completing at least two years of foreign language study will match the percentage of students entering college. There will be no decline in the commitment nor the momentum to provide equal opportunity, special help to the disadvantaged, or free and appropriate education to the handicapped.

In every state, the high school graduating class will surpass by 1989 the high school graduating class SAT/ACT scores attained by the class of 1965.

Every state by 1989 will increase the retention power and decrease the high school dropout rate so that no state will have a dropout rate in excess of 10 percent.

Every state will make teaching so attractive that entry level college graduates' salaries will be competitive with the average entry level salaries of college graduates with degrees in business and engineering.

Every state will establish career ladders and master teacher pay scales for experienced teachers that will make it possible for the highest salaries paid to the most outstanding teachers to range within 5 percent parity of school administrators.

Now, this is a big order for the nation's schools! We will have to solve many problems such as discipline, lack of parental commitment, adequate funding, and a changed and reordered life style for teen-age America. We will have to learn to stick to our priorities and to the basics that I have described. We will have to resist pressures that distort priorities. Our governors, state legislatures, teachers' organizations, and school administrators will have to work together with more harmony than we have seen in the past. Our nation's newspapers and media networks must be persuaded to continue to give us the tremendous support we have enjoyed during 1983—and our performance must merit that support. We must become the learning society described in the pages of the National Commission report and referred to in many other reports. But these goals are attainable, and I challenge all who have accepted our invitation to this forum to help us reach them.

Thank you for coming. Thank you for the contributions you have made. Thanks to Governor Orr and to Indiana for being such wonderful hosts. May you have a safe journey home. And most of all, may 1984 witness a magnificent renaissance in American education.

WHAT IS RIGHT WITH OUR PUBLIC SCHOOLS[1]

W. Ann Reynolds[2]

The year 1983 saw the publication of several studies highly critical of American education. Following the Chinese custom of naming years, Dr. W. Ann Reynolds, chancellor of the California State University system, dubbed 1983 as the "Year of the Secondary Schools." Acknowledging the seriousness of the educational situation in this country, Chancellor Reynolds nevertheless sought to provide a proper perspective in her keynote address to the annual National Assembly of the Council for the Advancement and Support of Education (CASE) on June 20, 1983.

The council, with more than ten thousand individual members, is an organization of colleges, universities, community colleges, and independent elementary and secondary schools. The members include senior professionals in the fields of fund-raising, institutional relations, alumni administration, and government relations. The organization sponsors training programs, conferences, and seminars and publishes works designed to promote education.

In her address, Dr. Reynolds told the delegates:

> At least part of the laxity of standards in the public schools and their preoccupation with things not directly related to education can be traced to the precedent set by higher education during the 1960s and early 1970s. In response to student demand for "relevance" and the right to "do their own thing," many institutions reduced their core academic requirements and added a host of lighter-weight courses designed to raise the students' social conscience or establish their personal identity. The result, in many cases, was neither enlightment nor enhanced morality but mediocrity, and that mediocrity eventually pervaded not only the schools but all phases of our public and private life.

"Despite the current outcry," Dr. Reynolds asserted, "there is much that is right with American education." She proceeded to support her contention with statistics, scholarly studies, and specific instances demonstrating progress and positive accomplishments. The speaker then outlined what she regarded as education's top priorities for the future.

Chancellor Reynolds delivered her address at the opening of the conference to an audience of approximately 1,000 in a large auditorium in

[1]Delivered at the opening of the annual National Assembly of the Council for the Advancement and Support of Education in an auditorium in the Town and Country Hotel, San Diego, California, at 1:30 P.M. on June 20, 1983.

[2]For biographical note, see Appendix.

the Town and Country Hotel in San Diego, California, at 1:30 P.M., on
June 20, 1983.

W. Ann Reynolds' speech: We in education have lately given a pe-
culiar twist to that old Chinese custom of naming the years. Early
in the decade, we had the "Year of the Demographic Decline."
Then came the "Year of the Crisis in Financial Aid." And this
year has become, indisputably, the "Year of the Secondary
Schools."

Once that would have been a rather peripheral concern for
those of us whose work is primarily in higher education. As Henry
Thoreau commented when he was told in the 1840s that a telegraph line would be run from Boston to Texas, "Are you sure that
Boston has anything to say to Texas?" But the schools do indeed
have a lot to say to higher education, and if we believe the recent
reports, most of it is bad.

"Our nation is at risk," declared the National Commission on
Excellence in Education, and it warned of "a rising tide of
mediocrity" in American education that is threatening our leadership in commerce, industry, science and technology, and our future as a nation and a people.

That has been the message, in slightly different words, of other
major reports this year as well. The National Task force on Education for Economic Growth and Twentieth Century Fund have
taken up the cause of the schools, telling us on network news and
in front-page headlines that something is drastically and fundamentally wrong with our system of education.

The statistics are no less chilling than the rhetoric. Among the
most alarming: 13 percent of all seventeen-year-olds are function-
ally illiterate; among minority youngsters, the figure may be as
high as 40 percent; average achievement of high school students
on most standardized tests, despite recent improvements, are still
lower than before Sputnik; nearly 40 percent of seventeen-year-
olds cannot draw inferences from written material; only 20 percent can write a persuasive essay; only a third can solve mathematics problems that require several steps; even among the brightest
students, those who score as "gifted" on standardized tests, only
half perform as well in school as their test scores would suggest.

And for a nation plagued by faltering manufacturing industries and dependent increasingly on high technology to sustain its economic base, it is sobering to realize that a third of the 21,000 secondary schools in the United States do not offer enough mathematics to qualify their graduates for admission to accredited engineering schools. Only a third teach calculus and less than that offer a course in physics taught by a certified teacher.

There is a somewhat apocryphal story about industry's reaction to tougher clean air laws. The first thing Japan did, the story goes, was to hire 2,000 more engineers. The first thing Detroit did was to hire 2,000 more lawyers. That says something about our national priorities; it says something about whose car Americans are more likely to buy; but it also says something about education. Engineers are not created overnight but rather through a long and arduous educational process that begins with a strong high school background in math and science. And for many young people that background is simply not available.

American children go to school, on average, only 180 days a year, with another twenty days usually lost to absences, while children in Japan attend for 240 days. Our school day is about five hours long, while in many other countries it is eight hours long. And much of the American school day for the teacher is taken up with activities that have little to do with education—attendance, grading papers, maintaining discipline.

As for our teachers, low pay, stressful working conditions, and better opportunities elsewhere—especially for talented women who were once the backbone of the profession—have taken their toll. Asked for three reasons why she had become a teacher, one replied, "June, July, and August."

Teaching has come to attract the least academically able college students and far fewer of them than even a decade ago. As recently as 1970, nearly 25 percent of college and university freshmen across the nation reported education as a career choice. By 1980, the figure had plummeted to 5 percent, with little sign of an upturn. The problem is particularly severe in the sciences and mathematics, where there are shortages of competent teachers in virtually every state and where nearly half of those hired to teach last year were not fully certified to teach the subjects they were assigned.

Add to this the growing list of services—from counseling to health care to nutrition—and the growing list of courses—from driver education to physical education to "preparation for marriage and family life"—which compete on equal footing with reading, writing, and 'rithmetic, and it is little wonder that the schools are in trouble.

But before you all leave to pack Junior's bags for Exeter, let's take a look at the other side. For despite the current outcry, there is much that is right with American education. And what isn't right is being worked on at many levels, in new and innovative ways, and through an expanded partnership that involves the schools, higher education, the private sector, and government at all levels.

First, let us look at the big picture, for there is much here of which we can be extremely proud. In 1950, less than half of America's young people graduated from high school. In 1977, it exceeded 80 percent and it is still increasing. In 1950, only 10 percent of black students graduated from high school; in 1977, it was 76 percent. And by 1980, the U.S. had more of its fifteen- to eighteen-year-olds enrolled in school than any other country in the world.

That higher level of education has had an impact on college and university attendance as well. In 1910, the average twenty-five-year-old American had completed 8.1 years of school. By 1950, the figure was 9.3, and by 1980, it was 12.5. In 1965, the percentage of black high school graduates going on to college was one-third that of whites. By 1980, the percentage of black high school graduates going on to college actually exceeded that of whites, although the proportion of high school graduates who were black had not decreased. In all, more that 12 million Americans are now enrolled in some form of postsecondary education.

That represents a massive national commitment to education, and it has brought us as a nation closer than ever before to the Jeffersonian ideal of as much education for each citizen as he or she has the desire and the determination to pursue. If it is in fact true that fifty years ago the nation's college students were brighter, it is hardly surprising. Most people of "college age" were not in college at all.

Perhaps even more impressive than sheer numbers is the variety of individuals—from the gifted to the economically disadvantaged to the developmentally disabled—for whom we have tried to provide the best possible education.

There is now little doubt that such programs as Head Start, which began in the Johnson administration to provide preschool education for the economically disadvantaged, have produced results. Lawrence Schweinhart and David Weikart (in *Phi Delta Kappan,* Nov. 1981) have estimated that the dollar return on early childhood education is 248 percent, and they have noted that "preschool not only prevents problems that, if unattended, cost society much more later on but increases the effectiveness and efficiency of the investment we already make in schooling."

Or take, as another example of success, the Madison, Wisconsin, public schools (reported in *American Education,* Jan.-Feb. 1981), which can claim among their 24,000 students all the many kinds of individuals identified as handicapped—the disadvantaged, the learning disabled, the emotionally disturbed, the autistic, the hearing-impaired, the visually impaired, the physically impaired, the speech- or language-impaired, the pregnant teenagers, the mildly or moderately mentally retarded, the multiply handicapped, and the severely or profoundly mentally retarded. There are some two thousand of these "special" students in Madison, and the district has a plan for each that provides education in the least restrictive environment possible.

With the help of the University of Wisconsin's School of Education, handicapped children are sought out from birth for individual and small group education, and by the time they reach kindergarten age, one out of three is ready to enter a regular classroom. The program is costly, with somewhere between $6,000 and $8,000 spent by the district per handicapped pupil per year. But, as supporters are quick to point out, keeping a handicapped child in an institution can cost the state $20,000 per year or more.

There are many other bright spots as well. As I read the depressing statistics and the damning reports, I am struck by the fact that, for the most part, my own children have had excellent teachers. And good teachers and good schools are not restricted to the more affluent school districts. In Los Angeles's Bret Harte Prepa-

ratory Intermediate School, just a few blocks from Watts, in P.S.
61 and Morris High School in the South Bronx, in Atlanta and
Chicago and Washington, D.C.—big cities where the problems
of public schools have been worst—things seem to be getting better. Children are doing as well, or almost as well, as others in their
age group, and the gap in performance between black and white
youngsters is narrowing.

In Atlanta last spring, three-quarters of the first graders
scored at or above the national norm on the verbal section of the
California Achievement Test, and 78 percent did that well on the
math. In Pittsburgh, 54 percent of elementary school children
scored above grade level in language skills last year, and 61 percent scored above grade in math. In California last year (as reported in the *San Jose Mercury,* June 10, 1982), test scores for third
graders improved for the fourteenth consecutive year, and twelfth
graders had better scores in every content area for the first time
ever.

Moreover, the formula for success seems surprisingly simple:
a commitment to teaching basic skills, a belief in the ability of all
children to learn, and a willingness to set high standards and enforce them. In Houston, which has already set up promotional
gates at grades one through eight and grade level standards all the
way through high school, computer literacy will be added next
year to the state's graduation requirements.

And at Morris High School in the South Bronx, which President Reagan cited recently as a school turned around by leadership and a return to the basics, students have a nine-period day,
with time for enrichment or remediation. They are obliged to do
a half hour of homework each night in each subject, and if they
plan to attend college, they must meet standards that exceed the
state requirements for science, math, and languages. The results
speak for themselves: 86 percent of this year's senior class are going to college, and they have offers of $1.3 million in financial aid.

There has been a return to the stick in enforcing high expectations, but there have been carrots as well. In Minnesota, virtually
every student from preschool through college has access to computer-based education, and in North Carolina, a residential campus for gifted eleventh and twelfth graders was opened three years

ago to provide high-level math and science instruction that is beyond the means of most individual districts.

Teaching, too, should be getting better now that some twenty states have instituted competency tests, and educators are coming to value substance in subject matter above methods and style. In Kentucky, for example, students in math and science who agree to take minimum certification courses and teach for three years in the state's public schools will have their college loans forgiven. The rationale is that even if these teachers then leave for other professions, Kentucky's students will have had at least three years of instruction from teachers who really know their subjects.

Perhaps most significant for those of you in CASE, colleges and universities, the College Board, and various educational associations are taking a new and expanded interest in just what the schools are teaching and what the graduates of those schools can and cannot do.

This is as it should be, for at least part of the laxity of standards in the public schools and their preoccupation with things not directly related to education can be traced to the precedent set by higher education during the 1960s and early 1970s. In response to student demand for "relevance" and the right to "do their own thing," many institutions reduced their core academic requirements and added a host of lighter-weight courses designed to raise the students' social conscience or establish their personal identity. The result, in many cases, was neither enlightenment nor enhanced morality but mediocrity, and that mediocrity eventually pervaded not only the schools but all phases of our public and private life.

But higher education's expanded interest in the schools is not purely altruistic. Colleges and universities, especially those state institutions with "open" admissions policies, are finding that remedial courses, for too many students, have become the norm rather than the exception. Remediation on a large scale can drag down the intellectual life of a campus, demoralize the individual student, and, especially in the public sector, raise uncomfortable questions about why taxpayers should have to finance the same education twice. To deal with these problems, some twenty-seven states recently have made it harder for students to attend their state universities.

At Ohio State, where I served as provost before coming to California last year, the trustees approved the faculty's establishment of curriculum of college-preparatory courses that high school students will be expected to take. The curriculum includes four units of English, with an emphasis on writing; three units of mathematics; two units of social sciences; two units of natural sciences; two units of a foreign language; one unit of visual and performing arts; and an additional unit from any of the previous categories. Students not meeting those standards can be admitted conditionally, but they will have to satisfy the conditions of their admission before any degree or certificate is awarded.

Similar policies, which follow the recommendation of the Advisory Commission on Articulation Between Secondary Schools and Ohio Colleges, appointed by the Ohio Board of Regents and the State Board of Education, have already been adopted or are in the final stages of development at several other Ohio universities.

As Ohio's Chancellor Edward Moulton commented (*Newsweek*, My. 9, '83), "Anybody who has raised children knows that they would rather play basketball than mow the grass, but if they know that they *must* mow the grass they will." And by telling prospective college students what they must do to succeed, Ohio hopes not only to prevent later disappointments for the students but also to realize substantial savings on its $10 million-a-year bill for remediation.

Within the California State University, a reassessment of general education has been under way since 1977, and in January 1982 our trustees adopted more rigorous admission requirements for entering freshmen, including four years of college-preparatory math in addition to the standing grade and test score requirements. And just last month the trustees voted to strengthen requirements for students entering and completing teacher education programs on the university's nineteen campuses.

But establishing specific course requirements does not automatically ensure that students will be well prepared, because there is often little uniformity in what college-bound students learn. Four years of English, for example, may be completed in some high schools without doing any expository writing, without reading the classics, without learning grammar. For this reason, many states and individual institutions are providing, along with their lists of required courses, more specifics on what the outcomes of a college-preparatory curriculum should be.

The College Board's Educational Quality Project, which began three years ago, is taking that message not only to the high schools, but to the students and their parents as well. In a major report released this May ("What Students Need to Know and Be Able to Do"), the College Board outlined the skills and knowledge needed for success in college. Significantly, at a time when we have tended to glorify the sciences and mathematics, it gave equal weight to English, the arts, social studies, and foreign languages. The EQ Project is now being used as a framework to improve the preparation of high school students in ten states stretching from California to Rhode Island.

After a long slide, then, quality is in again, along with designer clothing, condominiums, and racquetball. It is trendy, up-scale, just the thing to capture the American imagination and launch a new era of excellence in our educational system, K through postgraduate.

There are challenges remaining, of course, in this Year of the Secondary Schools, and they will not be solved by the end of 1983 nor even perhaps by the end of the decade. But they are important challenges, and ones that the members of CASE, with their considerable talents in communications, government relations, and development, are uniquely qualified to address. Let me describe briefly what I see as some of our top priorities.

First, we need to maintain the balance between the arts and the sciences as we work to increase the rigor of our academic program. We need talented and creative scientists and engineers, of course, but we also need a much larger group of educated citizens who are comfortable with the concepts and methods of science and able to integrate them into a coherent philosophy of life.

Mortimer Adler's controversial "Paideia Proposal" is one approach to achieving this kind of broad and balanced education, and although his single-track, K to twelve plan may be too idealistic for most schools, its balance and its commitment to excellence are goals to which we can all aspire. For as David Reisman has said, "Only by hitching the rickety wagon of education to a star can it be made to budge an inch."

Second, we must continue to improve not only the central core of education, but also education at the margins so that all Americans, regardless of their racial or economic backgrounds, their special talents or special handicaps, may receive the highest quality education that is suited to their needs.

But cutbacks, at the federal level especially, threaten our continued progress here. Let me cite an example from one of my own campuses, California State University, Northridge. Northridge operates the largest mainstreaming education program for deaf students in the country, and it has opened for these students many career paths that are not widely available. Yet we may soon face a shortage of interpreters, counselors, and note-takers due to uncertainties in federal funding. The situation is all the more unfortunate because we are seeing an upsurge in the number of deaf college students, who are the indirect victims of an outbreak of rubella that affected their mothers twenty years ago.

Likewise we can expect an increase in the number of blind students on college campuses, due in part to our success in controlling juvenile-onset diabetes and our lesser degree of success in controlling the blindness that often accompanies the disease.

And we are just beginning to identify other groups with special educational needs—the students of non-English speaking parents, children who are themselves parents, the mildly handicapped, the gifted, and many others for whom suitable educational programs are in the very early stages of development.

Third, we need to determine more precisely which kinds of improvements can be effected without new resources and which cannot, and then we must work to allocate our resources effectively.

Things like more homework, more instruction—and less administration—in the classroom, more integrated and sequential curricula, more challenging textbooks, more parental involvement, and higher expectations on the part of principals, teachers, and the students themselves are relatively cheap and indisputably effective. But better prepared and better paid teachers, adequate laboratory facilities, special programs for special students are just as important and much more costly.

Our colleges and universities, not only through their schools of education but also through their expertise in management, sociology, political science, and a host of other disciplines, can help us set our priorities here. And with that information in hand, I would urge you to seek the necessary support not only from government but from the private sector as well. It is naive to hope that we can solve all our problems by throwing money at them, but it is equally naive to expect to solve a great many of them without spending money.

Fourth, and most important, we need to reaffirm, and perhaps rediscover, the importance of teaching as a profession. We need to attract more talented young people to the field, and we need to reward them with the salaries and the respect they deserve. We who offer teaching training programs must provide a firm grounding not only in the methods of education but also in the disciplines our students will one day teach. And we must work with those teachers long after graduation to keep their skills current and their enthusiasm high.

Within the California State University, professors in English, math, and social sciences already work closely with their counterparts in local high schools to devise curriculums, and they sometimes exchange classes to get a better understanding of each other's problems. Many public school teachers come to our campuses for summer institutes such as the California Mathematics project and the California Writing Project, where they can not only improve their skills but also gain a sense that what they are doing is important.

But there is more that can be done, not only through more secondary–postsecondary collaboration, but also through the involvement of the private sector. In California, two corporate foundations, the Atlantic Richfield Foundation and the Bank-America Foundation, have provided funds to produce a special booklet for eighth graders on "Making High School Count." This booklet is one of the projects of the California Round Table for Educational Opportunity. The Round Table is an association of the chief executives of the systems of higher education, public and private, the State Superintendent of Public Instruction, and the director of California's coordinating agency.

And California's corporate leaders are working with the state's educational leaders to improve secondary school education, especially in math and science. Among the ideas we are now exploring are these:

The use of postsecondary instructors, including professor emeriti and graduate students, to teach math and science in the schools, with support from the business community;
special postsecondary "crash courses" in classroom techniques for business employees released to teach math or science on a part-time basis;
dual careers for math and science teachers, including joint business–education programs in colleges and universities that would be supported by the business community through employment opportunities and active recruiting.

Other activities along these lines are also being explored here in California, and I would suggest that with the imagination and resourcefulness that you in CASE can bring to the task, these sorts of initiatives could be carried out in other states and in other subject areas as well.

"The future of education," Robert Hutchins once said, "is the future of everything else." We in education have long been believers, and, thanks to the shocking reports of this spring, a large proportion of the American public is now on our side. As a people, we have come to recognize the crisis in American education, and, as the Chinese symbols for that word indicate, crisis is danger combined with opportunity.

Let us turn the new national perception of danger and the renewed concern into a broadly based and adequately funded commitment to the young people of this nation. For they are, quite literally, our greatest natural resource.

AN AMERICAN CHALLENGE IN A NEW AGE: FAIRNESS AND RESPONSIBILITY[1]

FRANK R. LAUTENBERG[2]

When the Founding Fathers proclaimed our independence and embarked on the task of creating a new government, not surprisingly they borrowed heavily from what they knew best: established English law, institutions, and tradition. One British custom they inherited was that of the maiden speech, on the basis of which new members of Parliament were judged as to their abilities. Dating back to the eighteenth century, the maiden, or first, speech by a new member was regarded as crucial to his future parliamentary career. Even today, the maiden speech in the House of Commons can be a terrible ordeal:

> Some friends advise him [the new member] to "get it over quickly"; others urge him to bide his time; he must not speak too quietly, nor should he shout; he must not be provocative or controversial, but his speech should not be colorless, and so on. (Roberts Rhodes James, *An Introduction to the House of Commons*, London, 1961, p 50)

Unlike the British Parliament, the United States Senate today attaches little importance to the maiden speech or to speaking ability in general. This attitude is illustrated by the occasion of the first speech by Senator Frank Lautenberg of New Jersey, delivered on June 7, 1983. Reporter Jane Perlez described the occasion:

> Mr. Lautenberg, standing in the rear row of desks on the Democratic side, spoke to an empty chamber—so commonplace have maiden speeches become, according to the Senate minority leader, Robert C. Byrd, Democrat of West Virginia. But he was welcomed before he began his oratory by the majority leader, Howard H. Baker, Jr., of Tennessee, and Mr. Byrd, who escorted the new Senator off the floor at the end of his 10-minute speech. . . . Following tradition, Mr. Lautenberg had made no substantive remarks on the floor until his maiden speech today. (*New York Times*, Je. 8, '83, p 13)

Since the Senate was empty except for the majority and minority party leaders, was Lautenberg's maiden speech of any importance? Why bother to deliver it? The answer probably is that the occasion provided him an opportunity, through publication in the *Congressional Record* and perhaps media coverage, to reach his constituents and the general public.

---

[1]Delivered to the United States Senate on June 7, 1983.
[2]For biographical note, see Appendix.

In fact, the *New York Times* covered the speech in a substantial article, and the senator reproduced the speech as printed in the *Record* for distribution to New Jersey voters.

The speech also attracted attention because Lautenberg—the son of immigrants—who had built a personal fortune by founding the largest data processing company in the nation, warned that computers threatened to create a new class of poor people. He was concerned that computers were proliferating more rapidly in wealthy districts and schools, leaving the poor to become illiterate in the new technology. He warned that computer illiteracy had the potential for creating new and distressing divisions in our society.

Senator Lautenberg's speech: Mr. President, I rise today to make my first speech on the Senate floor and I do so with gratitude and awe.

I am deeply grateful to my fellow citizens in the state of New Jersey for entrusting me to serve them in this great center of debate and decision.

I am in awe of the brilliance of our forefathers who wrote the Constitution for a nation that welcomed those seeking freedom and a new way of life. Their wisdom enabled my parents to be brought here by their families searching for refuge and oportunity.

It was their critical learning experience. All that followed, whether at university, business, or life in general was molded by the framework provided by these new citizens.

I am grateful also to those who preceded me in this chamber for their contribution to this beloved democracy, and to those colleagues with whom I presently share this honor for the advice and encouragement they regularly impart to me.

In particular, I am deeply indebted to the senior senator from the state of New Jersey, Senator Bradley, with whom I share common interest and goals, and to the Democratic leader, Senator Byrd, who has extended to me every courtesy and whose respect for the history and traditions of this institution set a high standard for a new member like myself.

Mr. President, not very long ago, our nation entered what many call the information age, a period during which information-service industries have become predominant in our economy. They have eclipsed manufacturing, just as manufacturing surpassed farming decades ago. The change has been gradual, but undeniable. Some 60 percent of our work force is employed in creating, storing, processing, or distributing information. Who does that include? Office workers, salespeople, secretaries, people at work in telecommunications, computers, in education, research and science, financial services, and insurance to name a few. People applying information technology to make the production of goods more efficient.

Technological innovation has brought vast changes in our society, in our work places, in our homes and schools.

Innovation and change is accelerating. This will drive the future growth of our economy and alter the character of our society. Mr. President, this nation can ride the wave of the information age, or can be swamped by it. Great challenges accompany the promises of change. In responding to those challenges, we must draw on the best of our values and ideals. In a nation that is plugged into computers, questions of success and failure may become questions of who is on-line and who is off-line. In an economy where technology will dominate our future, how do we cope with businesses, people and places still tied to the past?

Mr. President, these are issues I hope to address in the Senate. They are issues of equity and opportunity in the 1980s and the 1990s and beyond. They are issues that trouble my state. I am proud that New Jersey has been the home of many of the inventions that are the foundation of this new age. But New Jersey was also the birthplace of American manufacturing—and many of its factories and plants are in decline. New Jersey was third in the nation in new patents last year. But it lost 46,000 jobs in manufacturing. For those workers there is no end to recession.

The suburbs of my state are enjoying great growth, tied to service- and research-based industries on the rise. But New Jersey's cities are being stripped of the industry around which they were built. The unemployment in some of our cities is about the highest in the nation.

In reflecting on these contrasts, I feel compelled to offer a personal note. I myself am the son of a millworker. My father worked in textile mills that have long since shut down. But I made my mark in a computer-based company, a company that advanced in tandem with technology. I crossed into that future because my country gave me the chance. It gave me an education. It afforded me opportunity.

I pledged to the people of my state that one of my main missions would be to work to provide employment and economic opportunity. We must work to insure that everyone shares in what is to come. Already, we can see the kinds of challenges we face. Already, we can identify the tasks that lie ahead, to insure that the promises of the future are promises for all of us.

There is a broad consensus that we must place increased emphasis on training in math and science. There are proposals to enhance the quality of teaching, to enrich the opportunities for students at all levels. Most of our new jobs will be information-related. They will require new skills, constantly upgraded over a worker's lifetime. New demands will be placed on our educational training systems and on our people. The capacity to use and work with computers is becoming essential, almost as essential as being able to read and write clearly.

The concept of computer literacy in turn defines a new type of illiteracy, and the potential for new and distressing divisions in our society. From the fall of 1980 to the spring of 1982, the number of microcomputers and computers available to public school students tripled. Growth in the use of computers in the schools is accelerating. By January 1983, more than half of all people in the United States were using microcomputers in instruction. But where is the growth occurring?

According to one study, Title I schools—schools with programs for the economically and socially disadvantaged—average 25 percent fewer computers than non–Title I schools. Almost 70 percent of wealthy schools have microcomputers, almost 60 percent of poor schools have not. These statistics are ominous.

Numbers raise other questions as well. The same schools that lack the resources to buy computers very likely lack the resources to enrich the skills of their teachers, to buy the software, and design the programs and provide the faculty necessary for effective teaching. In an age that demands computer literacy, a school without a computer is like a school without a library. And the same patterns extend to the home. The Office of Technology Assessment says the number of computers in homes has doubled from

1982 to 1983. Those computers are being acquired by the affluent, reinforcing disparties in opportunity.

As we address the issue of education in an information age, we must address the question of equal opportunity. There will continue to be debate over what is the appropriate federal role when it comes to education. I believe that a major responsibility is to even out the inequities, to insure equal opportunity. The Congress is considering various proposals to insure an education appropriate to our times. We must see to it that all our children have an equal chance to get the education they need to grow and succeed in America today.

Mr. President, we face other issues of equity. Telecommunications networks will be the new infrastructure: satellite networks to conquer the physical isolation of rural communities; networks that link computers and businesses in a national web; networks that channel more information, at faster speeds, than ever before. Who will be connected, and who will not?

The American Telephone & Telegraph Company, our national phone system, is being broken up. Local telephone companies will be spun off and will provide basic telephone service.

For years, profits from long-distance and equipment charges have held down the cost of local telephone rates. But that day is ending. We are fast approaching a time when local telephone users will have to pay the full cost of local service. Local rates may double or triple. In my state, regulatory officials predict that basic telephone rates could rise as much as 150 percent by early 1984.

The effect could be devastating. For every 10 percent rise in price, we can expect that 1 percent of telephone users will drop service. Projected price increases would lead to a fall off of telephone service to more than 10 percent of the population. Further increases will cut millions more from the most basic of our information networks—the telephone system.

Cut off will be the poor, the sick, and the elderly, in need of telephone service for emergencies, for contact with the ouside world.

Cut off will be the unemployed, who will become further isolated from job opportunities.

Cut off will be whole areas of our poorest cities, adding another impediment to their revival.

Our concern for equity in the information age must also extend to heavy industry and industrial workers. While we should encourage the growth of service opportunities, we cannot turn our backs on basic industries or the people and places affected by job loss. Monumental changes occur in the life of an individual and his or her family when unemployment hits, when new skills must be acquired, when a new job must be found and a new life made, perhaps far from a person's home. And substantial distress is experienced by old cities with so-called sunset industries when the tax base and infrastructure built around declining industries erode.

Advance notice, information about job markets, and opportunities for retraining help workers adjust more easily to change. Targeted incentives and appropriate planning help many cities attract the makings of new industry—information-based, service industry, and new jobs. As a matter of responsibility, we must ease the process of adjustment.

We cannot stand back and permit our industrial base to disappear. We cannot concede these jobs to our foreign competitors. We must encourage change in our manufacturing and industrial plants to make them competitive. This can be done through changes in tax policy, in trade policy, and other incentives—and by promoting partnership among management, workers, and government. The Democratic industrial policy task force, on which I serve, is studying these questions to shape a legislative agenda to address them.

Mr. President, in my own state, there is growth and prosperity directly tied to the coming of the information age—jobs in research, science, financial services. But at the same time, there are areas in deep decline, cities where unemployment is pervasive, and industry on the wane.

In welcoming the information age, we must not leave these people and communities behind.

Mr. President, our nation has long stood for opportunity, equality, and fairness. I would not be here today were it not for the opportunities granted me. A child of the Depression, I was given the chance to get an education, to go forth, and make a mark. We are in the midst of substantial changes in our economy and our society. Industries are transforming. Tasks are changing. Demands are shifting. In our efforts to seize the best the new age has to offer, we must not ignore the call of our conscience, to insure that we go forward together, as a united people sharing the potential of this new age.

THE AMERICAN SCHOLAR[1]

ERNEST G. BORMANN[2]

It is a tradition at the University of Minnesota for the president of the local chapter of Phi Beta Kappa to address the new members after their initiation into the national honor society. On the last day of May 1983, Ernest G. Bormann, a distinguished scholar and professor of speech communication at the university, delivered the traditional address. Rejecting the idea that the occasion was trivial and that a speech commemorating it demanded nothing more than "mere rhetoric," Bormann told the initiates, "What you have done to gain membership in this society is a vital and integral part of who you are and indicative of what you may yet become. This is an important occasion. It deserves suitable commemoration and celebration. . . . I, therefore, approach the opportunity to deliver the Phi Beta Kappa oration . . . with great reverence and a high sense of its importance."

Dr. Bormann delivered his address to approximately 450 persons in the Mayo Auditorium of the medical school complex on the university's main campus in Minneapolis. The audience of 150 new initiates into Phi Beta Kappa, members of their families and friends, and interested students and faculty nearly filled the auditorium.

The meeting began at 7:30 P.M. Bormann's speech was preceded by a brief initiation ceremony that included an explanation of the history and purposes of the honorary society, administration of the pledge to the candidates, and the reading of pertinent articles from the organization's constitution. Professor Bormann was introduced at approximately 8 P.M.

In his address, Bormann traced the attitudes toward scholarly pursuit throughout the history of the country and sought to determine what are the values, if any, of study of the humanities. The worth of studying the humanities, he concluded, has nothing to do with whether they are useful,

[1]Delivered to the University of Minnesota chapter of Phi Beta Kappa in the Mayo Auditorium in Minneapolis at approximately 8:00 P.M. on May 31, 1983.
[2]For biographical note, see Appendix.

practical, or will result in a dollar-and-cents profit. "The humanities are ends in themselves; they relate not to those things that make life possible, but to those intellectual and artistic pursuits that make life worth living."

Ernest G. Bormann's speech: Fellow members of Phi Beta Kappa, relatives, and friends: It has been the tradition at Minnesota for the presidents of your society to speak to you on this occasion on topics drawn from their scholarly interests. My scholarship has been in the study of the history and criticism of great speeches and speakers and in the critical evaluation of mass persuasion.

What you have done to gain membership in this society is a vital and integral part of who you are and indicative of what you may yet become. This is an important occasion. It deserves suitable commemoration and celebration. I reject the notion that a speech on such an occasion as this is a frill or trivial. I reject that idea of "mere" rhetoric that is so popular today. I know of no better way to celebrate your accomplishments than the saying of appropriate words publicly. I, therefore, approach the opportunity to deliver the Phi Beta Kappa oration at the University of Minnesota in the year 1983 with great reverence and a high sense of its importance.

The genre of the Phi Beta Kappa oration is an enduring and honorable one in the United States. All over the country such orations have been given down through the years. I am deeply cognizant of the long line of great speakers stretching back toward Harvard College and that afternoon in August 1837 when Ralph Waldo Emerson journeyed to the First Parish Church in Cambridge, Massachusetts, a plain wooden meeting house that was used sometimes to serve the needs of Harvard University on anniversary occasions, and spoke to the title *The American Scholar*.

The audience was composed of the Phi Beta Kappa society of Harvard University and its guests and thus included some of the leading scholars, teachers, university officials, and literary people of the time.

It was a speech that set the learned community abuzz. Oliver Wendell Holmes called it "our intellectual Declaration of Independence," and noted that "young men went out from it as if a prophet had been proclaiming to them 'Thus saith the Lord.'" You can understand why I've spent so many sleepless nights the last month trying to live up to that tradition and this occasion.

The subject was, in Emerson's words "the topic which not only usage but the nature of our association seem to prescribe to this day: The American Scholar."

Forty-four years after Emerson spoke to the title of *The American Scholar,* Wendell Phillips—the Boston Brahmin, graduate of Boston Latin School and Harvard College, who married the ardent reformer, Ellen Terry, who had looked out of his window at the mobbing of William Lloyd Garrison, had become the foremost orator of the Garrisonian wing of the abolitionists, had endorsed the temperance reform and was one of the few who continued on after the Civil War in support of the women's suffrage movement, —forty-four years later this old agitator at the age of seventy was surprisingly asked to deliver the Phi Beta Kappa oration at Harvard and he took as his title, *The Scholar in a Republic.* Between Emerson and Phillips had been four decades of revolution, reform, reaction, crisis, Civil War, emancipation, and reconstruction. Yet the question was as pertinent for Wendell Phillips as it had been for Emerson.

The topic is an enduring one. It is the subject that I take for myself this evening, 146 years after Emerson gave his answer, Where stands the American scholar today? Or more to the point, What role should you take in the republic as the best and brightest of 1983? You probably recognize the phrase as the ironic title of Halberstam's book that delineates the way the best and the brightest of the political leadership of the 1960s led us down the path to economic troubles, war, and social and political chaos.

Why was Emerson's speech considered an intellectual Declaration of Independence? Because in his introduction he said of the intellectual life of America that, "Perhaps the time is already come when it ought to be, and will be something else; when the sluggard intellect of this continent will look from under its iron lids and fill the postponed expectation of the world with something better than the exertions of mechanical skill. Our day of dependence, our long apprenticeship to the learning of other lands, draws to a close."

He reiterated the theme in his conclusion. "We have listened too long to the courtly muses of Europe. The spirit of the American freeman is already suspected to be timid, imitative, tame. Public avarice makes the air we breathe thick and fat. The scholar is decent, indolent, complaisant. See already the tragic consequence. The mind of this country, taught to aim at low objects, eats upon itself." But he closed on a note of hope. "Please God, ours shall not be so. We will walk on our own feet; we will work with our own hands; we will speak our own minds. The study of letters shall be no longer a name for pity, for doubt, and for sensual indulgence."

Where stands the American scholar today? Our scholarship, like our popular culture, sweeps the globe. Foreign students are drawn to our universities to study; our science, social science, and humanities are read and incorporated not only in developing countries but in the intellectual centers of Europe. My daughter spent a year abroad studying in Vienna. The second semester, with her German improved to the point where she could attend lectures, she took a course in psychology thinking that here in the home of Sigmund Freud she would learn something she could not get on her American campus. What she got was a diluted dose of Skinnerian behaviorism and a survey of the latest psychological research in the United States reminiscent of Psychology 101.

In my sabbatical abroad some years ago, I attended a convention of the *Deutsche Gesellshaft fur Sprechkunde und Sprecherzieshung*—the German equivalent of our Speech Communication Association. They asked for suggestions on the latest and best books from the United States in all areas of my discipline.

I could multiply the examples. Not to be chauvinistic, to be sure scholarship thrives around the world, we borrow from the scholars of many lands, but on balance, Emerson's concerns are an anachronism. But old rhetorical grooves are hard to erase. In our national consciousness the inferiority complex about art and learning that Emerson fought to eliminate and Mark Twain satirized in *Innocents Abroad* dies hard.

In the late 1950s, as a young associate professor, I went through a series of soul-searching faculty meetings dedicated to a crisis in education. The Sputnik had become a rhetorical symbol of Communist superiority, a major victory in the Cold War. How were we to accommodate that shocking fact into our national consciousness? Our answer was that American education was inferior to European education. Our students were, to borrow Emerson's characterization, "decent indolent, complaisant." Russian students worked long hours, studied tough subjects. They knew their math, physics, and chemistry, while American students were electing easy subjects under the indulgent eyes of teachers who coddled them, and the result was they could not read, do arithmetic, nor become engineers and scientists.

We tooled up. The federal government poured billions of dollars into education. We tightened up our requirements. We established tough discipline in our schools. Some high schools had such tight security the doors were locked after the bells rang, and students had to have passes to move in the halls.

By the late 1960s we had turned up the pressure so high that when the whole thing burst there was a great movement to reform education. We were teaching by rote. There was no opportunity for creativity, no experimentation with new ways of education, no understanding of the meaninglessness of grades to the educational process. Requirements were relaxed, independent study encouraged, grading reformed, sometimes eliminated. You yourselves experienced some of the legacy of that period in terms of a grading system that allowed a liberal portion of S-N grades and that rather strange notation on your transcript, an N. The official interpretation of which, as near as I can tell, is N means nothing.

Now I again hear the familiar echoes of Emerson's charge of indolent and complaisant scholars. We no longer rule the world with that mechanical skill that Emerson noted as our only claim to intellectual fame. Even the legacy of such as Henry Ford and Thomas Edison cannot keep our automobiles as the world's cynosure—not even in the United States.

How are we to accommodate this shocking fact to our national consciousness. Will the script this time be different? Or will the rhetorical drama again contrast our indolent scholars with those dedicated and hard-working students of other lands who work many hours a day and who study the tough subjects. Recently I saw an article in the *Minneapolis Star and Tribune* reporting that "American schools have been increasingly criticized in the past few years as mediocre . . . they have been often compared unfavorably with those in Japan, whose rapid economic recovery after World War II is linked partly to the excellence of its educational system." Fortunately this article went on to point out that a number of American educators who are knowledgeable about the Japanese system "caution against concluding that the country is an educational utopia."

My point is not that American scholars and the American educational institutions are the best in the world, because such comparisons are often meaningless oversimplifications and I often, in moments of cynicism as my own children pursued their education, recalled with approval the comment of my philosophy professor at the University of Iowa. He was a Viennese immigrant who escaped ahead of Hitler's takeover. Perhaps as brilliant a man as I have ever known, he was trained in law and mathematics; a hanger-on at the Vienna Circle of logical positives who was interested in film, theater, literature. He once said to me, "Even this piggish American school system can't ruin the best minds."

My point is that when Emerson spoke on the life of the mind in America, he was much concerned with the perception that life was derivative of European thought and culture. We no longer need concern ourselves with such issues.

There is much about Emerson's speech that I applaud. With Wendell Phillips's advice on the role of the scholar in a republic, on the other hand, I take issue. His position has a long and powerful history in our country, but I take it as a foil for what I want to say to you tonight.

First, Phillips argues that scholarship, the life of the mind, has contributed hardly at all to the economic well-being of society. Second, Phillips chides the scholars in his audience because they have not become agitators for the great reforms, such as the abolition of slavery and women's suffrage, to which he had dedicated his life.

In regard to the first charge of economic irrelevance he said:

But what of education? Of course it is not book learning. Book learning does not make 5 percent of that mass of common sense that "runs" the world, transacts its business, secures its progress, trebles it power over nature, works out in the long run a rough average justice. . . . The ideal Yankee, who "has more brains in his hand than others have in their skulls," is not a scholar; and two-thirds of the inventions that enable France to double the world's sunshine, and make Old and New England the workshops of the world, did not come from colleges or from minds trained in the schools of science, but struggled up, forcing their way against giant obstacles from the irrepressible instinct of untrained natural power. Her workshops, not her colleges, made England, for a while, the mistress of the world; and the hardest job her workman had was to make Oxford willing he should work his wonders.

As we meet tonight, a society dedicated to the tradition of liberal learning, I would wager that each and every one of us has run into the pervasive and debilitating power of Wendell Phillips's argument. It is the argument of the bottom line, that fearful numerical bottom line expressed in dollars and cents.

Students come to me with the plaintive question, "I'm considering majoring in speech communication. What can I do? What kind of job can I get with a major in speech communication?" I hear the question everywhere. What good is a degree in history? In English language and literature? What kind of a job will the study of a foreign language and culture prepare me for?

I recall my first job right after World War II, when we were living in faculty barracks and we overheard a small child explaining to another that his father was a doctor too, but not the kind of doctor that did anybody any good. He was a scholar and not a practitioner of medicine.

We have had in this country a continuing rhetoric in the public press, from lecterns and podiums, from radio and television, that celebrates the practical, the pragmatic, the bottom line—how much per annum is that idea worth? We even spawned a school of philosophy, one of whose advocates expressed its position in the aphorism, "the cash value of an idea."

So pervasive has been the influence of the fantasy of the bottom line that many have tried to twist the liberal arts into practical skills. Taking Latin will help future doctors of medicine and lawyers use Latin terms and phrases more effectively. Music, poetry, history will enrich your conversation and enable you to sell more real estate.

As you contemplate your future, I would like to inoculate you against the virus of the rhetoric of the bottom line—inure you to the continual poundings you will receive from those who demamd utilitarian outcomes. We here, in this society, should be a bastion not only to publicly defend our commitment to the liberal arts but to so live our own lives that we enact their virtues.

Take the study of the humanities, the core of the liberal arts. You do not defend the humanities because they are useful. You defend them on the grounds that they are of no practical use whatsoever. The very notion of a dollars-and-cents bottom line in regard to the humanities is not only unfeasible because you cannot measure quality of life involved in them, but a perversion.

The basic defense of the humanities, to my mind, is that they are useless—they are not the means to other more important utilitarian ends. The humanities are ends in themselves; they relate not to those things that make life possible, but to those intellectual and artistic pursuits that make life worth living.

Years ago I was teaching courses in radio and television at an institution where the curriculum was shared by several schools and departments. We had a committee to deal with integrating our joint instruction. One of the members was from a professional school and as we talked he kept asking the question, "What kinds of jobs will our graduates take? For what kinds of jobs are we training them? Until we find out what kinds of jobs they are getting, we won't know what kinds of courses to require." I went on a tour of television stations to find out what jobs were available and what kind of training they wanted people to have. I was horrified to discover that in that region most television station managers were of the opinion that they would rather not have university graduates working for them at all. They preferred docile people who had practical experience. University-trained people were always asking embarrassing questions and thinking for themselves.

It finally struck me that we had been asking the wrong question. If we were in the liberal arts, it was foolish to ask for what jobs were we training the students. The question should be, How can we provide the best possible liberal education for our students?

The difference between training and education is essentially this: The trained individual has a recipe to meet stereotypical situations. Education, by contrast, prepares the individual to make wise decisions when confronted with the need to do so no matter how strange or unexpected these challenges may be. Liberal arts education enables the person to bring moral judgment to bear on pressing problems. Training a liberally educated person is simple and can take place efficiently on the job. Educating a trained person is difficult and cannot be done on the job.

The dangers of training were brought home to me graphically when I heard a lecture by Robert Maynard Hutchins. Hutchins was appointed president of the University of Chicago at a young age. He promoted the notion that a thorough study of one hundred great books was a good way to become educated. He applauded the abolition of Big Ten football at Chicago and maintained that extracurricular activities were no responsibility of the university. Indeed, he said that judging from the number of late night telephone calls he got from various outraged people and law enforcement officials, the students at the University of Chicago were more than competent to create for themselves a rich diversity of extracurricular activities.

In reply to a question that implied the bottom line mentality, Hutchins said that there was a snare in such thinking, too, for he said that shortly after one of the great southern California universities had instituted its college of cosmetology, Toni came out with home permanents, thus rendering much of the curriculum obsolete.

Training is ephemeral but a liberal education is enduring. If you learn how to listen actively and creatively, to speak with precision, power, and eloquence, to read creatively, and with comprehension, to write with clarity and elegance, these earmarks of a liberally educated person endure whether you are listening to a speech delivered by Demosthenes before the birth of Christ or messages bounced off satellites in the year 2000.

All of you have fulfilled the language requirement for membership in Phi Beta Kappa and all of you, I hope, have learned to think in another language. The moment when you first begin to think in a foreign language is an exciting one, for it allows you break out of the linguistic cocoon of your native speech and understand how influential that language and its associated culture is on your version of reality. That's the real reason you should study a foreign language, not so you can get a job with Control Data or 3-M in their overseas division.

Throughout Phillips's attack on scholars runs a persistent line of rhetoric that can be traced back in our country at least as far

at the revolt against the learned preachers during the great religious revival of the 1730s and 1740s. Over the years a substantial
community of people in the United States have had a strange
love–hate relationship with scholarship and intelligence.

Peter Cartwright, the uneducated circuit-riding Methodist
minister of the early nineteenth century, said the learned ministers
from the East who came to the frontier regions reminded him of
a "gosling that had got the straddles by wading in the dew." Yet
one eulogist of Cartwright, after praising him for being educated
in brush college and the school of hard knocks, said Cartwright's
main ability was to read the book of human nature, and went on
to praise him for having "sold more books than probably any man
ever did in a new country," and noted that "many a youth, who,
but for him might have slumbered on without intelligence or
education" owed the circuit rider a debt of gratitude. Indeed, the
uneducated circuit-riding satirizers of scholars founded a host of
Wesleyan colleges across the country.

From Cartwright to the modern-day George Wallace ridicul-
ing fuzzy-thinking intellectuals who don't know enough to park
a bicycle, the rhetoric has been the same. It is said we should hate
sin and love the sinner. This is a case of loving education and hating the educated.

Many, if not all, of us have faced again and again that time
of decision. We have felt the force of that ridicule. We have had
to make a choice. I still recall that day as a freshman in a little
South Dakota high school when the class advisor slid into my seat
to talk to me about my progress at the end of the first term. I felt
good about the first term. I loved algebra, I liked to write, I had
been answering questions while others dozed. He praised me for
the right things and then he said, maybe you shouldn't talk up so
much, answer so many questions, dominate the class discussions
as you do.

It came as a bombshell to me. I thought that was what it was
all about. The answers seemed to jump into my mind in an exciting way. I never did understand how all of these exciting ideas
could leave so many of my classmates bored and sleepy. In those
days I read the *Encyclopaedia Britannica* for recreation. But it
was soon borne in upon me, the cutting comments about "the

brain." In my high school it was no compliment to be called a brain.

When Professor Paul Torrance was at the University of Minnesota studying creativity in children, he documented a strange drop in creativity at approximately the fourth grade. His conclusion was that at about the fourth grade children became more interested in their peers and in popularity and discovered that they were strangely different. In his test for creativity, one of the tasks was to write a passage about an elephant that could fly. I still remember one selection in which the child wrote about the elephant that could fly and how exciting it was until the other elephants began to make fun of him and ridicule him and then he was sorry he could fly and he decided to stop flying altogether.

We have all, I suspect, faced the same issue. Do you want to be part of the dance line? Part of the popular clique? Part of the hockey team? Will you mask your intelligence, pretend to be interested in the banalities of your colleagues? Or will you push on with the life of the mind? If you do, then be prepared for the slings and arrows of outraged anti-intellectualism. You have to develop a tough hide and forego the rewards of social popularity and often of leadership. I recall a study by the University of Iowa indicating that the alumni leaders of politics, business, and industry had been for the most part the average students, in those days the C students, today the B students—not the A students.

Even at the university, where if anywhere in the culture there should be a congenial environment for those of us dedicated to the liberalizing arts, you have not escaped the pervasiveness of the tradition of Phillips's rhetoric. How often have the brightest and the best students in my classes been quiet during discussion periods? Quiet because they did not want to become troublemakers. How often have you been pressured with the bottom line fantasy: What are you going to do when you graduate? What kind of job can you get? And, of course, at last, at the end of the discussion—because last is always where we put the most weighty questions in any meeting or conference—at last comes the bottom line: How much money will you make? How I used to cringe when I would read those statistics about how much money education was worth. You recall those—a high school education is worth so many thousand more than a grade school education over a lifetime, a college education is worth so many thousand more than a high school education, and so forth.

Here within the confines of Phi Beta Kappa, a society dedicated to the celebration and perpetuation of scholarship, of the liberal arts, of the life of the mind, here in this sheltered enclave, do I dare to say that it is all right to be intelligent, it is all right to follow the excitement of creativity, innovation, of artistic creation, and the challenge of ideas? I'll say it. I'll say more. Be proud that you are such a person and that you have earned the right to take a place in the long line of intelligence leading back to those who heard Wendell Phillips speak and further back to those who heard Ralph Waldo Emerson delineate the ideal American scholar. I dare to say it is all right to turn your back on the bottom line and dedicate a substantial proportion of your life to those useless and impractical concerns that make it worth living.

VALUES AND CHALLENGES

IS AMERICA A LEADER?[1]

Terry Sanford[2]

Every spring the campuses of the country's colleges and universities provide a forum for the discussion by prominent spokesmen of significant issues. The occasion is the annual commencement exercise. In its June 20, 1983, issue, *Time* magazine reported, "Addressing the 1,378,400 members of this year's college graduating class, the largest in U.S. history, speakers across the land have warned of the dangers of nuclear war, reaffirmed the need to maintain high standards in life, and pondered the challenges of adjusting to a high-tech tomorrow." Unlike in the not-too-distant past, when the commencement address usually was an inspirational speech on the theme of passing the torch from one generation to the next, today's speakers often use the occasion to set forth their views on major issues of the day. Since the speakers include many of the nation's most prominent leaders and authorities, their remarks are widely reported and discussed.

A speech singled out by the media for attention in the spring of 1983 was that of Duke University president and former North Carolina governor Terry Sanford to the graduates of Emory University in Atlanta. Sanford's topic was, "Is America a Leader?"

In his address, Sanford said, "Our imminent danger is that today there is no world leader. The only nation which could exercise the leadership, the United States, does not know itself or its mission. . . . The United States, rather than a natural and confident leader that stands above the turmoil and the crowd, has been behaving like one of the ruffians in the schoolyard." Instead, we should be acting with boldness and the confidence that we are a leader, according to President Sanford:

> Our ultimate strength is an eternal idea, not a gun. . . . We breed distrust by our own distrust. . . . We do not need to be a petty, selfish nation seeking our narrow safety and security. . . . We are the only great nation which can first extend the hand of friendship, first slacken the bowstring, first give assurances of dedication to real peace.

[1]Delivered at the 138th commencement exercises of Emory University, Atlanta, Georgia, in the Quadrangle at approximately 9:30 A.M., May 16, 1983.

[2]For biographical note, see Appendix.

The 138th commencement at Emory University was held on the Quadrangle at the school, an area surrounded by the oldest buildings on campus. The exercises began at 9 A.M. on May 16, 1983, with a musical prelude, followed by the processional, a welcome by university President James T. Laney, and the singing of the hymn "God of Our Fathers." President Sanford then delivered his address, which was followed by the conferring of degrees, the closing hymn and benediction, and the recessional. In the audience of 8,500 were 1,700 graduating students, as well as faculty, guests, parents, and friends.

Excerpts from Sanford's address were reprinted in *Time, U. S. News and World Report,* and several major newspapers.

Terry Sanford's speech: President Laney, whose inspired leadership has meant and continues to mean so much to this outstanding university, distinguished trustees and faculty, honored graduates, and long-suffering parents, I am delighted to be taking part in the ceremonies of Emory University, which I am pleased to claim as a sister institution, similar in history, tradition, and purpose to my own.

Communicating with college students is always somewhat of a challenge. It is not that I have too much difficulty understanding your changing expressions and attitudes. It is that I forget what you never saw. I recently read in a church magazine that when preparing a sermon, one should remember to assume that ten is the age at which an event creates an impression, which means that of today's 200 million Americans:

> 86% cannot recall Charles Lindbergh's solo flight to Paris;
> 68% cannot recollect Hitler;
> 65% cannot remember life without television;
> 58% cannot remember Senator Joe McCarthy (so listen when I mention him later);
> 53% cannot remember a Studebaker or think it is a German pudding.

And 64,345,092 people don't know what a church key is; they started life with Coca-Cola's pop-top cans.

I started my speech aware that 100 percent of you keenly know that I am the last, big obstacle between you and your diploma, and that a diploma, even after all your work, doesn't come without pain. So stick with me. I am not going to give you all the advice there is. I will try to make only one point, that ought to be enough for one commencement.

I wish I could start this talk with the words of Charles Dickens, that it is the best of times, it is the worst of times. That sort of statement gives the speaker a lot of leeway. In the long sweep of American history, today likely is the worst of times. But a happy commencement is not a time to dwell on the pervading pessimism in the world today. The point of my talk is that it need not be the worst of times.

One could contend that there have been worse times in American history—for example, the long, bleak winter of Valley Forge, when the world's new and exciting experiment of self-government hung in awful suspense; or the spring of 1862, when General McClellan was locked in mortal checkmate with General Lee and the survival of our nation was daily doubt. Or more recently, one might cite the dark days of Pearl Harbor, when the Pacific fleet was wiped out in one swift attack.

Those were all bad times. Those were the times, as Thomas Paine reminded the patriots at Valley Forge, that tried men's souls. But in each of those times, as well as during the ordeal of the Great Depression of the 1930s, America had not lost its way, not lost sight of itself. It knew where it had to go. It knew what it had to do.

Now, in 1983, we are not sure who we are or where we are going, and do not seem to know what we have to do. The road signs point to "extermination of mankind." Our military leaders and commander in chief tell us, almost daily, that the Russians can blow us off the globe and imply that they are likely to do so. They keep us scared. Instead of calm confidence in our system and sturdy determination that we can surmount our problems, they are frantically spending the bulk of our earnings for weapons and more weapons. I do not believe our leaders know how to avoid war. That is why it is the worst of times.

We might not avoid war. Wars have always been with us. In ancient times war was heroic, as far back as when Achilles urged Amagemnon on to Troy. All wars, somehow, have been absorbed and tolerated by civilization, and there has long been a widespread conviction that wars are inevitable. As put by Sigmund Freud in his time and place, "War is not to be abolished; so long as the conditions of existence among the nations are so varied, and the repulsions between people so intense, there will be, there must be, wars."

Today it is different. It was in this century that the first world wars were fought, and that weapons capable of literal world destruction were invented. It was in this century that it had to be concluded for the first time that wars could no longer be absorbed and tolerated and had to be abolished; so it follows that history will record that this was the century when wars were of necessity permanently abandoned. Then why is it the worst of times? Because there might not be any history to record and nobody left on Earth to record it. Our imminent danger is that today there is no world leader. The only nation which could exercise the leadership, the United States, does not know itself or its mission.

The United States, rather than a natural and confident leader that stands above the turmoil and the crowd, has been behaving like one of the ruffians in the schoolyard. We have methodically reduced our status to that of being just one more of the big, mean, thick-headed troublemakers. By adopting such a belligerent posture, we have destroyed our capacity for world leadership and have created for ourselves the image of an insecure and ineffective bully.

Our President publicly proclaims that the Soviet Union is the "evil empire" and snarls at its leaders. The Soviet leaders respond in kind. That is why most of the people of the world see the United States and the Soviet Union as two of a kind, the two superpowers to be feared or to be played against one another. We are in an insatiate military competition with a people as rich or richer in natural resources, a society older than ours, a nation with more people. They can create as many weapons as we can. No one can win that race.

There is a race the United States can win. The difference is that the Soviet Union is a nation whose revolution, unlike America's, lacked the benevolent touch of the hand of Providence which gave our nation the thrust of self-governance, human dignity and value, and individual freedom. There are some understandable reasons for the Soviet Union's paranoia and internal distrust. Theirs is a repressive government, and only the internal police power holds back the people who would throw off their dictator's yoke. Witness Poland. They do fear that we might attack them. They have been invaded too many times. They do not have our inherent sense of security which comes from internal freedom.

Circumstances, history, heritage, and good luck made our nation distinct, a natural leader with unique powers that come to a free nation. There is no way that this nation of free and freedom-loving people can be conquered and regimented and enslaved. Contemplate that there is no power on Earth capable of that kind of conquest, occupation, and conversion. Nor do we, as a government or as a society, need to fear internal revolt. We cannot look on ourselves as merely one more powerful nation competing on the same level with another powerful nation, a people struggling merely for national supremacy, as roughs and toughs on the same schoolyard. We are different. We hold a trust for destiny.

The fearsome fact is that we may not be smart enough to fulfill our destiny. "The Russians are coming" is a paranoia that has engulfed the great, strong, free people of America for more than fifty years. The dread of the "yellow peril" kept us from speaking to the people of China for some forty years. This national hysteria was exploited by Joe McCarthy to make himself a national figure, and it is our rationale for the present mindless buildup of military overkill. It is a blinding fear. Why should the people of the United States react in blindness to any challenge?

Instead of lurking behind the edge of the school building, peeking around the corner, picking up brickbats, looking nervously over our shoulders, screaming at the little ones who will not cluster around us with their own little pile of rocks and broken bottles, we should be walking across the yard with boldness and confidence in the sure knowledge that we were created to be a leader, not just another one of the pugnacious bullies of the schoolyard.

Our ultimate strength is an eternal idea, not a gun. The constant lamentations from Washington that Russia has more weapons, that we must arm and arm and arm to protect ourselves from annihilation or subjugation, fails to ask the ultimate question, Arm for what purpose? Ultimate war? This dubious reliance on military strength overlooks the fact that the United States, itself, is contributing mightily to the creation of the dreadful, frightful, dangerous world. We breed distrust by our own distrust.

Not for a minute do I suggest that American sweetness and light will free the world of the warlike tensions, or disarm the Soviet Union, or take away their dreams, if any, of world grandeur. Of course, we must have weapons to protect ourselves against possible aggression. We do need to brace ourselves against some ambitious or frightened opponent who could blow our part of the world away while getting themselves blown away. Our weapons policy should be to deter that. Not for a moment do I suggest that we should disarm unilaterally. But we must find the voice, the will, the intelligence, the faith to stop the arms race.

We must find our unique way to speak with assurance and reassurance to the Soviet people, letting them and the rest of the world clearly understand that we are not warlike, that we do not hate them or fear them. It profits us nothing to cut out grain suplies or pipelines or truck factories. They get these things anyway. We breed more ill will for no useful purpose.

The end mission of the people of the United States is not to build an armed camp to face the other armed camps of the world. And yet that is what we are doing. We can do better than that. We should not be slamming doors in the faces of the Soviet Union and China. We should be promoting massive programs of cultural, commercial, and education exchange, as well as commerce and tourism.

If you accept what I say, you will be criticized by some, as will I, as being "blind to Russia's avowed purpose of world conquest," for ignoring their conquest of Afghanistan, their repression of human rights. Don't worry. You will be right if you understand the best way to protect ourselves and to promote an expansion of freedom, and, indeed, an acceptance of more freedom by Russia, is to act now like free people, confident that we can lead.

We do not need to be a petty, selfish nation seeking our own narrow safety and security. The way we have been going is the least likely to assure safety and security. We are the only great nation which can first extend the hand of friendship, first slacken the bowstring, first give assurances of dedication to real peace.

I do now know where to find the precise path of leadership we should follow in this difficult world. If I did, I couldn't tell you in eighteen minutes. I can only tell you there is one, or many, which can be found by intelligence and faith and self-confidence.

I have mentioned massive exchange programs. That is the first move—to have, ultimately, tens of thousands of citizens conversing and talking and sharing concerns and experiences.

Second, we could utilize, as we have not, the United Nations as a place of true resolution of aggression and conflict. It could also be better used to champion the devices of peace. The United States could make it more effective by taking it more seriously, and by continually insisting that the members live up to the charter.

Third, we could do better in aiming material and technical aid toward people of developing countries and their opportunities, their education, their training, their health, and their hopes, avoiding diversion by the petty dictators, and not invariably linking it to military assistance. World banking, with our encouragement, can give support to development of the human capital throughout the world. I still believe hunger and poverty can be eliminated and that human opportunities can be opened for people in all parts of the world. We have, in our preoccupation with armaments and our participation in conflicts, lost our focus on what the world needs.

Freud's concern about the lack of understanding and comprehension of different cultures as being one of the breeding forces of war might well be overcome now that we have the physical capacity for worldwide satellite communication. This is only one illustration of the creative approaches to peace that your generation might design. Satellites provide a rapidly developing, connecting link that has never before been available for bringing simultaneously to all parts of the world communication, entertainment, education, health information, and conversation. The United States could be the first to foster the now necessary international second language that has been a dream since the time of the Tower of Babel. Several such existing languages, including Esperanto, have never been widely embraced because there has been no compelling reason for people to learn them. Part of the resistance has been the haughty response that English is already the international language. That attitude is one of our problems.

The United States could initiate the promotion of an international second language, which might be known as the "satellite language." The satellite would provide the strong motivation as

well as the means for learning it. In short order the people of all
cultures and tongues could understand it and communicate more
readily. Symbolically, it would tie together the humanity of the
Earth as a people with one destiny. For this to be done, the ener-
getic leadership of a nation would be required. Far better that we
embark on some such venture as this, challenging China, the Soviet Union, the African nations, and others to join with us, as one
of our evidences of leadership, than to spend our time snarling and
bickering about who has what in place to blow up the others.

This is one project. It is the spirit and the attitude that I am
talking about. There are many creative ideas of American leadership—of world conciliation—that you can think of.

America can lead. If you of this age—who do not remember
the two great wars, who do understand the arms race—develop
a determination that America, if we are to avoid nuclear extermination, must move, unafraid, with the confidence of free people,
then history looking back will judge your time as one of the best
of times.

Congratulations and best wishes!

TOLERANCE AND TRUTH IN AMERICA[1]

EDWARD M. KENNEDY[2]

To the surprise of liberals and conservatives alike, on October 3,
1983, Senator Edward M. Kennedy of Massachusetts addressed an audience of 5,000 at Liberty Baptist College in Lynchburg, Virginia, an institution founded by the Reverend Jerry Falwell. The surprise was
occasioned by the fact that the Reverend Falwell, the television evangelist
and founder of the Moral Majority, invited the liberal senator to deliver
an address to the college.

Falwell, whose "Old Time Gospel Hour" is carried by nearly 700 radio and television stations and reaches an audience of 18 million or more
viewers (the statistics are for 1980), organized the Moral Majority in

---

[1]Delivered at 8:00 P.M. in an auditorium on the Liberty Baptist College Campus, Lynchburg, Virginia,
on October 3, 1983.

[2]For biographical note, see Appendix.

1978 with the avowed purpose of electing to office politicians who would serve their conservative cause and defeat those who disagreed with their stand. Moral Majority set out to mobilize from 30 million to 65 million evangelical Christians, many of whom seldom voted, into a potent force at the polls. (See Patricia Roberts Harris's speech, "Political Pluralism and Religious Absolutism," in *Representative American Speeches, 1980-1981,* pp 35-48, for additional background information.) Buoyed by their successes in defeating liberals in the 1978, 1980, and 1982 elections, Moral Majority leaders made Kennedy a target of their attacks because of his prominence among liberals.

The events leading to Kennedy's invitation to speak began with a computer-generated error that inadvertently sent the senator a letter inviting him to join the Moral Majority and help in its work against "ultraliberals such as Ted Kennedy" and including a plastic Moral Majority membership card. When the fact was reported in newspapers, Cal Thomas, communications director for the Moral Majority, sent the senator a facetious note telling him he did not have to surrender the card. As an afterthought, Thomas said that he should stop by at the college for a tour if ever he was in the area. Kennedy replied that he would be delighted to visit and would like to address Liberty Baptist's students while on campus. (*Chronicle of Higher Education,* O. 12, '83, p 4) According to another version, the senator accepted an invitation by Thomas to address the students, and when his acceptance was reported to Falwell "he turned white as a sheet and said 'What!' He said that some of his people thought Ted Kennedy was the Devil incarnate." However, Thomas was able to persuade Falwell that, aside from being a "public relations stroke," having Kennedy on campus would help dispel the idea held by critics of the Moral Majority that its members were intolerant, close-minded bigots. (Phil Gailey, *New York Times,* O. 4, '83, p 7)

So persuaded, Falwell not only sent his private jet plane to Washington to pick up Senator Kennedy, his daughter, and sister, but also played host to a dinner party for the Kennedy and Falwell families preceding the address.

Kennedy delivered his speech at 8:00 P.M. in a multipurpose auditorium building on the Liberty Baptist College campus. His audience consisted of students, faculty, administrators, and residents of Lynchburg. His appearance was billed as the first half of a "liberal-conservative" debate, sponsored by the Political Science Department, in which Representative Jack Kemp would speak for the conservative side the following month. The evening began with a welcome from Falwell and an introduction of the senator by Jerry Combee, chairman of the History and Political Science departments. The address was well covered by media, including the three major television networks, the *New York Times,* the *Washington Post,* the *Los Angeles Times, Time, Newsweek,* and *U. S. News and World Report.*

In advance of his arrival, the college chapter of the Young Americans for Freedom had distributed several hundred leaflets attacking the senator's record on such issues as abortion, the nuclear freeze, and homosexual rights. Before the speech, one student was asked for his thoughts on the event. "Well," he replied, his mind scanning the scriptures for something appropriate, "I guess if Daniel survived the lion's den, Ted Kennedy won't have any trouble here. The Lord locked the jaws of the lions and the college has locked the mouths of the students." (Phil Gailey, *New York Times,* O. 4, '83, p 7) The student was referring to the fact that, to make sure Kennedy was not subjected to treatment that might embarrass the college, Falwell and college administrators had taken the precaution of permitting only junior and senior political science students to ask questions following the speech.

The *Chronicle of Higher Education* reported that Kennedy was received "politely but not warmly by members of his audience." (O. 12, '83, p 3) The *Washington Post* described his reception as "polite but restrained." (O. 4, '83, p 1) *Newsweek* observed that "Kennedy did not trim his rhetoric for the religious right . . . and he was getting applause—for one of the best speeches he has ever given." (O. 17, '83, p 63) Falwell said to Kennedy after the speech, "You might have gotten to a few of them tonight, but I'll get them back." (*Newsweek,* O. 17, '83, p 30)

Kennedy's opening remarks provide an excellent example of a speaker's attempt to overcome the hostility of an unfriendly audience through the use of humor and through this candid admission:

> I know we begin with certain disagreements; I strongly suspect that at the end of the evening some of our disagreements will remain. But I also hope that tonight and in the months and years ahead, we will always respect the right of others to differ.

Later, he attempts to create a favorable attitude by associating his cause with the Constitution and the Founding Fathers.

Senator Kennedy's speech: Let me thank Dr. Jerry Falwell for that generous introduction. I never expected to hear such kind words from him. So, in return, I have an invitation of my own: On January 20, 1985, I hope Dr. Falwell will say a prayer—at the inauguration of the next Democratic president of the United States. Now, Dr. Falwell, I'm not sure exactly how you feel about that. You might not appreciate the president, but the Democrats certainly would appreciate the prayer.

Actually, a number of people in Washington were surprised that I was invited to speak here—and even more surprised when I accepted the invitation. They seem to think that it is easier for a camel to pass through the eye of a needle than for a Kennedy to come to the campus of Liberty Baptist College.

In honor of our meeting, I have asked Dr. Falwell, as your chancellor, to permit all the students an extra hour next Saturday night before curfew. In return, I have promised to watch "The Old Time Gospel Hour" next Sunday morning.

I realize that my visit may be a little controversial. But as many of you have heard, Dr. Falwell recently sent me a membership card in the Moral Majority—and I didn't even apply for it. I wonder if that means I am a member in good standing.

This is, of course, a nonpolitical speech—which is probably best under the circumstances.

Since I am not a candidate for president, it certainly would be inappropriate to ask for your support in this election—and probably inaccurate to thank you for it in the last one.

I have come here to discuss my beliefs about faith and country, tolerance and truth in America. I know we begin with certain disagreements; I strongly suspect that at the end of the evening some of our disagreements will remain. But I also hope that tonight and in the months and years ahead, we will always respect the right of others to differ—that we will view ourselves with a sense of perspective and a sense of humor. After all, in the New Testament, even the disciples had to be taught to look first to the beam in their own eyes, and only then to the mote in their neighbor's eye.

I am mindful of that counsel. I am an American and a Catholic; I love my country and treasure my faith. But I do not assume that my conception of patriotism or policy is invariably correct—or that my convictions about religion should command any greater respect than any other faith in this pluralistic society. I believe there surely is such a thing as truth, but who among us can claim a monopoly on it?

There are those who do, and their own words testify to their intolerance. For example, because the Moral Majority has worked with members of different denominations, one fundamentalist group has denounced Dr. Falwell for hastening the ecumenical church and for "yoking together with Roman Catholics, Mormons, and others." I am relieved that Dr. Falwell does not regard that as a sin—and on this issue, he himself has become the target of narrow prejudice. When people agree on public policy, they ought to be able to work together, even while they worship in diverse ways. For truly we are all yoked together as Americans—and the yoke is the happy one of individual freedom and mutual respect.

But in saying that, we cannot and should not turn aside from a deeper, more pressing question—which is whether and how religion should influence government. A generation ago, a presidential candidate had to prove his independence of undue religious influence in public life, and he had to do so partly at the insistence of evangelical protestants. John Kennedy said at that time, "I believe in an America where there is no (religious) bloc voting of any kind." Only twenty years later, another candidate was appealing to an evangelical meeting as a religious bloc. Ronald Reagan said to fifteen thousand evangelicals at The Roundtable in Dallas, "I know that you can't endorse me. I want you to know that I endorse you and what you are doing."

To many Americans, that pledge was a sign and a symbol of a dangerous breakdown in the separation of church and state. Yet this principle, as vital as it is, is not a simplistic and rigid command. Separation of church and state cannot mean an absolute separation between moral principles and political power. The challenge today is to recall the origin of the principle, to define its purpose, and refine its application to the politics of the present.

The founders of our nation had long and bitter experience with the state as both the agent and the adversary of particular religious views. In colonial Maryland, Catholics paid a double land tax and in Pennsylvania they had to list their names on a public roll—an ominous precursor of the first Nazi laws against the Jews. And Jews in turn faced discrimination in all the thirteen original colonies. Massachusetts exiled Roger Williams and his congregation for contending that civil government had no right to enforce the Ten Commandments. Virginia harassed Baptist preachers and also established a religious test for public service, writing into the law that no "Popish followers" could hold any office.

But during the revolution, Catholics, Jews and nonconformists all rallied to the cause and fought valiantly for the American commonwealth—for John Winthrop's "city upon a hill." Afterwards, when the Constitution was ratified and then amended, the framers gave freedom for all religion—and from any established religion—the very first place in the Bill of Rights.

Indeed the framers themselves professed very different faiths—and in the case of Benjamin Franklin, hardly any at all. Washington was an Episcopalian, Jefferson a deist, and Adams a Calvinist. And although he had earlier opposed toleration, John Adams later contributed to the building of Catholic churches—and so did George Washington. Thomas Jefferson said his proudest achievement was not the presidency, or writing the Declaration of Independence, but drafting the Virginia Statute of Religious Freedom. He stated the vision of the first Americans and the First Amendment very clearly: "The God who gave us life gave us liberty at the same time."

The separation of church and state can sometimes be frustrating for women and men of deep religious faith. They may be tempted to misuse government in order to impose a value which they cannot persuade others to accept. But once we succumb to that temptation, we step onto a slippery slope where everyone's freedom is at risk. Those who favor censorship should recall that one of the first books ever burned was the first English translation of the Bible. As President Eisenhower warned in 1953, "Don't join the bookburners . . . the right to say ideas, the right to record them and the right to have them accessible to others is unquestioned—or this isn't America." And if that right is denied, at some future day the torch can be turned against any other book or any other belief. Let us never forget, today's Moral Majority could become tomorrow's persecuted minority.

The danger is as great now as when the founders of the nation first saw it. In 1789 their fear was of factional strife among dozens of denominations. Today there are hundreds—and perhaps thousands—of faiths and millions of Americans who are outside any fold. Pluralism obviously does not and cannot mean that all of them are right; but it does mean that there are areas where government cannot and should not decide what it is wrong to believe, to think, to read, and to do. As Professor Laurence Tribe, one of the nation's leading constitutional scholars has written, "Law in a nontheocratic state cannot measure religious truth"—nor can the state impose it.

The real transgression occurs when religion wants government to tell citizens how to live uniquely personal parts of their lives. The failure of Prohibition proves the futility of such an attempt when a majority or even a substantial minority happens to disagree. Some questions may be inherently individual ones or people may be sharply divided about whether they are. In such cases—cases like Prohibition and abortion—the proper role of religion is to appeal to the conscience of the individual, not the coercive power of the state.

But there are other questions which are inherently public in nature, which we must decide together as a nation, and where religion and religious values can and should speak to our common conscience. The issue of nuclear war is a compelling example. It is a moral issue; it will be decided by government, not by each individual; and to give any effect to the moral values of their creed, people of faith must speak directly about public policy. The Catholic bishops and the Reverend Billy Graham have every right to stand for the nuclear freeze—and Dr. Falwell has every right to stand against it.

There must be standards for the exercise of such leadership, so that the obligations of belief will not be debased into an opportunity for mere political advantage. But to take a stand at all when a question is both properly public and truly moral is to stand in a long and honored tradition. Many of the great evangelists of the 1800s were in the forefront of the abolitionist movement. In our own time, the Reverend William Sloane Coffin challenged the morality of the war in Vietnam. Pope John XXIII renewed the Gospel's call to social justice. And Dr. Martin Luther King, Jr., who was the greatest prophet of this century, awakened our national conscience to the evil of racial segregation.

Their words have blessed our world. And who now wishes they had all been silent? Who would bid Pope John Paul to quiet his voice about the oppression in eastern Europe; the violence in Central America; or the crying needs of the landless, the hungry, and those who are tortured in so many of the dark political prisons of our time?

President Kennedy, who said that "no religious body should seek to impose its will," also urged religious leaders to state their views and give their commitment when the public debate involved ethical issues. In drawing the line between imposed will and essential witness, we keep church and state separate—and at the same time, we recognize that the city of God should speak to the civic duties of men and women.

There are four tests which draw that line and define the difference.

First, we must respect the integrity of religion itself. People of conscience should be careful how they deal in the word of their Lord. In our own history, religion has been falsely invoked to sanction prejudice and even slavery, to condemn labor unions and public spending for the poor. I believe that the prophecy "the poor you have always with you" is an indictment, not a commandment. I respectfully suggest that God has taken no position on the Department of Education—and that a balanced budget constitutional amendment is a matter for economic analysis, not heavenly appeals.

Religious values cannot be excluded from every public issue—but not every public issue involves religious values. And how ironic it is when those very values are denied in the name of religion. For example, we are sometimes told that it is wrong to feed the hungry, but that mission is an explicit mandate given to us in the twenty-fifth chapter of Matthew.

Second, we must respect the independent judgments of conscience. Those who proclaim moral and religious values can offer counsel, but they should not casually treat a position on a public issue as a test of fealty to faith. Just as I disagree with the Catholic bishops on tuition tax credits, which I oppose, so other Catholics can and do disagree with the hierarchy, on the basis of honest conviction, on the question of the nuclear freeze.

Thus, the controversy about the Moral Majority arises not only from its views, but from its name, which in the minds of many seems to imply that only one set of public policies is moral—and only one majority can possibly be right. Similarly, people are and should be perplexed when the religious lobbying group Christian Voice publishes a morality index of congressional voting records, which judges the morality of senators by their attitude toward Zimbabwe and Taiwan.

Let me offer another illustration. Dr. Falwell has written, and I quote, "To stand against Israel is to stand against God." Now there is no one in the Senate who has stood more firmly for Israel than I have. Yet I do not doubt the faith of those on the other side. Their error is not one of religion, but of policy, and I hope to persuade them that they are wrong in terms of both America's interest and the justice of Israel's cause.

Respect for conscience is most in jeopardy—and the harmony of our diverse society is most at risk—when we reestablish, directly or indirectly, a religious test for public office. That relic of the colonial era, which is specifically prohibited in the Constitution, has reappeared in recent years. After the last election, the Reverend James Robison warned President Reagan not to surround himself, as presidents before him had, "with the counsel of the ungodly." I utterly reject any such standard for any position anywhere in public service. Two centuries ago, the victims were Catholics and Jews. In the 1980s, the victims could be atheists; in some other day or decade, they could be the members of the Thomas Road Baptist Chruch. Indeed, in 1976 I regarded it as unworthy and un-American when some people said or hinted that Jimmy Carter should not be president because he was a born again Christian. We must never judge the fitness of individuals to govern on the basis of where they worship, whether they follow Christ or Moses, whether they are called "born again" or "ungodly." Where it is right to apply moral values to public life, let all of us avoid the temptation to be self-righteous and absolutely certain of ourselves. And if that temptation ever comes, let us recall Winston Churchill's humbling description of an intolerant and inflexible colleague: "There but for the grace of God—goes God."

Third, in applying religious values, we must respect the integrity of public debate. In that debate, faith is no substitute for facts. Critics may oppose the nuclear freeze for what they regard as moral reasons. They have every right to argue that any negotiation with the Soviets is wrong, or that any accommodation with them sanctions their crimes, or that no agreement can be good enough and therefore all agreements only increase the chance of war. I do not believe that, but it surely does not violate the standard of fair public debate to say it. What does violate that standard, what the opponents of the nuclear freeze have no right to do, is to assume that they are infallible—and so any argument against the freeze will do, whether it is false or true.

The nuclear freeze proposal is not unilateral, but bilateral—with equal restraints on the United States and the Soviet Union.

The nuclear freeze does not require that we trust the Russians, but demands full and effective verification.

The nuclear freeze does not concede a Soviet lead in nuclear weapons, but recognizes that human beings in each great power already have in their fallible hands the overwhelming capacity to remake into a pile of radioactive rubble the Earth which God has made.

There is no morality in the mushroom cloud. The black rain of nuclear ashes will fall alike on the just and unjust. And then it will be too late to wish that we had done the real work of this atomic age—which is to seek a world that is neither Red nor dead.

I am perfectly prepared to debate the nuclear freeze on policy grounds or moral ones. But we should not be forced to discuss phantom issues or false charges. They only deflect us from the urgent task of deciding how best to prevent a planet divided from becoming a planet destroyed.

And it does not advance the debate to contend that the arms race is more divine punishment than human problem, or that in any event, the final days are near. As Pope John said two decades ago, at the opening of the Second Vatican Council, "We must beware of those who burn with zeal, but are not endowed with much sense . . . we must disagree with the prophets of doom, who are always forecasting disasters, as though the end of the Earth was at hand." The message which echoes across the years since then is clear: The Earth is still here; and if we wish to keep it, a prophecy of doom is no alternative to a policy of arms control.

Fourth, and finally, we must respect the motives of those who exercise their right to disagree. We sorely test our ability to live together if we too readily question each other's integrity. It may be harder to restrain our feelings when moral principles are at stake, for they go to the deepest wellsprings of our being. But the more our feelings diverge, the more deeply felt they are, the greater is our obligation to grant the sincerity and essential decency of our fellow citizens on the other side.

Those who favor E.R.A. are not "antifamily" or "blasphemers" and their purpose is not "an attack on the Bible." Rather we believe this is the best way to fix in our national firmament the ideal that not only all men, but all people, are created equal. Indeed, my mother—who strongly favors E.R.A.—would be surprised to hear that she is antifamily. For my part, I think of the amendment's opponents as wrong on the issue, but not as lacking in moral character.

I could multiply the instances of name-calling, sometimes on both sides. Dr. Falwell is not a "warmonger" and "liberal clergymen" are not, as the Moral Majority suggested in a recent letter, equivalent to "Soviet sympathizers." The critics of official prayer in public schools are not "Pharisees"; many of them are both civil libertarians and believers, who think that families should pray more at home with their children and attend church and synagogue more faithfully. And people are not "sexist" because they stand against abortion; they are not "murderers" because they believe in free choice. Nor does it help anyone's cause to shout such epithets or try to shout a speaker down, which is what happened last April when Dr. Falwell was hissed and heckled at Harvard. So I am doubly grateful for your courtesy here today. That was not Harvard's finest hour, but I am happy to say that the loudest applause from the Harvard audience came in defense of Dr. Falwell's right to speak.

In short, I hope for an America where neither fundamentalist nor humanist will be a dirty word, but a fair description of the different ways in which people of goodwill look at life and into their own souls.

I hope for an America where no president, no public official, and no individual will ever be deemed a greater or lesser American because of religious doubt—or religious belief.

I hope for an America where we can all contend freely and vigorously, but where we will treasure and guard those standards of civility which alone make this nation safe for both democracy and diversity.

Twenty years ago this fall, in New York City, President Kennedy met for the last time with a Protestant assembly. The atmosphere had been transformed since his earlier address during the

1960 campaign to the Houston Ministerial Association. He had spoken there to allay suspicions about his Catholicism, and to answer those who claimed that on the day of his baptism, he was somehow disqualified from becoming president. His speech in Houston and then his election drove that prejudice from the center of our national life. Now, three years later, in November 1963, he was appearing before the Protestant Council of New York City to reaffirm what he regarded as some fundamental truths. On that occasion, John Kennedy said, "The family of man is not limited to a single race or religion, to a single city or country. . . . The family of man is nearly 3 billion strong. Most of its members are not white—and most of them are not Christian." And as President Kennedy reflected on that reality, he restated an ideal for which he had lived his life, that "the members of this family should be at peace with one another."

That ideal shines across all the generations of our history and all the ages of our faith, carrying with it the most ancient dream. For as the apostle Paul wrote long ago in Romans, "If it be possible, as much as it lieth in you, live peaceably with all men."

I believe it is possible; the choice lies within us. As fellow citizens, let us live peaceably with each other; as fellow human beings, let us strive to live peaceably with men and women everywhere. Let that be our prayer—yours and mine—for ourselves, for our country, and for all the world.

THE LONG-TERM WORLDWIDE BIOLOGICAL CONSEQUENCES OF NUCLEAR WAR[1]
Donald Kennedy[2]

In his column in the *Christian Science Monitor,* veteran journalist Richard L. Strout wrote early in 1984:

[1]Delivered to the Conference on the Long-Term Biological Consequences of Nuclear War in a meeting room at the Sheraton Washington Hotel, Washington, D.C., on the afternoon of October 31, 1983.

[2]For biographical note, see Appendix.

As a newspaper reporter you get used to all sorts of funny assignments and mine have included politics, debates, and wars, but the most arresting, I believe, was a conference this winter of noted scientists (Oct. 31-Nov. 1) on "The World After Nuclear War." It was at a conventional hotel; the uniformed doorman let us in at the revolving door; the half hundred or so celebrities looked quiet, normal, and everyday enough, only they were forecasting that civilization might end. Not merely civilization, but all life on planet Earth. They were serious about it. How do you cover a story like that?

They had satellite images projected on triple screens coming from Moscow with translated statements from members of the Soviet Academy of Scientists. Four Soviet and four U.S. scientists asserted that "a nuclear attack would be suicide for the nation that launched it, even if there were no retaliatory strike."

The U.S. scientists were quiet and matter-of-fact. They were reporting on studies that had been made in the last year or so. They were authorities like Carl Sagan of Cornell University and Donald Kennedy, president of Stanford University. . . . Maybe these experts knew what they were talking about; maybe it was exaggerated.

But the difficulty for the ordinary listener was adjustment: how to go from this creepy hearing into the everyday world. . . . How is man supposed to keep pace with this strange new world? (Ja. 6, '84, p 15)

Strout's was just one more report on the growing concern throughout the globe of the possibility of nuclear annihilation. In the United States in the early 1980s, this fear was reflected in the dramatic increase of support for a nuclear freeze among scientists, physicians, religious leaders, and other concerned citizens. In 1983, 13,000 physicists called for a halt to the nuclear arms race and Roman Catholic bishops in the United States by a vote of 238 to 9 called upon Catholics to help rid the world of nuclear weapons, while Protestant clergymen, artists, musicians, medical practitioners, and members of other professions established organizations designed specifically to try to prevent nuclear holocaust.

Until October 1983, antinuclear groups had emphasized the immediate widespread devastation and chaos that would result from nuclear war. However, the Conference on the Long-Term Biological Consequences of Nuclear War introduced a new concept, the frightening prospect of "nuclear winter." The conference, attended by more than a hundred physicists, biologists, and atmospheric scientists, presented the findings of a two-year study of the effects of a nuclear holocaust on the ecosphere as a whole. The study's principal new finding was that in a nuclear war in which five thousand megatons of explosive power was released (less than half the explosive power of the world's nuclear arsenals), "dust from the explosions and soot from the world's burning cities and forests would create a blanket over the whole earth, first over the Northern Hemisphere, where it was assumed that the explosions would occur, but then also over the Southern Hemisphere." This blanket would "block as much as ninety-five percent of the sunlight from reaching the ground, and this would reduce temperatures, even in summer, to thirteen degrees below zero, or even lower." (*New Yorker,* N. 21, '83, p 41) The scientists were telling the world—not for the first time, but with more compelling supporting evidence than ever before—that our species is in imminent peril of extinction in a nuclear holocaust.

Keynote speaker at the conference was the distinguished president of Stanford University and biologist Donald Kennedy. In his address, Kennedy stressed as a central theme that in the development of knowledge about the possible consequences of nuclear war, much of what we know is a result of erratic, accidental, and unplanned revelations, not systematic study. "We must learn to expect the unexpected."

Dr. Kennedy delivered his remarks at the special conference held in a meeting room of the Sheraton Washington Hotel on the afternoon of October 31, 1983, to an audience of some one hundred scientists and media representatives.

Although Kennedy's address and the significant findings of the conference eventually found their way into the debate over a nuclear freeze, the mass media gave them scant attention at the time. The *New Yorker* observed:

> As far as we know, no major newspaper in this country put the story at the top of its front page. (*The Washington Post,* to its credit, did run it on the front page, though at the bottom.) ABC gave it a minute and forty seconds, well into the evening news. The NBC Nightly news mentioned it briefly near the end of the broadcast. The CBS Evening News had nothing. The world had just been given the most authoritative warning it has ever had that its doom is an urgent and present danger, but the viewers of this news program never heard a thing about it. . . . Nor did the political community respond. The President had nothing to say. Congress was mute. (*New Yorker,* N. 21, '83, p 41)

Donald Kennedy's speech: There is a convention that applies to all so-called keynote speeches, and it requires that I begin by telling you how happy I am to be here. Actually, I am not happy at all; ours is *anything* but a happy subject. In the first place, the consequences of nuclear war are dire indeed, and it can be no great pleasure to assemble for the purpose of telling people that they are even more dire that they have been told. Furthermore, there is unfortunately no *simple* way out of the problems posed for us by the nuclear arms problem—though some people insist that there is. Instead, there is a continuing need to deal with danger, and to struggle with a national security policy that seems terribly refractory to rational design. It is against this depressing background that we meet to discuss the long-range biological consequences of nuclear war.

Before beginning, I want to acquaint you with some qualifications I *lack* for my role of introducer, and then announce one or two convictions. I am not a veteran of the antinuclear movement, nor am I experienced in matters of arms control and disarmament. I am, moreover, happy to concede to others' technical mastery of the inexact discipline of nuclear strategy, the technological and game-theoretic background of detente. As to convictions, I must tell you that I hold the old-fashioned belief that we shall continue to require a defense establishment in this country, that whether we like it or not nuclear weapons will continue for some time to play an integral role in our national security strategy and that of others, and that, accordingly, we shall need to continue efforts to understand such weapons if we are ultimately to control them and deal sensibly with one another.

Those disclosures should convince you, I would think, that I am neither a likely technical resource for an arms control conference nor a promising candidate for cheerleader at a peace rally. Fortunately, unless I have been seriously misled, this meeting is *neither* of the above. Rather, it is an occasion for reporting some serious scientific analyses of the consequences of nuclear war. And to introduce *that* subject, I do have one perspective that I think may be relevant. During a period of service in government, I was head of a federal regulatory agency much concerned with the hazards associated with toxic chemicals, and more generally with the consequences of premature introduction of new technologies. During those years, and in the time immediately preceding and following them, I found myself deeply involved in the business of risk assessment: evaluating the consequences of the use of agricultural chemicals, setting tolerances for contamination by industrial pollutants, estimating the effect of food additives, and so forth. In that role I worried a good deal about how to estimate risks, even under circumstances in which the data are necessarily incomplete.

I think three lessons from that experience are applicable to the subject matter of this conference. First, one of the great policy challenges in risk evaluation is to formulate the soundest possible decisions in the face of large uncertainties. To meet it successfully, it is essential that one be as aware of what one does not know as one is of what one knows.

That challenge is made enormously more difficult by public attitudes about risk. That is the second lesson: people are ambivalent about risk. We will devote enormous personal and social resources to the saving of an identified life in danger, but we will appropriate very much less to confer a statistically much larger protection of unidentified individuals in the general population. We will enthusiastically pass laws that avert very small, involuntary risks; but we will quickly repeal them if they curtail personal freedoms. In short, we will spend a great deal to get little Kathy out of the well she has fallen into, but we have trouble lowering the speed limit, or even banning some cancer-causing substances if people like them enough.

The ambivalence becomes even more marked when probability and severity of risk are considered separately. There is a difference between attitudes toward modest, broadly distributed statistical risk—like extra cancer deaths due to an environmental toxin—and low-probability risks with widespread disastrous consequences—like a nuclear weapons exchange. Although we are only beginning to develop a science of human attitudes about risk aversion, the results so far suggest that people treat low-probability events with highly negative consequences in a way that departs significantly from the choices we would predict under standard "expected utility" theories. Such research may eventually have something quite useful to say about public attitudes on nuclear war. And it may be even *more* important with respect to the crucial matter of how the decision-makers, in those awful last moments, will be making their decisions.

The third and final lesson I should like to take from the more conventional domain of risk assessment has to do with the time scale on which we recognize consequences. Here, the analogy from the world of toxic substances is actually quite exact.

When the postwar revolution in industrial chemistry first began to generate concern about the human risks associated with toxic substances, the worry was almost entirely confined to immediate or "acute" effects. The first toxicological testing programs devised to evaluate these hazards were the so-called LD_{50} tests, which measured the amount of some compound that would constitute a lethal dose for 50 percent of the organisms employed in the test. Later on, it was gradually recognized that long-term, "chronic" effects—the potential to cause cancer, or to make one more prone to heart disease and stroke, or to produce birth defects—were substantially more important, and quite impossible to measure using the conventional short-term tests. Subsequent experience has confirmed that these chronic hazards are much larger worries than the acute ones, and today we would not even consider evaluating the safety of a new chemical without undertaking long-term experiments to evaluate its carcinogenic potential, the possibility that it might produce effects on the fetus, and so on.

That is where we now stand with respect to nuclear war: just beginning to understand the long-term effects—just beginning to understand the environmental equivalents of cancer, heart disease, and stroke.

I now want to turn to a central theme in the development of our knowledge about these chronic consequences of nuclear war. *It is the erratic and accidental character of our discoveries.* What we now understand, and it is certainly much less than we wish we understood, we have come to know largely as a result of unplanned revelation, not systematic study. As a result of the weapons detonated over Japanese cities at the end of World War II, we came to a grim reckoning of the acute effects: the devastation caused by the primary blast and by shock waves and the human impact of local radioactivity. But it was not until the tests at Bikini Atoll in 1954 that we learned of the dangers of distant contamination by radioactive fallout following atmospheric transport. Even now, nearly three decades later, we find ourselves surprised by the significance and range of this phenomenon. For example, the celebrated escape of radiation from the damaged reactor at Three Mile Island, an incident that generated widespread concern and hundreds of pages of congressional testimony, deposited less than one-tenth the amount of radiation (as ^{131}I) as had been deposited in the same part of Pennsylvania by fallout from the cloud produced by a single bomb test in China two years earlier. Other de-

layed and accidental revelations have included the Van Allen belt
effects, the electromagnetic pulse (EMP) and its effects on elec-
tronic communications, and, more recently the injection of NO_x
into the ozone layer. In reviewing these events, one observer commented as follows: "Uncertainty is one of the major conclusions
. . as the haphazard and unpredicted derivation of many of our
discoveries emphasizes." Those words were not written by an academic critic of government policy; they came from a present un-
dersecretary of defense in the Reagan administration.

The conclusion is clear, and it is not very comforting. *We must
learn to expect the unexpected.* This conference places us squarely
in the midst of another and even more significant set of revelations
about the chronic risks associated with nuclear war. In an important sense, the genealogy of this conference begins with the extraordinary work of the organization called Physicians for Social
Responsibility. They made the first quantitative evaluations of the
medical circumstances that would prevail immediately following
a nuclear exchange, and demonstrated the inadequacy of present
medical institutions, programs, and plans to deal with those circumstances. Their revelations raised serious questions about the
entire structure of civil defense preparedness, and cast grave doubt
over the confident assertions of defense planners that recovery following a nuclear attack could be complete in a relatively small
number of years.

The results presented in this conference summarize more serious scientific analyses of the long-range ecological and climatolog-
ical consequences of nuclear weapons exchanges. Ecological risks,
in particular, were originally given remarkably short shrift in the
evaluation of nuclear strategies. Early studies done under Department of Defense support (for example, that by Mitchell) consisted
of little more than analogies with natural catastrophe. The summary conclusion from Mitchell's Rand study will illustrate the
genre: "The large-scale damage due to fire, drought, flood, and
other things has already presented the world with problems of reconstruction and reconstitution of biotic communities which are
similar to those envisioned in the post-attack environment." How
that similarity might provide a useful assessment of real risks is
left to the reader.

It is, of course, not entirely fair to criticize these earlier studies; our present view has become both more explicit and more somber, for a variety of reasons. First, some specific recent discoveries (for example, the sensitivity of some natural ecosystems to acid rain, and the paticular sensitivity of plants to radioactivity and temperature) have tended to worsen the estimates. Second, our general view of the complexity and delicacy of ecological systems has changed a great deal over the past two decades; we now understand their vulnerability in a much more thoroughgoing way. Finally, the numbers and the accuracy of our weapons systems have changed in ways that may increase the highly destructive character of weapons exchanges.

How perplexing it is, then, that even today we are being offered reassurances based upon much earlier estimates. A pamphlet still being distributed by emergency agencies was prepared in 1979 by the Defense Civil Preparedness Agency. In it, the following conclusion appears—precisely echoing the metaphor of the 1963 report: "No logical weight of nuclear attack could induce gross changes in the balance of nature that approach in type or degree the ones that human civilization has already produced." Even if it were true that the magnitude of ecological change that could result from the largest plausible nuclear attack is less than that produced by human civilization over all of history, there is surely a vast difference between the impact of large changes wrought in milliseconds and ones accomplished over millennia.

Elsewhere, the same pamphlet quotes from a 1963 National Academy of Sciences study the comforting news that "ecological imbalances that would make normal life impossible are not to be expected." There is no mention whatever of a much more recent National Academy of Sciences study on the long-term worldwide effects of multiple nuclear weapons detonations. This latter report was issued in 1975, four years *before* the disaster agency's pamphlet was prepared. Its conclusions are much harsher, as one might expect: the effects of nitrous oxides on the ozone layer had been recognized, and the prospects for climatic change had been taken more seriously into account. Yet the more recent information was bypassed. We ought to worry whenever obsolete data are driving public policy choices.

By themselves, the newer ecological estimates give substantial cause for greater concern. But I think it is fair to say that the most striking new information presented at this conference, and indeed the most potentially disturbing of all of the chronic effects of nuclear war so far described, is the prospect of major climatic consequences. Those consequences are so profound that they could dwarf all of the other long-range effects so far described.

This new view results in part from a new general paradigm in scientific thinking about the processes that have influenced the Earth's history and shaped its present form. In the eighteenth and early nineteenth centuries, major landforms were thought to have resulted from catastrophic processes visited upon the Earth and its occupants by an angry Maker. A major revolution against this view, led by the British geologist Charles Lyell, recognized the importance of such gradual processes as erosion, sedimentation, and reef-building, and substituted for the catastrophic view one based upon a doctrine of uniformitarianism. Today the earth sciences are in the middle of a second revolution, triggered by the remarkable discoveries of plate tectonics; and the emphasis has moved back toward more dramatic events. Increasingly, it is recognized that major discontinuous interventions such as volcanic eruptions and asteroid collisions may have had profound effects on the history of the Earth and of the life on it. A particularly controversial hypothesis, for example, is that an asteroid collision with the Earth 65 million years ago and the long-lived atmospheric dust cloud it produced led to climatic changes that caused the massive extinctions at the end of the Cretaceous age. When it was first announced, the notion that the dinosaurs might have died in the dark evoked great skepticism from my fellow biologists; although they may be right, it is widely recognized that significant events of the same kind have occurred in historic time as the result of volcanic eruptions. "Years without summer" in ancient records have been associated in time with glacial deposits of acid rain, for example, and more contemporary meteorological vagaries have been associated with eruptions like that of El Chincon in Mexico, eighteen months ago.

Findings such as these have made us much more conscious of the sensitivity of world climate to sudden perturbations. It has been known for some time that nuclear explosions can inject dust and aerosol into long-term circulation in the upper atmosphere. Recent calculations indicate that large-scale fires will add a synergistic effect, supplying additional particulates and adding substantially to the convective forces that distribute material into the circulation of the upper atmosphere. This new information has made real for the very first time the prospect that changes in temperature and ambient light, lasting for one or several seasons in the Northern Hemisphere, could result from a major nuclear exchange. It is a prospect of alarming magnitude.

Taken together, all this information *should* signal a major shift in the way in which we as citizens evaluate our risks and the way in which our national strategists should view them. No longer is it acceptable to think of the *sequelae* of nuclear war in terms of minutes, day, or even months. That would be like evaluating a toxic chemical, in this day and age, in terms of what it did to one after five minutes. What we have learned from the things biologists and atmospheric physicists are telling us today is that the proper time scale is *years,* and that the processes to which we must look are unfamiliar both in kind and in scale. They show that the risk estimates on which our strategists have been working and citing to our citizens are disturbingly optimistic.

I want to turn before closing to one other aspect of risk analysis. It is one I mentioned briefly earlier: the notion of "rationality" on the part of decision-makers in confronting questions of probability and severity of risk. Not only are there reasons to doubt that decision-makers confronted with risks of great severity and low probability behave according to rational, utilitarian models of choice; there are also explicit historical precedents for believing that they are going to behave in more political—and human— ways than the "rational actor" model would suggest. In his splendid book, *The Essence of Decision,* Graham Allison looks at the management by the United States Government of the Cuban missile crisis in 1962 from the perspective of different behavioral models. On reading it, one cannot escape the conclusion that no chief of state, no government official, no senior military officer behaves like a "rational actor" in making decisions when the fate of nations and the world hangs in the balance. Bureaucratic structures, political allegiances, background—as well as the other behavioral nonlinearities we are just beginning to probe—play large roles. Yet the structure of military preparedness and the strategic balance are built on the expectation of rational response and rational counterresponse. Rationality will be especially hard to conserve in the early stages of nuclear conflict, where uncertainty and the need for rapid decisions dominate. That is why it seems so unlikely to experienced military leaders as well as to others that a nuclear war can ever remain limited.

Risk assessment ought to proceed, in any event, under worst-case assumptions. That is why the scenarios used by the panels in this conference, like most others, involve the detonation of substantial proportions of the world's nuclear stockpile. But there is an additional reason as well, and that is the likelihood that in the real decision-making context of nuclear combat, it will be so difficult to confine retaliation and response that the *expected course* of such a conflict is to proceed without limit.

I want, finally, to talk a little about what is new and what is not in the presentations you will hear today and tomorrow. It is highly significant that a large group of distinguished biologists has reached a thoughtful consensus on the ecological consequences of nuclear war. (You may not know how difficult it is for biologists, *especially* distinguished ones, to agree on anything.) The group working on atmospheric and climatic effects, in its companion report, raises some new and chilling possibilities with respect to these aspects of the nuclear aftermath. But as I have tried to illustrate, these findings are part of an orderly process in the evolution of scientific thought through which we have gradually refocused our attention from the immediate and obvious to the more long-term and complex *sequelae*. That transition also moves us into a zone in which the effects are potentially even more serious, yet much more difficult to estimate with accuracy. Indeed, the history of our development of nuclear knowledge, as well as the complexity of many of the longer-range effects that will be discussed here, suggest that uncertainty ought be a thematic warning to the policy planners. What our most thoughtful projections show is that a major nuclear exchange will have, among its plausible effects, the greatest biological and physical disruptions of this planet in its last

65 million years—a period more than thirty thousand times longer than the time that has elapsed since the birth of Christ and more than one hundred times the lifespan of our species so far. That assessment of prospective risk needs to form a background for everyone who bears responsibility for national security decisions, here and elsewhere.

Just as there is continuity between today's findings and the outcomes of earlier scientific work, I would emphasize that there is continuity also between the views of the scientists you will be hearing today and those of their distinguished colleagues who are not here. I want to close by stressing the latter, since it is sometimes so easy to dismiss bad news by mistrusting the messenger. Earlier projections of the long-range effects of nuclear war, based on then-available information, were made in 1975 by the National Academy of Sciences and in 1979 by the Congressional Office of Technology Assessment. The academy, which was chartered by Abraham Lincoln to give advice to the United States government on scientific matters, consists of nearly thirteen hundred of America's most distinguished scientists. In addition to the 1975 study on long-term effects, it now has under way an analysis of atmospheric and climatic consequences, which we all hope will extend and draw further attention to the problems to be described next by Professor Sagan. As a consequence of such efforts, the membership of the academy, a year ago this past April, passed an unprecedented resolution—unprecedented in that it overcame a rather characteristic academy caution on such matters. Although this is a conference devoted to scientific findings and *not* to policy recommendations, I do want you to know the judgment reached by my academy colleagues on this matter, so I shall close by quoting the National Academy of Sciences Resolution on Nuclear War and Arms Control:

—Whereas nuclear war is an unprecedented threat to humanity;

—Whereas a general nuclear war could kill hundreds of millions and destroy civilization as we know it;

—Whereas any use of nuclear weapons, including use in so-called "limited wars," would very likely escalate to general nuclear war;

—Whereas science offers no prospect of effective defense against nuclear war and mutual destruction;

—Whereas the proliferation of nuclear weapons to additional countries with unstable governments in areas of high tension would substantially increase the risk of nuclear war;

—Whereas there has been no progress for over two years toward achieving limitations and reductions in strategic arms, either through ratification of SALT II or the resumption of negotiation on strategic nuclear arms;

Be it therefore resolved that the National Academy of Sciences calls on the President and Congress of the United States, and their counterparts in the Soviet Union and other countries which have a similar stake in these vital matters;

—To intensify substantially, without preconditions and with a sense of urgency, efforts to achieve an equitable and verifiable agreement between the United States and the Soviet Union and other countries which have a similar stake in these vital matters;

—To take all practical actions that could reduce the risk of nuclear way by accident or miscalculation;

—To take all practical measures to inhibit the further proliferation of nuclear weapons to additional countries;

—To continue to observe all existing arms control agreements, including SALT II; and

—To avoid military doctrines that treat nuclear explosives as ordinary weapons of war.

1984 AND 2001: A NEW YEAR'S RESOLUTION[1]

CARL E. SAGAN[2]

On New Year's Eve, December 31, 1983, one of America's most distinguished scientists, Dr. Carl E. Sagan, delivered an address to an extraordinary meeting. The speaker, a Pulitzer Prize winner and author

[1]Delivered on New Year's Eve, December 31, 1983, at the Cathedral of St. John the Divine in New York City.
[2]For biographical note, see Appendix.

of more than a dozen books and 400 papers and articles, is probably this country's best-known scientist as a result of his Emmy and Peabody award-winning television program, "Cosmos," which became the most widely watched series in the history of American public television.

The unusual occasion of his address was a "Concert for Peace" at the Cathedral of St. John the Divine in New York City. The performance was part of a series of free public concerts, emphasizing united efforts for world peace. An audience, estimated at between twelve thousand and fifteen thousand people, attended the concert, which featured the distinguished musical artists Frederica Von Stade, William Warfield, Caroline Stoessinger, and Dora Schwarzberg, with Leonard Bernstein conducting the Soviet Emigré Orchestra in a program of Haydn and Bach.

The audience consisted of a broad cross-section of New Yorkers, from senior citizens to teen-agers. Dr. Sagan delivered his address during the concert, which began at 7:30 P.M. He was introduced by the Very Reverend James Parks Morton, dean of the cathedral, who spoke briefly about the purposes of the "Concerts for Peace."

Sagan's topic was the long-term consequences of nuclear war. Less than two months earlier, he had been one of two principal speakers (along with Stanford University President Donald Kennedy, whose address appears on pp. 63–75 at a special conference of forty biologists and physicists on the consequences of nuclear war. The speech by Dr. Sagan on New Year's Eve was a shorter version of his remarks at the conference.

The standing-room-only audience on a night when many persons celebrate at private parties was considered remarkable and was interpreted by the sponsors of the event as reflecting the depth of interest in world peace efforts.

Carl E. Sagan's speech: There was once a time when humans were newly evolved, when all life on the planet was in a nearly perfect ecological harmony, and when the uranium was still in the rocks. (Doubtless there was music then because all human cultures make music, but it is unlikely that the music then was as lovely as the music we have heard and are about to hear tonight.) If anyone thought about such things then, the future must have seemed bright. There were conflicts perhaps, although they are surprisingly rare among hunter–gatherer societies. Simple weapons were stockpiled, perhaps. Leaders surely were chosen for demonstrated qualities, including a real and tested understanding of the world. In any case, the worst a leader could do was destroy a tribe. There were many tribes. The human species was not then in jeopardy, no matter what the leaders did.

Today it is different. The uranium is no longer entirely in the rocks. Some of it is in nuclear warheads. There are almost eighteen thousand strategic warheads in the arsenals of the United States and the Soviet Union, each of them far more devasting than the weapons that destroyed Hiroshima and Nagasaki. The strategic inventories contain enough destructive power to devastate a million Hiroshimas. But there are only about twenty-five hundred large cities on the planet. We now know that the detonation of even a small fraction of those nuclear stockpiles is sufficient to imperil the human species by triggering a nuclear winter. The clouds of smoke and dust that would be raised would block out the sun, and, according to recent scientific studies, turn all the Northern Hemisphere into a dark, subfreezing radioactive wasteland. Nor would the Southern Hemisphere be spared. By tearing the delicate ecological fabric that sustains life on Earth, it is possible that a nuclear war, even a rather small one, would carry the human species to extinction.

Because we now realize that the steady accumulation of nuclear weapons has placed our species in real jeopardy, it is clear that there must be changes in what passes for conventional wisdom. The Soviet Union has, without doubt, made significant contributions to the nuclear arms race. But, for the moment, consider the United States. In 1945 the U.S. had the most powerful military force on the planet. It was bordered, east and west, by immense oceans, and, north and south, by weak and friendly neighbors. The U.S. had little to fear in 1945. But in an effort to enhance our security, to save lives, we invented things. The U.S. produced the first atomic bomb in 1945. The U.S. was first to use these bombs on civilian populations, again in 1945. The first intercontinental strategic bomber was invented by the U.S. in 1948. The first hydrogen bomb was devised by the U.S. in 1954. The Soviet Union was first to develop the intercontinental ballistic missile in 1957, followed by the first U.S. ICBM one year later. The first submarine-launched ballistic missile was invented by the U.S. in 1960. The first multiple independently targeted reentry vehicle (MIRV) was invented by the U.S. in 1970. The first long-range cruise missile was invented by the U.S. in 1982. Each of these American strategic innovations was evenly matched by the Soviet

Union. The total cost to the planet of these nuclear strategic systems has been well in excess of a trillion contemporary dollars.

For what? For the first time in the history of our nation, every American could be killed following the outbreak of a major war. The U.S. is now far less secure than it was in 1945, and so is the Soviet Union. Every step in this mad nuclear arms race had its momentary justification. The mutual recriminations of the U.S. and the Soviet Union are endless. But step back and examine the broad picture. Embrace a planetary perspective. Then you will find that we, the human species, but in particular the U.S. and S.U. [Soviet Union] have done something supremely foolish. The nation states have failed in the most fundamental responsibility of government: to guarantee the well-being, the safety, the future of their citizens. Our governments have wired our lives to a fuse about thirty minutes long. Our survival now depends on the good judgment, the sobriety, the sanity, the mutual sensitivity of the leaders of several nations, and the absolute reliability of machines, all projected into the indefinite future. That is surely taking a very grave risk.

Because the threat of nuclear war engenders a sense of hopelessness, a turning away from the future, it is already claiming its casualties. When our young people find themselves reluctant to work hard to prepare for the future, we are endangering the future, even if there never is a nuclear war. The threat of a nuclear holocaust has already done significant damage to our children and our grandchildren and to the human future.

There are two books, each bearing as title a year. Both are famous in our time. They present two very different visions of the future. In about three hours, 1984 will be upon us. George Orwell's novel *1984* has become a symbol of state suppression of individual growth, of freedom and joy, a code word for a government decoupled from the will and well-being of its people. By contrast, Arthur Clarke's novel *2001* has come to be a symbol of hope for an exploratory future, a future in which humans take a giant stride toward maturity. One pictures a world in which we are robbed of hopeful future, the other in which we are on our way to attaining it. From Orwell's time to our own, the strategic stockpiles have been rising. In the early 1950s, only a few years after

1984 was written, the global nuclear arsenal (almost all of which was then in the United States) reached a kind of threshold beyond which the nuclear winter could be triggered. But no one in either nation had performed the appropriate calculations, and the global confrontation between the two superpowers continued in utter ignorance of the world climatic catastrophe that their actions might unleash.

Conventional wisdom and schoolyard experience teach that stronger is safer, that more weapons mean more security. When, in the early sixties, it became clear that the U.S. and the Soviet Union could each utterly annihilate the other, the idea of saturation or "overkill" arose, the notion that it was pointless to be able to destroy your adversary more than once, the feeling that enough is enough, the suspicion that more nuclear weapons did not buy more security. But this perception was not converted into national policy. The implications of nuclear winter represent a still further departure from the conventional wisdom. It now appears that, beyond a certain point, more nuclear weapons buy dramatically less security, that above a threshold, which is very roughly around a thousand strategic warheads, the world is in significantly greater danger. If the world's strategic arsenals were to be reduced from their present inventory of eighteen thousand weapons to something below one thousand weapons, below the threshold for nuclear winter, the posture of strategic deterrence could still be maintained. But there would be no possibility of destroying the human species. No concatenation of computer malfunction, unauthorized acts, communications failure, miscalculation, or madness in high office could unleash the nuclear winter.

If we begin today, on the threshold of 1984, we can get below this doomsday threshold safely, verifiably, mutually, multilaterally, while preserving the security of all nuclear powers by the year 2001. I am talking about reclaiming our future. In the process there are additional things to do. We can temper childish invective. We can resist the temptation to demonize the adversary. We can reduce the likelihood of strategic confrontations arising from accidents or miscalculations. We can stabilize old and new weapons systems—for example by de-MIRVing missiles. We can abandon nuclear war fighting strategies, and the foolish illusion that it is possible to fight or contain, much less to win, a nuclear war. We can consider, because the nuclear arsenals are so grotesquely bloated, safe unilateral steps, such as the retiring of certain old weapons systems with very high-yield warheads. We can improve communication at all levels, especially between general staffs and between heads of governments. And we can make public declarations of relevant policy changes. I wonder. Does not the nation that invented nuclear weapons, does not the nation that first used nuclear weapons on civilian populations have some special responsibility to reverse the nuclear arms race?

So this is my New Year's resolution, a resolution on the eve of 1984. I invite you to share it with me. We will devote a significant part of 1984 to educating ourselves and our public officials on the apocalyptic implications of nuclear war. We will make certain that every candidate for the House of Representatives, for the Senate, and for the presidency has made a clear public statement, a clear position on the nuclear arms race. And then we will work to elect those who are committed—not to some vague and fence-straddling generalities, but to specific and consistent proposals for major and verifiable reductions mutual in the world inventories of strategic weapons. This does not involve "trusting" the Soviet Union about anything except their commitment to their own survival. Let us convert "1984" from a code word for a government-managed nightmare, to a year in which we start freeing ourselves from the trap that we have carelessly and foolishly set for ourselves. I would like 2001 to dawn on a world that will truly initiate a new millennium, liberated from the danger of nuclear annihilation of the human species.

Let us act this year, so that in 2001 we can look our children and our grandchildren in the eye and say, "Here, we made the world a better place for you. We continued the tradition of the forty thousand generations of humans who came before us. Do the same for your children."

THE QUEST FOR EQUALITY

STRUGGLE ON[1]

Benjamin L. Hooks[2]

The National Association for the Advancement of Colored People assembled in New Orleans on July 12, 1983 for its seventy-fourth annual convention amid internal strife, uncertainty about the future, and disillusionment with the effects of the Reagan administration's policies upon black Americans.

The internal conflict was the result of an attempt earlier in the year to have Executive Director Benjamin L. Hooks removed from his position. Although Hooks was retained, the dispute had engendered bitterness.

The infighting came at a critical time in the NAACP's history, a time when it was working to overcome dwindling membership and disorganized management. Kelly M. Alexander, Sr., vice chairman of the board, summed up the problem as follows:

> It's not like it was twenty to thirty years ago when segregation was a way of life. . . . We are still selling freedom and justice but many people, the third generation of blacks, have to be educated that they are where they are because the NAACP made it possible for them to have opportunities. (Sheila Rule, *New York Times,* Je. 11, '83, p 7)

Frustration was widespread and deep among civil rights groups as they witnessed the policies of the Reagan administration, which had reduced spending for social programs and had turned away from such remedies as busing, lawsuits, and affirmative action. (For example, see John Jacob's speech to the National Urban League, January 12, 1982, *Representative American Speeches, 1981-1982,* pp. 145-149.)

In his keynote address to the association at 8:00 P.M., Mr. Hooks paid tribute to past leaders in the struggle for equal rights for blacks, announced plans for programs to reinvigorate the movement, and challenged President Reagan to meet and talk with him and other black leaders. He issued the challenge in the following terms:

[1]Keynote address delivered to the 74th annual convention of the National Association for the Advancement of Colored People at 8:00 P.M., July 12, 1983, at the Rivergate convention center in New Orleans, Louisiana.

[2]For biographical note, see Appendix.

As the executive director of the nation's largest, oldest, and most powerful civil rights organization, I challenge Ronald Reagan to sit and communicate the logic of his policies.

He has insisted that his policies are aimed at changing this nation for the better. Our evidence—our experiences—have shown that they are changing America for the worse. Black people, poor people, elderly people, and women—we have all felt the brunt of an administration's policies that have rewarded the rich and punished the poor, helped the powerful and ignored the weak. Ronald Reagan must be held accountable for his policies that now threaten to set this nation's social concerns back for fifty years.

I challenge you, Mr. President, to meet and to talk about how some of your citizens are suffering in these United States. I challenge you, Mr. President.

Mr. Hooks concluded his speech with an emotional plea to "struggle on" that was highly reminiscent of the verbal style of Martin Luther King, Jr., and other earlier civil rights leaders. John Herbers described Hooks as "one of the few speakers employing the old-fashioned preaching style that galvanized audiences in the 1960s." (*New York Times*, Ag. 29, '83, p 1) Regarding audience response, Sheila Rule reported:

> There did not seem to be the high level of enthusiasm among delegates that was evident at some past meetings. In delivering his address, Mr. Hooks excited them only after he invoked the words of the Rev. Martin Luther King, Jr. (*New York Times*, Jl. 18, '83, p 7)

Hooks delivered his address at the Rivergate convention center to an audience of approximately 300.

Benjamin L. Hooks's speech: Supporters and members of the NAACP, Chairman Wilson, Mayor Morial, Vice Chairman Kelly Alexander, Sr., branch President Shirley Porter, state President Rupert Richardson, and national President James Kemp, members of the Board of Directors, presidents of our thirty-six state conferences, and representatives of more than 1,800 branches, youth councils, and college chapters, I am pleased and privileged to have this opportunity to address your seventy-fourth annual convention.

It is with a deep sense of humility and pride that I come to this place tonight, a city of great struggle and sacrifice, yet a city that prides itself on electing to the office of mayor the grandson of a former slave; a city that is slowly, but surely, ending the disparity between the races and working toward becoming a model of what America can be.

I come humbled by the knowledge that as we assemble in this convention center, we stand on the shoulders of many giants who put their lives on the line in order that the racial progress we now enjoy could be made. We pay tribute to our own martyred Medgar Evers who, twenty years ago on June 12, was cut down by an assassin's bullet. Medgar realized better than most that to stand up for justice in Mississippi in the sixties was a dangerous and potentially fatal endeavor. Yet he stood boldly and tall, declaring to the world that it is better to die in dignity for a just cause than to live on one's knees as a supplicant. He loved Merlie and the children in a unique way, but he was conscious of the fact that life is a struggle and that the sacrifices of one generation are the foundation stones upon which we build a future for our race. Let us not forget other martyrs who gave their lives: Harry T. Moore, Vernon Dahmer, George Lee, and others.

Today, there are more elected black public officials in the state of Mississippi than any state in the nation. Today, the face of race relations has been drastically altered by the surgical knife of self-denial and self-sacrifice by the thousands of men and women who met in churches off lonely roads, assembled around dining room tables of shacks and shanties, and who marched until the Ross Barnetts gave way to elect officials who helped to bring that state into the twentieth century. *Life is a struggle.*

One does not have to be a confirmed evolutionist to understand that life is a struggle. The evolving nature of life and the changes that take place all around us ought to convince each of us of this sobering reality. From the moment of conception to the time of our demise, we struggle from one state of existence to another. The miracle of birth is wrapped in a mysterious enigma of struggle. The act of birth itself is a struggle of the baby to leave the secure warmth of its mother's womb. From its first breath, there is a struggle for attention, for nourishment and affection. Then there is a struggle through early childhood to grasp the language, to learn to walk, and to coordinate extremities. In school there is a struggle to comprehend and to master the required skills of grammar, of penmanship. There is a struggle which takes place in adolescence, that strange and somewhat confused state between childhood and adulthood. There is a struggle which takes place in all of us as we determine our ethical and moral priorities. There is a struggle to find a job and to develop our careers. There is a struggle to make ends meet, to pay for the roof over our heads, the clothes on our backs, the food that we eat, and the very comforts which we as a society have taken for granted. There is a struggle of rearing our children and preparing for retirement; and then when all of this is completed, there is a struggle against the inevitability of life's end, the desire to go on living in spite of the inevitability of death. Yes, from the womb to the tomb, life is a struggle.

So it should come as no surprise that even though slavery has been officially over for more than 118 years, we still find ourselves struggling against slavery under new guises: racial discrimination in this country, apartheid and colonialism abroad. But as far back as we can read recorded history, life for every group of people has been a struggle. From the dusty crypts of the past, from the towering pyramids built by slave labor to honor dead pharaohs, the hanging gardens of Babylon amidst the glory and grandeur which was Rome under the Caesars; amidst the philosophical enlightenment of the Greeks in ancient Greece; amidst the spendor of Notre Dame in France, the Gothic structures of Germany, and the bell towers of pre-Cromwell England. Life has been a struggle.

Here in America, from the Mayflower at Plymouth Rock to the Men-of-War at Jamestown, life for the earliest settlers and the first slaves has been a struggle.

One out of every three blacks in this country is officially listed below the poverty line.

One out of every three blacks lives in substandard housing

One out of five black adults is unemployed.

One out of two black youths can't find work.

Black infant mortality is twice as high as that of whites.

Despite the progress we have made in the area of voter participation, less than one percent of the more than 500,000 elected officials are black.

In the House of Representatives there are a total of twenty-one black congresspersons, including the nonvoting delegate from the District of Columbia, out of 435.

In the United States Senate, since the defeat of Senator Edward Brooke, there are no blacks in the U.S. Senate out of one hundred senators.

Of the top Fortune 500 corporations, less than 125 have blacks on their boards of directors.

Black enrollment in medical schools is less than 4 percent, in dental school less than 3 percent, in law schools less than 4 percent of the totals.

In the area of business, according to the most recent survey, there are a total of 321,203 black firms, but they have a combined gross receipt of only $8.6 billion. This, in a nation with over a trillion dollars gross national product. The life expectancy for black Americans is 6.1 years less than that of whites. The black median family income is 56 percent of that of white families.

I cite these figures to highlight the fact that although we have made tremendous progress in the area of race relations, we still have a long way to go; and contrary to the glib assertions of the present administration, much remains to be done if blacks are to share in the economic wealth and prosperity of this nation.

We disagree with most of the major initiatives of the Reagan administration. We think that their position on enforcement of affirmative action, busing, tuition tax credits are wrong. Nevertheless, we shall continue to alert the president and his officers about our concerns. We shall explain and talk to them through the press, radio, TV, or in person when afforded the chance.

Tonight we challenge the present administration to meet with us, to talk with us, to dialogue with us. We are concerned, Mr. President, about your policies. You say we do not understand you, you say that we misinterpret you, so let us sit down and together talk about the problems that we see, the solutions we propose, and see whether or not we indeed do have much to offer that would help move this nation forward. I mean, Mr. President, sit down and talk with Ben Hooks. Come let us reason together.

Like all of us, Ronald Reagan must be held accountable for his actions. I agree with the mass media that Ronald Reagan is a great communicator and I am calling upon Ronald Reagan to communicate with me. As the executive director of the nation's largest, oldest, and most powerful civil rights organization, I challenge Ronald Reagan to sit and communicate the logic of his policies.

He has insisted that his policies are aimed at changing this nation for the better. Our evidence—our experiences—have shown that they are changing America for the worse. Black people, poor people, elderly people, and women—we have all felt the brunt of an administration's policies that have rewarded the rich and punished the poor, helped the powerful and ignored the weak. Ronald Reagan must be held accountable for his policies that now threaten to set this nation's social concerns back for fifty years.

I challenge you, Mr. President, to meet and to talk about how some of your citizens are suffering in these United States. I challenge you, Mr. President. So many of your citizens need the help that only the national administration can give.

I challenge you, Ronald Reagan, to communicate with me, Ben Hooks, to communicate to me how your citizens in this country—and especially your racial minorities, the poor, the elderly, and this nation's womenfolk—can expect to be made a part of this nation's mainstream.

I challenge you, Mr. President, to meet with me and to communicate.

But we must say to this administration, unless you change your course and show more concern for our interest, we will meet you at the ballot, and there, in the classic American fashion, we will express our dissatisfaction. But we do not come here merely to express gloom and doom or to criticize.

We have a program! Voter registration, education, and participation are the keystones of our program. Last year we registered more than 850,000 voters. Between now and November of 1984, we plan to register 2 million additional voters.

We will kick off a mammoth "Overground Railroad" march on August 14 under the leadership of Joseph Madison. Starting at the Kentucky side of the Cincinnati Bridge, we will march through Ohio to Toledo, culminating with a mass rally on Labor Day weekend in Detroit, Michigan. Along the way, thirteen young people representing each of thirteen southern states will be active participants.

Our second cornerstone is "Economic Development" or "Fair Share." This program is designed to radically alter the nature of unemployment and economic imbalance among blacks. We want representation on boards of directors. We will insist on blacks in senior management positions, an aggressive affirmative action program, and a minority procurement program.

Our young people are walking the streets, hopeless and in despair. We can and we must redeem this imbalance.

The third cornerstone of our program is building support for our own institutions. Blacks have a gross national product of over $150 billion. We must support our churches, our colleges, our black newspapers, our fraternal orders, our civil rights groups. We must build a strong, viable, and efficient network of NAACP units across the nation. Dr. T. J. Jeminson, president of the 7-million-member National Baptist Convention, USA, Inc., has given us the torch and has presented us with a map for helping the NAACP become the organization that destiny has called us to be.

I shall within a few days convene a meeting of key national religious leaders to personalize a massive nationwide effort to engender support for the NAACP.

President Lincoln said that a nation cannot exist half slave and half free. Whitney Young said that we may have come over on different ships, some on the Mayflower and others on slave ships, but we are now all in the same boat. Frederick Douglass said no man can put a chain about the ankle of his fellow man without at least finding the other end of the chain fastened about his own neck. President Lyndon Johnson said, prophetically, that America must come to grips with the fact that it has historically mistreated the Negro, and that if we are to ever, as a nation, realize our fullest potential, we must now find ways to include those in who were systematically excluded.

Mr. Reagan, our quest as a nation for greatness must not be built upon the foundations of MX missiles or B-1 bombers, not even upon the cornerstones of a mythical Star War-type defense system; not upon hundreds of individuals becoming billionaires, or corporate profits; not upon the stock market indicators of Wall Street, but upon the well-being of over 200 million people from all parts of the world who now call themselves Americans.

Yes, my friends, we are in the midst of a fierce struggle, one that becomes more difficult seemingly with the passing of each day.

Nineteen eighty-four is the seventy-fifth anniversary of the association. For all this time the NAACP has been without a permanent headquarters it owned. With this in mind, I propose a three-point program which will be designated "4,004" to give a thousand or more in '84. This creative and innovative effort envisions 4,004 or more individuals, branches, youth councils, college chapters, state conferences, organizations, churches, fraternal groups, and others giving $1,000 or more to the NAACP for three specific purposes: $2 million for a purchase of a building; $1 million to retire our debt; $1 million for a permanent endowment for the NAACP.

I believe, no I know, that there are at least 4,000 individuals who will join us in this effort. We will have a commemorative plaque in your national headquarters listing the names of those who joined in this noble effort.

Anyone who has an appreciation for history should be cognizant of the fact that nations and great civilizations were not destroyed from without but from within. When hopes are blasted, when expectations are doomed, when respect for government is shattered by the disparate treatment of groups of individuals; when people are left out, then a social order is doomed to destruction. Yes, social and economic destruction from within, not foreign aggressors, constitute the greatest threat to our system of government.

While we must protect ourselves against those who may choose to be our adversaries, we must also work incessantly to defeat the age-old triplets of hunger, of poverty, and of disease. To do less is to doom our future and seal our fate.

Fortunately for us, and for our nation I might add, there is the NAACP, strong and vibrant. Although we are put upon as ineffective and outmoded by the nattering nabobs of negativism, ostracized, vilified by cynics from both inside and outside, nonetheless, the NAACP stands today as it stood for the past seventy-four years as a bastion of hope for black Americans.

What other organization has a history of fighting through the courts, marching in the streets, lobbying on Capitol Hill and in state capitals in fifty states for the advancement of civil and human rights?

What other organization has a mass membership base, verifiable by certified public accountants, of almost 400,000 members?

The NAACP, for more than half a century, has been the most effective vehicle for black Americans in the struggle for full human rights. The NAACP worked in the quarry when the rock was hard, and thank God we offered bold, imaginative leadership to those Americans who had little reason to believe in the hollow promises of this society. We must not lose the respect and confidence of the black masses.

Like a tree planted by the waters, in this struggle, I shall not—we shall not—be moved! We have not, since 1909, faltered or failed to be the faithful advocate of our people. We intend to turn out of city halls mayors who do not concern themselves with the plight of the poor, who won't appoint blacks to positions of responsibility, or who neglect our neighborhoods. We intend to send into retirement governors whose policies adversely impact blacks, women, Hispanics, and other minorities. We intend to drive from the hallowed halls of the Senate and from the exalted chambers of the House of Representatives men and women who are not representative of those of us who are caught at the bottom of the economic ladders. And unless there are major changes in the current direction of this administration, we intend to march on the ballot box in November of 1984 and send President Ronald Wilson Reagan back to the sunshine, solitude, and placid seaside of California.

On Labor Day weekend, we are calling upon blacks around the country to demonstrate to merchants throughout the land that we have enormous economic clout which cannot be taken for granted. Under the leadership of L. R. Byrd, our "Fair Share" consultant, we are launching this effort, calling upon blacks to use Susan B. Anthony silver dollars and $2 bills for the purchases of goods and services they make that weekend. By so doing, we will say to the economic movers and shakers, businessmen and merchants, that a significant portion of their income is derived from the black community and that we are insisting upon our "Fair Share" of the job and entrepreneurial opportunities which are available.

My brothers and sisters, as I close tonight I want you to know that the struggle that we will face through the remaining period of the eighties and on through the twenty-first century will not be an easy one. It is fraught with pitfalls and plagued with setbacks, but we as a people have developed a resiliency which has made it possible for us to survive slavery and vicious discrimination. We must never tire or become frustrated by difficulties. We must transform stumbling blocks into stepping stones and march on with the determination that we will make America a better nation for all to live in.

I know what it is like to be put upon. As leaders of branches, state conferences, you too know what it is like to be vilified and abused. You know what it is like not to have your efforts appreciated and to have your motives questioned. But struggle on.

When the school boards and boards of education are reticent to provide the kind of education that our children desperately need in the decade of the eighties, go to the school board meetings, let your voice be heard, and struggle on. When you sit down with corporations and institutions and negotiate for more job opportunities for blacks and you are told that they cannot find blacks who are qualified, do not give up, but struggle on.

We in the NAACP want no more nor no less than the same opportunities which have been afforded to the other groups that have landed on these shores.

Struggle on: We want more schoohouses and less jail houses,

Struggle on: We want more books and less weapons,

Struggle on: We want more learning and less vice,

Struggle on: We want more employment and less crime in our communities,

Struggle on: We want more help for the needy and less breaks for the greedy,

Struggle on: We want more justice and less vengeance,

Struggle on: We want more of our children to graduate from high school able to read and write, not more on unemployment lines,

Struggle on: We want more statesmen and less politicians,

Struggle on: We want more workers in our ranks and less cynics,

Struggle on: We want more hope and less dope,

Struggle on: We want more faith and less despair,

Struggle on: We shall struggle on until justice "rolls down like waters and righteousness, like a mighty stream"; we shall struggle on until every valley be exalted, every hill and mountain shall be made low, and rough places shall be made smooth, and the crooked places, straight, and the glory of the Lord shall be revealed and all flesh shall see it together; we shall struggle on until those who languish at the bottom rung of the economic ladder shall be able to enjoy the fruits of this democracy,

Struggle on: We shall struggle on until blacks are in representative and proportionate numbers in the corporate board rooms,

Struggle on: We shall work until the Congress, the state legislatures, mayors, governors, and presidents are committed to the notion that either this nation will afford to all of its citizens opportunity for justice for all of its citizens or there shall be justice for none.

We will fight to our last breath to build a world where men and women, boys and girls, Protestant and Catholic, Jew and Arab, can exist in the absence of hunger, in the absence of social and economic deprivation, and in the presence of a new world order where every man is accorded the dignity that his personhood entitles him to as the son or the daughter of the living God.

> Lift ev'ry voice and sing:
> Till earth and heaven ring.
> Ring with the harmonies of liberty;
> Let our rejoicing rise
> High as the list'ning skies
> Let it resound loud as the rolling sea. Struggle on.
> Sing a song full of the faith that the dark past has taught us,
> Sing a song full of the hope that the present has brought us.
> Facing the rising sun of our new day begun,
> Let us march on till victory is won.

Struggle on, struggle on, struggle on.

A WALL OF MISUNDERSTANDING[1]

GEORGE H. W. BUSH[2]

Regardless of whether one disagreed with Vice President George Bush and the Reagan administration policies which he sought to defend, even his severest critics must have felt a tinge of respect for his courage in addressing the National Association for the Advancement of Colored People July 15, 1983, on the closing day of its annual convention. For four days, association leaders, including Executive Director Benjamin Hooks (see pp. 81–91), had denounced the president and his Republican supporters in the strongest language for supporting policies they believed to be detrimental to blacks. A string of Democratic candidates for the presidential nomination had appeared and met with reactions ranging from positive but unexciting, to warm, to "an exuberant display of affection" for former Vice President Walter F. Mondale. (Sheila Rule, *New York Times,* Jl. 16, '83, p 7)

Of the speakers appearing at the convention, Mr. Bush clearly had the toughest time of it. The vice president, battling a chorus of "hisses and boos," contended that there was a "wall of misunderstanding between most members of this audience and the Reagan administration," but insisted that President Reagan was making progress in civil rights. Although he had campaigned against Ronald Reagan for the Republican presidential nomination in 1980, Bush as vice president had become a staunch supporter of the administration. According to Louise Sweeney, "If a Heisman Trophy were awarded for the most loyal team player in politics, Bush would win it . . . for his unswerving loyalty to the President's position and his loyalty to the administration stance even when it overrode his earlier criticisms as presidential candidate." (*Christian Science Monitor,* Ja. 26, '84, p 18)

Confronted with an antagonistic audience, the vice president chose candor as the best way to reduce hostility. "Well, I'm here," he said. "After looking at the TV coverage that's come out of this convention since Monday, there were a lot of people betting I wouldn't show up. They wonder what could possibly be accomplished by my coming to speak to a convention whose leadership has already indicated that their top priority next year is to defeat the administration I serve."

He went on to say:

---

[1]Delivered to the annual convention of the National Association for the Advancement of Colored People, 12:30 P.M., at the Rivergate convention center in New Orleans, July 15, 1983.

[2]For biographical note, see Appendix.

I heard those statements, too. And the more I heard, the more I wanted to come here because I believe, just as President Reagan does, that a national administration can't carry out its responsibility just by talking and listening to its supporters. The president and I both believe we need to talk and listen to our critics, too. That's why he was at your convention two years ago. That's why I'm here today.

Vice President Bush delivered his speech at 12:30 P.M. to an audience of approximately 150 convention delegates at the Rivergate convention center in New Orleans.

Vice President Bush's speech: Well, I'm here.

After looking at the TV coverage that's come out of this convention since Monday, there were a lot of people betting I wouldn't show up. They wonder what could possibly be accomplished by my coming to speak to a convention whose leadership has already indicated that their top priority next year is to defeat the administration I serve.

But I'll tell you something. I heard those statements too. And the more I heard, the more I wanted to come here because I believe, just as President Reagan does, that a national administration can't carry out its responsibility just by talking and listening to its supporters. The president and I both believe we need to talk and listen to our critics, too. That's why he was at your convention two years ago. That's why I'm here today.

Do I expect to make any converts? Let me be frank. I think a wall of misunderstanding exists between most members of this audience and the Reagan administration, and no single speech or action is going to break that wall down. But you know, despite what my good friend Ben Hooks here was quoted as saying recently—that this administration doesn't care about the plight of blacks in America—we do care, and we care deeply.

The charge has been made that this administration has shut its ears to the voices of black Americans. But that just isn't so. Don't take my word for it. Just ask Ben whether he's ever had any trouble contacting or visiting me at the White House, where we've talked long and hard about the issues and problems facing black Americans.

Or ask Vernon Jordan. Or ask Jesse Jackson. Or Dorothy Height, John Jacobs, Leon Sullivan, or Ralph Abernathy. Or ask

Carl Holman or Pat Jacob's about our discussions about how we can work together to provide jobs, education, equal opportunity, and improved living standards for minority Americans. Or ask Maynard Jackson, or Ben Payton, or Margaret Bush Wilson, or James Cheek.

Ask any of these black leaders if my office isn't always open to representatives of the black community. We may not agree on how to resolve these issues and problems, but the dialogue goes on. Progress can and in fact is being made, and the charge that this administration has written off the black segment of American society is dead wrong. The door to the Reagan White House is open to leaders of the black community. It's been open and will always remain open. But let me say this, too. Open doors are fine, but we've also got to have open minds, on both sides of the dialogue between the administration and America's black leadership.

No, we're not going to write off any group. But we don't want to be written off, either. And when I hear it said that the aim of the NAACP next year is to defeat the Reagan administration, I find it hard to believe that the better part of your responsibility as leaders is to foreclose your options and let black Americans be taken for granted by the opposition party.

Let's take a look at those options, a fair look, with open minds. Who knows? We might even make a small crack in that wall of misunderstanding.

What about the charge that this administration has been lax on civil rights enforcement?

Wrong. Dead wrong. The fact is—and again, don't take my word for it, just check the record—this administration is actually ahead of past administrations in what we've done to enforce civil rights.

You doubt it? Well then, let's get a little historical perspective on the subject. Check back to see how much the Carter administration achieved in civil rights enforcement after three years in office. You'll find that the Reagan administration is far ahead of the Carter administration in terms of criminal prosecutions for civil rights violations. We've had more grand jury presentments and the Justice Department has pursued more prosecutions of people who violate the civil rights of others than its predecessor or any other administration. I'm talking about combatting racial violence, about fighting hate organizations like the Ku Klux Klan, and prosecuting cases against those who brutalize or seek to terrorize black and minority Americans.

What about the area of equal opportunity in the working place? Again, it's been charged that the Reagan administration has been lax in carrying out its duties to guarantee and protect equal opportunity. And again, that charge is dead wrong. Check our record against the Carter administration's. You'll find that we have 116 ongoing cases against public employers who've been discriminating against blacks and we're fighting these cases in courts across the country, from New York and Wisconsin to Alabama and Texas.

What about housing discrimination? We've just sent Congress proposed new amendments that would put real teeth into the Fair Housing Law. If our amendments are passed by Congress, for the first time you'll see heavy financial fines levied against those who practice housing discrimination.

I'm not talking rhetoric here. I'm talking record.

School desegregation. Charges have been made that this administration has been dragging its feet in that area. Again, those charges are dead wrong. The Justice Department has taken legal action against both Mississippi and Alabama, charging discriminatin in those states' higher education systems. At the same time, the department is actively investigating such discriminatory practices in Ohio.

Check our record in this area against the Carter administration's or any other administration's. You'll find that once the TV rhetoric is set aside, our record is second to none in trying to uproot discrimination in our schools.

What about voting rights? During our first year in office, the Reagan Justice Department took action to remedy thirty-one election law changes found to be racially discriminatory, it took action to remedy eighty-nine election law changes last year, and forty-five election law changes so far this year. That's 165 separate enforcement actions in all. Our record on voting rights is better than any past administration in this area of black and minority concerns.

All right, let's be candid about our disagreements in other areas—these are disagreements not in goals, but in methods to achieve those goals. It's hardly news that the NAACP and the Reagan administration don't see eye to eye on the issue of school busing. But to put that disagreement in perspective, this actually reflects the division of opinion on the issue inside the black community.

We differ on quotas, too. Our position is that we just don't think the way to fight racism is by setting up race as a criterion. Our approach is to fight racism and discrimination not by seeking quotas, but by seeking justice, and that's the principle on which the NAACP itself was formed.

So far I've been talking about the gap between rhetoric and record in the area of civil rights. Our common goal is to provide equal opportunity for black and minority Americans. But beyond the legal framework, what about the problems facing black and minority Americans who want to take advantage of that opportunity? After all, what good is equal opportunity if you don't have the skills to compete? Which leads us to the most critical problem facing black America today, unemployment.

We just don't think past programs, programs like those of the Carter administration, were effective in meeting the black community's long-range employment needs. And I think the record backs us up. In fact, it wasn't that long ago—in the late 1970s—that leaders of the black community, including members of this organization, were criticizing the Carter administration's inability to cope with the problem of black and minority unemployment. And for good reason. The burden of unemployment has always been disproportionately heavy on the country's black working population, particularly among black youths. That was true a decade ago—it was true during the Carter years—and I don't have to tell this audience that this tragic waste of young lives and human potential is still with us.

We came into office convinced that a new, long-range approach is needed if we're going to break the back of this chronic national problem, not for a year or even a decade, but once and for all.

Our approach is to target money to those who need it most. Our voucher program to retrain the long-term unemployed—a program in which private employers are given incentives to train workers on the job—is in dramatic contrast to previous programs where money went not to training people but to funding government agencies.

We've also created the Jobs Partnership Training Program to provide jobs and training to 165,000 displaced workers, victims of structural unemployment. And in the area of minority enterprise, under the 8A program, funds contracted to black-owned firms have increased to $2.7 billion, up more than 40 percent over the last two years of the Carter administration.

Make no mistake, I'm glad to have the opportunity to be here today, because I welcome the chance to cut through the TV smoke and talk about this administration's real record in dealing with black issues and problems.

That record on assisting black business is a case in point. Fact: This administration has the best—that's right, the best—record of *any* administration in history in providing direct and indirect assistance to black business. Through 8A contracts, loans, and by other means, we've provided some $18.7 billion to minority businesses, and we've increased deposits in minority banks by some 75 percent over the Carter years.

Finally, let's look beyond the present to the future and talk about an issue of special concern to our country's black community, the issue of educating our young people so that every American has the opportunity to fulfill his or her God-given potential. We're all familiar with the recent report of the National Commission on Excellence—a report that noted glaring failures in our current educational system—failures that affect students of all races and regions. In any case, it's as true today as it ever was that education is the real key to solving the problems of our society, particularly the problems of inequality and discrimination. This administration is committed to removing every obstacle that stands in the way of young people getting the education they need and want. And our record bears out that commitment.

Student assistance grants in the 1984 budget have been increased by $300 million, and the number of students receiving Guaranteed Student Loans next year will increase to 2.9 million.

In the area of America's historically black colleges, the Reagan administration is giving more money to these institutions directly, along with working to increase their participation in federally sponsored programs. And let's not forget that some of the best news for hard-pressed colleges and universities in recent years has been the decline in inflation. Every 1 percent reduction in inflation buys a total of $2 billion in educational services.

As I've said, a wall of misunderstanding exists between most members of your organization and the Reagan administration, and that wall does neither of us any good. For our part, we're determined, if we can't break it down, to keep chipping away at it. We'll keep at it because we think that's our job, and regardless of what our critics say, because we care. I'm not saying our record is perfect, that we haven't made mistakes. Sure, we've made errors in judgment. But let me say this: When we've seen that we're in error, we've moved to correct our mistakes and we're always open to constructive criticism.

It was exactly ten years ago, at your convention in Indianapolis, that Roy Wilkins spoke of black people having an investment in America, as he put it, "an investment in blood and tears, in lives dead and revered, and in lives which are triumphant over insults and barriers and persecution. . . . This is our land," Roy Wilkins said. "For good or bad, it owns us, and we own it. We bought it and our futures here with sacrifices and heroism, with humility and love. It belongs to us and we shall never give up our claim and run away."

So spoke a great black leader a decade ago. As followers in his tradition, you aren't going to run away from the challenges and problems facing black and minority Americans and, speaking for the Reagan administration, neither are we.

That's why I'm here today. And that's why the doors to the White House are open and will remain open to those who, whether they vote for us or not, seek a dialogue to help meet the challenges and solve the problems that affect America's black community.

WOMEN IN POLITICS: TIME FOR A CHANGE[1]

DIANNE FEINSTEIN[2]

Women play a more important part in political life today than at any previous time in American history. In increasing numbers, they serve in government positions ranging from local, county, and state offices to membership in Congress, presidential Cabinet positions, and even the Supreme Court. In 1983 there were seventy-six women mayors of United States cities. The most prominent probably was Dianne Feinstein, the first woman mayor of San Francisco.

Mayor Feinstein was the closing keynote speaker at a three-day meeting entitled, "Impact '84: A Leadership Conference for Democratic Women," sponsored by the Women's National Democratic Club in Washington, D.C., from September 26–28, 1983. Among the subjects covered at the conference was the possibility of a woman as the Democratic Party's vice-presidential candidate, a topic receiving considerable publicity as the campaign progressed. Two prominent speakers at the meeting—both women state lieutenant governors—urged the conferees to work for a woman as vice president on the ticket. Senator Edward M. Kennedy, who also addressed the conference, went a step further, telling them that it was time for Democrats to "talk seriously about women candidates," not only for the vice presidency, but for the top job as well. (*Washington Post*, S. 29, '83)

Among the women most frequently mentioned as possible vice-presidential candidates was Mayor Feinstein (Sheila Caudle, *USA Today*, S. 28, '83), so it is not surprising that the conference chose her to deliver one of the main addresses at its meeting.

The mayor has been described as "a 5-foot-9-inch political dynamo with a mixture of dignity and sparkle . . . someone with a passionate desire to succeed, to do right," and "an articulate and capable communicator." (Linda-Marie Singer, King Features, Baton Rouge *State Times*, O. 3, '83, p 8) She delivered this address, immediately following the morning session at which the final conference report was adopted, at noon to an audience of 225 delegates at the Women's National Democratic Club.

Mayor Feinstein's speech: About thirty years ago, Senator Margaret Chase Smith was asked by *Time* magazine what she would

---

[1]Keynote speech at a three-day conference entitled, "Impact '84: A Leadership Conference for Democratic Women," delivered at noon on September 28, 1983, at the Women's National Democratic Club in Washington, D. C.
[2]For biographical note, see Appendix.

do if one day she woke up in the White House? She replied that she would apologize to Bess Truman and leave immediately.

Women in politics, particularly in positions of major authority, have carried that kind of gender burden traditionally in our country. There is an incredulity and improbability that has surrounded women's rise to the top of the political ladder. I suggest to you that times and traditions have changed, and that women have changed, too.

I am delighted to be here today addressing women who have jumped into political life with both feet. Your program tells me you are setting new goals and articulating women's priorities for the next election year.

But what are women's issues? Many people consider women's issues to be those areas intrinsically related to women, their bodies, and their families—like abortion and school issues. The E.R.A. has been an interesting departure. The campaign for ratification and its subsequent setbacks presented women with the opportunity to become a major political force in the country.

In my view, the time has come for us to draw a broader agenda. The time has come for women to reach out and grapple with the major issues of our day.

I submit to you that it is time women realize they are not a minority. We are a majority—in virtually every state, every city in this country, and in this world. We are a majority of voters, too. Let us not forget that.

War and peace, the economy, the national defense, housing, and jobs are all our issues, issues we should join today—right now. Let us stop building fences around ourselves and the questions facing our society: the issues belong to all of us. Issues like mortgage revenue bonds, programs for the homeless, urban reconstruction banks, tax reform and indexing, health care, and other such programs should be as familiar to us as that simple twenty-four-word amendment to the Constitution.

There is good reason for our concern right now. Never in history have more people been made richer—or poorer—than during the current administration. Never since the Great Depression have we seen more people out of work. Even today, in the midst of a recovery, we have almost 10 million Americans without jobs.

Even on Jimmy Carter's old "misery index," the American people are no better off than they were four years ago. As a matter of fact, many millions are far worse off.

It is time for women to speak out on the economy—because it is our pocketbooks that are vitally affected every day. Half this nation's work force is women, and we are also half the unemployed.

It is time we women took up the issue of a balanced budget, social security reform, and the question of "defense versus the cities," which this administration has "lurched" us into.

It is time for women to take a strong stand on the nuclear question—to support a bilateral nuclear freeze—just as we stood strong against Vietnam. Who loses more in war than we women? Whose children, husbands, and sweethearts die? Who are condemned to the agony of uncertainty by that three-letter label, MIA, so familiar now to us all?

It is time for women to speak out for our cities. Seventy percent of Americans live and work in cities, and the cities and their people are hurting—oh, how they are hurting: soup kitchens blossoming, health centers closing, and hopes fading.

It is time for women to join the environmental movement in a major way, to see to it, once and for all, that toxic wastes do not inundate our neighborhoods, that our children and their children can breathe clean air and drink unpolluted water. This country's battle to protect the environment has suffered mightily in the last three years.

It is time for women to demand social justice for all minorities—for blacks, Hispanics, Asian-Americans, and all Americans. We have fought for our own rights. We know the problem.

In short, women of America must proclaim an agenda of conscience. It is our time to act, and we should do so boldly and with confidence.

In doing so, let us also pause to take stock of ourselves. Let us ask if we can accomplish the goals we are talking about. Let's see where we are, here in 1983.

In my view, our involvement in the political process has increased sharply as officeholders, registered voters, and party activists, and that new stature can be reflected more powerfully in national policies and platforms than ever before.

We live in an exciting time because increasingly, women are emerging in positions of power in our country and in the world. Consider in the last decade three women have served as prime ministers: Golda Meir, Margaret Thatcher, and Indira Gandhi.

Thousands of us now serve in local, state, and national offices, among them ninety-three mayors of big and little cities all across this land. And I'm proud to tell you those mayors are getting organized for the first time in history. Last June in Denver we had our first meeting, and in Washington in January we will convene our first caucus of women mayors.

I come from a city where the voters have seen fit to elect a woman mayor, both representatives in Congress, a majority of the Board of Supervisors, and its president. I am proud to have appointed a woman city treasurer, three department heads, and 110 women to boards and commissions. It pleases me greatly that the voters have given women authority in San Francisco. I believe that is because our women as officeholders are acceptable to the people of our city—and because we use our authority wisely.

It is important to all of us that when women get into office they concentrate on doing the job and doing it well. We should not let one success go to our heads and rush on to the next higher office. A most important realization is that success means doing a job well over a considerable period of time, with enthusiasm, motivation, and staying power. It means getting elected and reelected to the same job.

Women in office must develop staying power. We must have consistency. We must develop that sense of timing, that ability to convince, that substantive knowledge that only comes with time.

If we lose—an election or an issue—we must get right back up and try again. Abraham Lincoln, after all, lost six elections. I've lost a couple myself and it's tough, but it comes with the territory. I've often said, "Winning may not be everything in this arena, but losing has nothing to recommend it."

I repeat, it is time that we, as women, broaden our agenda. Let us become a more significant part of a more significant dialogue. The great issues of our time belong to us. And if we don't use this opportunity to add to the solutions, and not to the problems, we have only ourselves to blame for future failures.

Having heard all this, and agreed, you might well say, How?

How can I, a mother of small children?

How can I, who live in a remote area or small town?

How can I, who don't want to run for office?

How can I make a real difference in the public policy of my town, my city, state, or nation?

Let me suggest a way—and it's one I have learned the hard way—it is one that worked for me. Most of us are anxious to participate, and we spread ourselves too thin. We join too many organizations, go to too many meetings, feel frustrated and ineffectual. The key, I suggest to you, is not to do that. Instead, select an area—one area—of your interest and concern.

Is it party organization or platform, housing production, tax reform, health care, the aged, poor, and disabled, the environment? Whatever it is, figure out one major area, and then search out the organizations, the experts, the doers in the field, the pertinent literature and research on the subject. Identify with those effective and positive organizations and leaders.

Then learn, listen to points of view, be part of the consortium of action, be flexible in your thought, be open to new ideas and—yes—even compromises. Write and speak, whenever and wherever.

Again, listen, be flexible, amend your views until you reach a point where you are part of the wing of viable and constructive change. This is possible to achieve in a relatively short time. Why? Because so few do it.

I say it is time. Every issue that faces our world is a women's issue. It's time we do more about it.

Thank you very much.

THE FUTURE OF SPORTS

SPORT AS PART OF OUR SOCIETY[1]

Larry R. Gerlach[2]

The immense popularity of sports, especially with television viewers, has led to many abuses. Pressures to win on college coaches and athletic directors have led to altered grade transcripts, false course credits, forgeries, violations of recruitment guidelines, undercover payments to athletes, and even physical abuse of student competitors. Educators are concerned over the low percentage of college athletes who actually graduate and the fact that many athletes who are not offered professional contracts upon completion of their campus careers suddenly find themselves unemployable in any other area.

In recent years, college and university educators, administrators, and athletic officials have become increasingly concerned about these problems. In January 1983, the National Collegiate Athletic Association passed a proposal to toughen academic requirements for incoming athletes. Other recommendations, such as one to prevent the exploitation of student athletes, have been or are being considered by both college administrators and professional sports organizations.

On October 25, 1983, participants in the Warren P. Williamson, Jr., Symposium at Youngstown State University in Youngstown, Ohio, addressed the subject of "Sports and Television." The symposium is an annual forum for consideration of the relationship of television to other aspects of our lives and future. Among the speakers at the symposium was Dr. Larry R. Gerlach of the Department of History at the University of Utah, whose topic was "Sport as Part of Our Society." Dr. Gerlach delivered his remarks at 10:45 A.M., October 25, 1983, in a lecture hall to approximately 250 students from Youngstown and other universities in the tri-state area. Dr. Gerlach's speech followed an address by Charles Alexander of Ohio University.

Larry R. Gerlach's speech: In the fall of 1925 the Hearst newspaper syndicate dispatched one of its premier writers, Laurence Stallings, to Philadelphia to cover a college football game between the universities of Pennsylvania and Illinois. It was the first sports

---

[1]Delivered to a symposium on "Sports and Television" in a lecture hall at Youngstown State University, Youngstown, Ohio, at approximately 10:45 A.M. on October 25, 1983.

[2]For biographical note, see Appendix.

assignment for Stalings, and seemingly a rather frivolous one at that for a man who had achieved an international reputation as a novelist, journalist, dramatist, and war correspondent; only recently his literary talent had again been acclaimed when he published that classic play about World War I, *What Price Glory?* The game featured the first eastern appearance of a gifted halfback Harold "Red" Grange. Despite a muddy field, the "Galloping Ghost" slithered for three touchdowns to lead the Fighting Illini to a smashing victory over the Ivy Leaguers. At the end of the game, while the other sweaty literati pounded out copy on their typewriters, the man who had covered the Great War from front-line trenches nervously paced through the press box. Finally, he shouted in exasperation: "I can't. I can't do it. It's too big."

Whatever the actual magnitude of the contest, Stallings was right about one thing: It *was* big. Far more Americans would carefully and critically weigh every word of his account of the Big Game than had ever even skimmed his reports of the Big War.

As Laurence Stallings realized, sport had become the most pervasive activity in modern American society. It had become a social-cultural phenomenon that extended into politics, education, art, economics, literature, mass communications, even international diplomacy. Public opinion polls and box office receipts reveal the obvious: More Americans are involved in sport either directly as participants or indirectly as spectators than any other voluntary social-cultural activity.

Moreover, sport is more than business enterprise, more than recreational activity, more than entertainment spectacle. Sport has become the psychic nerve center of American culture. The composition of spectators at athletic events demonstrates that the passion for sport cuts across ethnic, racial, economic, education, regional, religious, sociological, philosophical, sexual, and occupational lines. What other public gathering is so truly a cross-section of the American populace? What other happening transcends so completely the socioeconomic groupings that have traditionally divided us? Why is the sports section the largest unit of the newspaper (aside from classified ads), and why do surveys show that most readers spend far more time perusing the sports pages than any other part of the paper? Why has sport long since replaced the weather as the primary topic of daily chitchat? Why has locker room jargon and sport apparel become the language and fashion of an entire society?

Each spring I teach a course entitled, "The History of Sport in America." The course draws extremely well, with 300 or 400 students. It is the only course I teach where the students come convinced of the importance of the subject at hand and are deeply interested in exploring the topic at great length.

The first day of class I ask two questions: What is sport? What is athletics? I am not especially bothered when most students respond to my questions by casting their eyes downward in the unmistakable, "please don't call on me" message of body language. But I am perplexed that without exception, my students who cover sports for the local campus newspaper have no idea as to the nature of that about which they write. And I am absolutely amazed that the forty or fifty varsity athletes in class have no intellectual comprehension of the activity which brought them to the university in the first place, and which constitutes the driving force of their collegiate lives.

Sport, I am convinced, is the best known yet least understood phenomenon in American society. Much of our misunderstanding and misconceptions about sports stems from our failure to make meaningful distinctions among the various components of the sport world. And I don't want to get into a long definitional discussion here, except to highlight the difference between our two major sport phenomena.

One is sport. Sport is an extension of play involving two or more persons. Sport turns on games and contests which are highly organized, competitive, characterized by the established rules; but like play, sport has as its primary purpose fun for the participant.

Athletics, on the other hand, derives not from play at all, but from work. Athletics, as they have been referred to from the ancient Greeks, on, refers to intensely competitive confrontation between especially trained performers whose primary objectives are (a) spectator entertainment and (b) victory. Although the game involved in sport and athletics may be the same, as, for example, basketball, the two activities are worlds apart in terms of purpose and attitude. And to make this very complicated thing exceedingly simple, I would simply call your attention to the obvious difference that we understand between intramural sport and intercollegiate athletics.

My reason for raising the definitional issue is not to confuse but to clarify. The fundamental truth is that modern American society is preoccupied not with sport but with athletics. This symposium is in fact misnamed. The telecommunications industry is interested in athletic contests, not sporting events. However, today I will defer to convention and use *sport* and *athletics* interchangeably.

Two fundamental and basically irreconcilable philosophical conflicts color our involvement with sport. First of these is while we extol the amateur sportsman, we insist that our performers be professional athletes. Second, we want sport to be fun and to be purposeful. Now the amateur/professional dichotomy we can talk about later if you'd like.

Today, in trying to determine the sort of role or why the emphasis on sport in American society, I would like to look at that second phenomenon, *purposeful sport*. Although we persist in paying lip service to the fun or the recreational dimension of sport, the historical record clearly shows that Americans have always considered sports to be primarily a serious, that is, a purposeful activity. The roots for purposeful play extend deep into our past to the inability of New England Puritans to distinguish between work and play, to the efforts of pre–Civil War reformers and child guidance writers to promote sport as a means of developing ethical values and character traits, discipline, courage, teamwork necessary for success in a modernizing society, to the attempts of the late nineteenth century to utilize sport as a means of Americanizing immigrants, controlling the frustrations of industrial laborers, and ensuring the physical fitness of a virile nation on the global make, and to the recent systematic efforts of the government to employ sport as the mechanism of chauvinism, military preparedness, and international diplomacy.

Surely our emphasis on sport in modern America stems in large measure from the basic fact that Americans view sport as a serious, purposeful, enterprise related to the fundamental well-being of society at large. We still hear, and this is why I had a fight with my son, *ad nauseam,* such mindless prattling as "sport builds character," when the very actions of the lords of sport give lie to that simple-minded rhetoric.

What is the larger significance of our insistence on purposeful sport? I would like to quote to you and then comment on two observations, one from a student of American culture and another from a sports writer. The first is the student of American culture, Christopher Lasch, who wrote an issue entitled, "The Corruption of Sport." And Chris Lasch made this observation:

> The degradation of sport consists in its subjugation to some ulterior purpose, such as profit making, patriotism, moral training or the pursuit of health. Sport may give rise to these things in abundance but ideally it produces them only as by-products having no essential connection with the game.

And second is Robert Lipsyte, former sports writer for the *New York Times*:

> For the past 100 years most Americans believe that playing and watching competitive games are not only healthful activities but represent a positive force on our national psyche. This faith in sport has been vigorously promoted by industry, the military government and the media. The values of the arena and the locker room have been imposed on our national life. Even for ball games these values with their implicit definitions of manhood, courage, and success are not necessarily in the individual's best interest, but for daily life they tend to create a dangerous and grotesque web of ethics and attitudes. The sport experience has been perverted into a Sport World state of mind in which the winner was good because he won and the loser, if not actually bad, was at least reduced and had to prove himself over again through competition (i.e. Roberto Duran). Sport World is a grotesque distortion of sport, it limits the pleasure of play for most Americans while concentrating on turning our best athletes into clowns. It makes the finish more important than the race.

Well, among modern students of sport and society, terms like corruption, distortion, grotesque, and degradation are watch words. Surely these are among the byproducts of purposeful sport in America today.

The problems associated with purposeful sport have always been with us, but as we moved during the past three centuries from informal folk games and recreations before the Civil War to organized commercial sport after the Civil War to the era of national sport industries today, those problems have been increasingly troublesome and even pernicious. Just as television is responsible for the creation of the modern sport industry, television has contributed fundamentally to the problem of modern sport. The impact of television is manifold.

First of all, promotional. The enormous capacity of television to reach people has sold sport. If TV moguls devote so much programming time to sport, then sport must be important. If television devotes virtually an entire day to covering the Super Bowl, then that contest must be important. And by extension, sport itself must be very important. I would suggest that sport is regarded as being much more influential in our society than it really is because of the attention that television pays to it.

The second is financial. Television, with its national marketing capabilities, has brought unbelievable wealth to the world of sport and created nothing short of a sport industry. The result has been an extraordinary proliferation of sprot franchises and leagues—the major leagues, baseball, the National Football League, the NBA. When I was a kid, that is, in the 1950s, there was no resemblance to these institutions today. The result is greatly expanded playing schedules and the domination of sport not by the gentlemen sportsmen of the pre–World War II era, but by corporate executives. Once there was a Tom Yawkey and now there is a George Steinbrenner. It is often said—it is a cliché—that money is the root of all evil, and so it is with the world of sport.

Television, third, has fundmentally intruded on sport by directly affecting the contests themselves. Baseball's league championship series and nighttime World Series, football's absurd playoffs, and the hyperbolic Super Bowl, even NCAA's utterly reprehensible mass postseason basketball tournament, is due to television payoffs. Contests start at times that conflict fundamentally with common sense and the interest of performers because of television payoffs. My friend, Bear Bryant, says, "I'll play anytime, anywhere, if the price is right." Basketball now incorporates TV time-outs in a way that fundamentally affects the strategy and execution of the game. The New York Jets defeated the San Diego Chargers earlier this season thanks in part to a referee's concern

about a TV commercial. Two-minute warnings in professional
football games are there simply to provide one more commercial
opportunity. The point is that television does not merely broadcast
games, television manipulates the games.

Fourth, television broadcasts a distorted image of sport. Television promotes an illusion of sport, its values, its importance, its
role in society that is at odds, I think, with reality. Television is
not concerned with sport but with professional athletics. Television made the National Football League. Television made the National Basketball Association. Television made the golf and
professional tours. At the time of World War II, there was no stable NFL, there was no systematic professional basketball in this
country, there was no golf tour, there was no tennis tour. And today, when most Americans think of sport, they think of professional televised sport. And it is not surprising, I think, that the
sports that are televised are the ones that televise best. The coverage of sport in your local newspaper is a far more accurate view
of Americans' interest in sport than the broadcast schedules of the
national networks. Although I keep complaining about the coverage in my local paper, the sports editors know the real world of
sport.

Fifth, television promotes a perverse concept of athleticism as
the norm in sport world. The pros have become the models and
the value of the pro game becomes the values of the sport generally. I think that is obvious to anyone who has watched youth or
high school sports and those youngsters slavishly imitating the
pros. The athlete is a conspicuous minority among the inhabitants
of Sport World, yet the athlete sets the tone due to television.
Moreover, the incredible hype of television promotes a larger-
than-life concept of sport in which winning triumphs over participation.

Do not underestimate sport-think, which has fundamentally
and, I think, cruelly defined my son's self-image and his world
view. Now, as to the future of this, the pro games will go on, albeit
in somewhat diminished form. I think we can put up with only
so much shock, so much pimping, so much hype, and frankly so
much bull. Ratings are down for Monday night football whether
it is Monday night football on Monday, Monday night football

on Wednesday, Monday night football on Thursday, Monday night football on Friday, Monday night football on Saturday, or Monday night football on Sunday. Television has made sport almost a caricature, a grotesqueness of cheap commercialism where the broadcast all too often overshadows the contest. Monday night football is only the most gross offender. The likelihood is that network coverage will diminish in favor of cable broadcasting, which focuses more closely on the contest per se.

The greatest impact of television has been on intercollegiate athletics. Television in the next decade promises to accomplish what university presidents, athletic directors, and coaches have been trying to do for the last hundred years, namely, destroy intercollegiate athletics as an academic amateur sports enterprise. The open professionalism of intercollegiate athletics will, if nothing else, end the rampant corruption and blatant hypocrisy that currently afflict the collegiate sport establishment.

In 1873 Andrew D. White, president of Cornell University, responded thusly to a request by Cornell footballers to travel to Michigan for a game. "I will not permit thirty men to travel 400 miles merely to agitate a bag of wind." Three years later John Bascom, president of the University of Wisconsin, responding to student and alumni pressure for increased athletic programs as entertainment, said, "If athletics is needed for amusement, we should hire a few persons as we do clowns to set themselves apart to do this work."

Well, in the intervening years, university presidents learned about the money to be made from intercollegiate sport, if not directly then indirectly through alumni donations and so on, and a hundred years later, my friend, Bear Bryant, made the following statement: "I used to go along with the idea that football players on scholarships were student athletes, which is what the NCAA calls them, meaning a student first, an athlete second." We are, of course, kidding ourselves trying to make it more palatable to the academician. We don't have to say that anymore and we shouldn't. At the level we play, the boy is really an athlete first and a student second. When men like Joe Paterno of Penn State and Tom Osborn of Nebraska agree to play a kickoff classic in August in East Rutherford, New Jersey, after publicly arguing

that the game was against the best interests of the program and
their players, the collegiate sport scene is in sad shape.

Well, I ducked the basic issue here, which is the great appeal
of sport today, and I wrote some remarks which are intended to
be provocative. And I wrote them after watching a Lite Beer commercial which kind of puts the whole thing together. Mr. Butkus
and Mr. Smith, trying to achieve a modicum of class and culture,
have gone to the opera. Well, I wonder why the great appeal of
sports today. I think it is very simple. Sport accurately reflects
American society, its frustrations, its fantasies, its cultural values.
The arena is at once apart from and a part of everyday life. But,
of course, the same thing is true for a variety of other activities,
i.e., the opera. So what is the special appeal of sport? My son
asked me about the comment he hears always that sport is simply
children's games played by adults. He said, "Is that right?" And
I think that is right, and I think that is why sport plays such a
very important role in our society.

Four reasons: Sport is pure. That is, sport is the only non-
ideological cultural activity in our society or any society. Literature, art, music, dance, all of these activities are value-laden. Sport
is only a kinetic enterprise. There is no value represented as two
athletes line up to run 100 meters. It is pure. It is innocent. It is
basic.

Second, sport is elemental and elementary. It involves confrontation between obvious good guys—my team—and obvious bad
guys—your team. That conflict is cleanly, finely, and clearly resolved through the use of physical force. The more physical the
game, the more popular the game. One defeats opponents literally
by beating them, and that is the basic mechanism of conflict resolution. It is, in a word, kind of Star Wars mentality.

The third, sport is simple and simplistic. It is the cultural activity in our society that is wholly intelligible to the lowest common denominators in society. My thirteen-year-old can discuss
basketball on an equal basis with me. It is the ideal cultural activity in a democracy, rather like the public school system. It is intelligible, too, and embraceable by all elements in the culture.

And fourth, sport, to continue the childhood metaphor, is fan-
tastic. That is, sport turns on illusion, on fantasy, on dreams,

whether dreams of future glory or nostalgic remembrances of glories that once were or might have been. I think it symbolic that the relationship between journalism, particularly broadcast journalism, and sport is so evident and that the majority of TV addicts, Star Wars freaks, fairy tale fanatics, and sports fans in this country are children. Sport represents in large part the maintenance of childlike innocence and values in a harsh, cynical adult world.

Speaking of kids, to wind up my formal remarks, whatever the reality of sport and sport personalities, in my youth there were perceived heroes, perceived exalted values to sport participation. That's why I ate and slept and breathed sport. As a youth, I viewed sport as a blissful refuge from everyday life. Today my son views sports as a component of the cheapness, tackiness, selfishness, corruption of everyday life. The tragedy is that where I once believed, my son and his friends have never believed. Fantasy has always been an essential, perhaps the essential, element in sport. If sport loses its illusions and becomes part and parcel of reality, I fear very much about the future of sport in American society.

SPORTS AND POLITICS[1]
James B. Reston[2]

When Walter W. ("Red") Smith passed away January 15, 1982, journalism lost a distinguished stylist whose writing set a standard for literary excellence that other members of his craft admired and emulated. Frequently called the Dean of American Sportswriters by fellow journalists, Smith shunned the label, modestly saying, "I'm just a newspaperman trying to write better than I can."

Shortly after Smith died, his alma mater, the University of Notre Dame, decided to honor his accomplishments and to promote the teaching of journalism and writing by instituting the Red Smith Lectureship in Journalism. The lectureship, sponsored by the Department of American Studies, brings a distinguished journalist to the campus annually for a public lecture, classes, and informal meetings with students and faculty.

On April 20, 1983, James B. Reston, the *New York Times* columnist,

---

[1]Delivered as the first Red Smith Lecture in the Auditorium of the Memorial Library at the University of Notre Dame, South Bend, Indiana, at 8 P.M., April 20, 1983.
[2]For biographical note, see Appendix.

delivered the first Red Smith Lecture. Reston, known as Scotty, who has
served the *Times* as a correspondent, columnist, Washington bureau
chief, associate editor, and executive editor, has earned two Pulitzer
Prizes, three Overseas Press Club awards, and many other honors. His
syndicated column appears in newspapers around the world.

The Reverend Theodore M. Hesburgh, C.S.C., president of Notre
Dame, delivered the opening remarks to inaugurate the lectureship.

Following Father Hesburgh's statement, Reston was introduced by
Smith's son, Terence, also a graduate of Notre Dame and at the time editor of the "Washington Talk Page" of the *New York Times*. Smith spoke
movingly of his father and expressed pleasure in the choice of Reston as
the inaugural speaker in the series, saying:

> When the idea of an annual Red Smith Lecture in Journalism was
> first mentioned to me, I thought immediately of Scotty Reston as the
> ideal person to give the first lecture. After all, Scotty is a reformed
> sportswriter himself. . . . In any event, Scotty has been first in just
> about everything he has done since. He has been a commanding fig-
> ure in American journalism for forty-five years and he remains that
> today.

The lecture was delivered to an audience of from 250 to 300 students,
faculty members, journalists, and residents of South Bend in the Auditorium of the Memorial Library on the Notre Dame campus at 8 P.M., April
20, 1983.

The lecture was published shortly after it was delivered. The reception to the publication was excellent, with several professors using the address in their classes.

James B. Reston's speech: Father Hesburgh, Mr. Chairman, Ladies and Gentlemen:

What we have just heard from Terry Smith tells us a lot about
his father and his mother, who didn't get a Pulitzer Prize but got
Terry and Terry's sister, Kit, who are with us this evening. Red
once delivered a brief eulogy at the funeral of a colleague. "Dying
is no big deal," he said. "The least of us can manage it. Living is
the trick." He knew the trick. And the proof lies at the end, when
your children become your friends, and sons can talk about their
fathers as Terry talked about Red.

I'm fairly sure Red Smith didn't like lectures. They are the
calisthenics most young reporters have to endure during the spring
practice of their youth. But later on we tend to doze off during lectures and wonder who is that old geezer reading this paper, and
who do you suppose wrote it for him, and how long will he go on?

I didn't really know Red very well. I broke into this business thinking of him as a *Herald Tribune* man—one of those cheeky poets on 40th Street in New York who got together at Bleeck's pub after work and wondered why the *Times* was so stuffy.

There were only three blocks between the *Times* on 43rd Street and the *Herald Tribune,* but that was quite a distance. We concentrated on the solemn aspects of life, and always boasted that our circulation was larger than theirs, maybe because a lot of obscure professors were always dying on the obit pages of the *Times,* whereas their departure never seemed to be noticed in the *Herald Tribune.* On 40th Street, they had more fun, though the saddest obit we ever ran in the *Times* was about the death of the *Herald Tribune,* and we didn't know how much we needed it until it was gone.

I envied Red. He stuck to sports reporting all his life and knew at the end of each day who won, whereas I drifted into the reporting of foreign affairs, where you have to wait twenty-five years to know how it all came out, and maybe not even then.

Our paths crossed from time to time, occasionally at the end of his life on Martha's Vineyard, but we had different tastes in sports. He loved fishing, which I thought was a sucker's game, because I never caught anything. I loved basketball, which I still think, next to ice-skating, is the nearest thing in sports to ballet. But Red mocked it as "round-ball," with a lot of giants running up and down a shiny floor in their underwear.

Fortunately, my prejudices weren't shared by Jim Roach, the sports editor of the *Times,* who thought Red was better than Grantland Rice or Westbrook Pegler or any of the other illustrious sportswriters who had gone before him, because he worked harder and wrote better than any of them. Somebody once asked Red whether it was "easy" to write. "Sure," he said, "All I do is cut open a vein and bleed." Anyway, Roach happily brought Red over to the *Times* in 1971, and that closed the gap between 40th and 43rd streets.

My guess is that Red would have preferred it if Notre Dame had not invested in the Department of American Studies but in the Sports Department and concentrated on getting another good quarterback. Maybe he will forgive me, however, if I talked, not too long, about sports, and politics, and newspapers, which were among the many American studies that amused him.

Sports play a more important part in our lives than we realize, because they are about the only thing left to us these days that are definite. They are played by rules that most folks understand. They have umpires and referees who settle disputes with a whistle and a wave of the hand. (I wish we could do that in Washington.) They have a beginning, a half-time for reflection, and a definite conclusion.

Also, they demand precision under stress. It is said that diplomacy requires the same. But anybody who watched Joe Theismann of Notre Dame passing the Washington Redskins to victory in the Super Bowl last year, with a charging line before him, and with inches between the receiver and the defender, and between victory and defeat, knows the difference.

H. G. Wells, who was no athlete, and probably never heard of Knute Rockne, made a point I think Red Smith would have liked. Despite all his success as a novelist and a prophet, Wells wrote, "I am a journalist all the time, and what I write goes now and will presently die."

Of course, Wells was wrong about Red Smith, who is still alive in this room today, but Wells said something about the difference between the physical and intellectual worlds that is worth remembering:

Are there no men of politics to think as earnestly as one climbs a mountain, and to write with the uttermost pride? Are there no men (in politics) to face the truth as those boys at Mons faced shrapnel, and to stick for the honor of the mind and for truth and beauty as those lads stuck to their trenches?

He would have liked Red.

Maybe this is a poor analogy, for it's a little easier to coach a team than to direct a foreign policy in a turbulent world without rules. But the physical struggle for excellence is not irrelevant to the political world of ideas.

Anybody who works in the nation's capital is constantly reminded of the difference between sports and politics. Coaches recruit the best talent available, and insist on performance. Presidents all too often settle for a pick-up team of friends and loyalists and tolerate incompetence. If a coach keeps losing more games than he wins, the head of the athletic department doesn't keep him on with the excuse that he's a nice guy who didn't mean to lose. He gets rid of him. Parliamentary governments do the same, but not under our system in Washington. There, recruiting and hiring are remarkably casual, and resigning, even among incompetents, almost unheard of.

When Argentina invaded the Falkland Islands to the surprise and embarrassment of the British government, Lord Carrington, the foreign secretary, resigned at once, but after the fiasco of the Bay of Pigs, the tragedy of Vietnam, and the aborted military raid in the desert of Iran, nobody quit and nobody was fired, with the exception of Cyrus Vance in the Iran affair. The administration of sports may be harsh and sometimes cruel, but in many ways it is preferable to our administration of government.

I believe in sports, with some reservations I will come to later, and I think Red Smith did too. For a time, I was in charge of sports publicity at Ohio State University in 1933. The next year, I was traveling secretary for the Cincinnati Reds and helped Larry MacPhail introduce night baseball into our national life. I'm not boasting, for in those two years, with my brilliant advice, Ohio State's football team had about the worst season in its history, and the Reds ended up in the National League cellar.

But I learned something in the process, though I remind you that I'm a Scotch Calvinist, and nothing makes us happier than misery. What I learned in Columbus, or so I believe, is something about the relationship between sports and academic opportunity in a university.

For the people and legislature of the state of Ohio paid more attention to its teams than to the university's Department of Liberal Arts and Sciences. They wanted a university equal to the best in the Big Ten or anywhere else, not only in sports but in *everything* else. And the legislature, populated mainly by Ohio State's graduates, voted the funds to keep the university in the forefront of American education.

One other point about the importance of sports to American studies. Some years ago, the late Paul Douglas, the senator from Illinois, was invited by the Touchdown Club of Washington,

D.C., to address the All-American high school, college, and professional football players, all arrayed uncomfortably in their starched shirts and black ties.

"You have done a wonderful thing for this country," he said. "You have brought back pageantry." When America revolted against the British crown, he argued, it rejected the pageantry of the monarchy. But pageantry, he insisted, is important, and you have restored it on the playing fields of America. In your conflicts, he said, you have made clear the pride of the states. You have given us heroes, now in short supply. But what will happen to the heroes after it's all over? he asked. This was a question that troubled Red Smith until the very end.

Sports reporting is by far the best discipline and school of journalism. It has an audience that has seen the game and instant replay on television on disputed points.

The political reporter may get an argument if he's wrong, but the sports reporter may get a punch in the nose. This encourages accuracy.

I don't want to get into the middle here between the English Department and the Sports Department, but I think they have more things in common than they realize. I have had the privilege of knowing, for many years, William Saltonstall, who was principal of one of our most distinguished academies at Exeter for two decades—a superb athlete and teacher, whom I admire as much as any person I have ever met. Just before he retired, he said he was proud of the academy's record in the teaching of mathematics and science, and, he hoped, in honest dealing, but he was disappointed in the record of teaching young people how to write. There was something wrong, he thought, at least for the rising generation, in the process of teaching kids to write through parsing sentences and juggling subjects, adverbs, and verbs. Was there another way? Could journalism help?

We never got around to testing that question, but I believe the simple arts of reporting may have something to contribute. If, for example, the teacher invites somebody to come into the classroom who says something, does something, and departs—and the question is put: "What happened? What did this character look like, and say, and do?"—and then lets the students write their answers, and challenge one another's reports, making the practical point that whatever they do in future life, as doctors, lawyers, or garage superintendents, they must know how to make their thought clear, especially when they are writing love letters, which I hope has not gone out of style.

Parenthetically, I wonder if it would not be useful to offer such a course in sports reporting at Notre Dame, with Red Smith's columns as a textbook. One of the things that troubles universitites is how to prepare their athletes for a career after their playing days are over. They are attracted to the world of communications, but most of them have little training for it.

As another subject for American Studies I would argue that sports in my generation have probably done as much to remove the stain of racial prejudice as anything else. I am just old enough to have known Branch Rickey and remember the fuss when he brought Jackie Robinson as the first black into the big leagues. And now to see the basketball playoffs for the national championship dominated by black players is a transformation in our time that could scarcely have been imagined a generation ago.

I don't want to get too silly or too romantic about this. I'll get to the bad news later, but meanwhile a few words about sports and politics. Red didn't write much about politics, but he was very good when he did and usually very funny. Once, by accident, when the Philadelphia Athletics were training in Mexico, he wrote about an interview with Leon Trotsky, then banished by Stalin to the suburbs outside Mexico City, and headlined: "Red Trotsky talks to Red Smith." It's a good example of Red's gifts of observation, description, and humor. You ought to look it up.

In 1956 he went to the Democratic presidential nominating convention in Chicago and described in sporting terms Harry Truman's entrance into the hall. This was after Mr. Truman had retired, if he ever did.

"The old champ," Red wrote, "came striding down the aisle with outriders in front of him and cops behind, and memory recaptured the classic lines which once described Jack Dempsey's entrance in a ring: 'Hail! The conquering hero comes/Surrounded by a bunch of bums.'"

There are some similarities between sports and politics in America. They are both very hard and even cruel in their temptations on the players and the families. I have come to believe that the ideal life should be a gradual ascending journey stretching across the decades until at last you reach the top with the respect of your colleagues, as Father Hesburgh has done in this university and as Red Smith did in journalism.

But that's not what normally happens in sports or politics. It is not a gradual ascending journey over the years even for the stars; not a marathon but a hundred-yard dash, marked by spectacular victories and defeats, often measured by inches and accidents. There is very little room at the top, and even for those who make it, the glory road is all too short and the rest of it "a treadmill to oblivion."

Some, of course, clear the hurdles from sports to politics and continue the journey. For example, Jack Kemp, the former pro quarterback from Buffalo on the Republican side, and Bill Bradley of the New York Knicks and New Jersey on the Democratic side—both among the most effective members of the Congress.

But in general, life for most of the big shots in both fields is almost too dramatic at the beginning and too lonely at the end. This was not true of Dwight Eisenhower, an indifferent football player who went from his triumph in the last world war to the White House, or of Jerry Ford, who went from center on Fielding Yost's Michigan football team to the Congress and the presidency. And it is certainly not true of that old sports announcer out of Illinois, Ronald Reagan, who went from the football bench to Hollywood, on to be governor of California and preside over the White House.

Even so, when you look at the political record as a whole, there is a different story. Since 1960, we have had six presidents. Kennedy, who came so fast, so early, was murdered. Johnson, who succeeded him, gave up in despair. Nixon, who did so many good things, made one terrible fumble and trick play at Watergate, and was run out of town. And Jimmy Carter, the triumphant underdog, had the misfortune to run into Iran, as Johnson ran into Vietnam, and is now, like Nixon, living with his memories and his regrets.

I won't bore you by recounting the sad stories of the many sports heroes, from Lou Gehrig, who was struck down by illness, to so many of his successors, who thought they could prolong their successes with drugs, or relieve their defeats with booze. All I'm saying is that success in sports and politics have one thing in common: It's a sometime thing, giving them more praise than they deserve and, often later, more pain than they can bear.

This is one of the many things that impressed me about Red Smith. He has a sense of pity for the sports heroes who were gone. He lived long enough to know them when they were rookies, described their skill at the height of their careers, but never forgot them when their knees gave out.

He gathered together on Martha's Vineyard, at the urging of some publisher and his son Terry, a collection of his columns, *To Absent Friends*. It is a beautiful book, and typical of Red. For it was a series of memories of the forgotten sports heroes, many of them written before the old boys died so that they would know that somebody remembered.

Yet there are differences between sports and politics in America, I think, that have affected public opinion, and not always in a good way.

We are coming down now to George Orwell's *1984,* and his fear that the corruption of politics began with the corruption of langauge. He thought that if we couldn't describe in words where we were going, we'd never get there. The English Department here would probably agree.

The language of sports is vivid. It deals with dramatic limited events, as on a stage. And in Red Smith's generation and mine, which has stretched from the days of our national isolation to the deepest involvement in the politics of the world, politicians and the political reporters have come to use the language of sports to describe the conflicts of politics at home and abroad.

We talk incessantly on the sports pages about "who's number one," and "who's ahead"; of "ancient rivalries" and "trick plays," and runs, hits, and errors; of pennant "races" and "throwing the bomb" on the football field—all natural terms in describing games.

We have come to use the same terms in our discussion of domestic and world politics. We are engaged in a momentous debate now about "who's number one" in the nuclear arms race, whether the "offense" or the "defense" is ahead in the development of these apocalyptic weapons. We measure "who's ahead" in the presidential "race" by statistics, like box scores—all in keeping with Frank Kent's book entitled *The Great Game of Politics*.

This box-score approach to politics expresses, I think, a national attitude, a way of looking at a complicated world in simplistic sports terms, which is easy but not very helpful. For world politics today is no game, if it ever was. It's not like sports, where the clear object is to win, tear down the goal posts, and go home. For there is seldom ever an end to conflict in world affairs, and often you dare not win, for the only home you can go home to is the world, which is increasingly demanding cooperation rather than confrontation.

Also in a changing world, there are no unavoidable, unchangeable rivalries. At the beginning of this century, there seemed no greater menace to peace than the rivalry between France and Great Britain, but within a little more than a decade, they had signed the Entente Cordiale, and a few years later were allies together in the terrible First World War. The enemies in the Second World War, Germany and Japan, are now allies, and the Soviet Union, our ally in World War II, is now our most serious adversary. And I remind you of the paradox and unpredictability of history, for both world wars were supposed to have been fought to defend the freedom of Poland and the other eastern European states that are now the satellites of the Soviet empire.

All this talk of who's ahead and who's behind reminds me of one of Adlai Stevenson's favorite stories from the last world war, when he was at the Pentagon in charge of shipping arms to the Russians in the early days of the struggle against Hitler and the Nazis. The Soviet minister in Washington complained to him that Washington was behind in delivering its weapons to Moscow. Stevenson said this was probably so because Moscow was behind in defining precisely what weapons were needed. "Look," the Soviet minister said, "I'm not here to discuss my behind but your behind."

But now I'm getting behind, so to go on. The English Department, I think is going to have to help us speak across the barriers of this complicated world in something other than the simplistic clichés of the sports press box.

Sports clichés are too simple, too combative, too dramatic, whereas the work of politics in the largest sense is to work away patiently until some honorable compromise is reached. The religious wars went on for hundreds of years, partly because of the unyielding language on both sides, and did not end until the spirit of toleration rescued both those who believed in the Cross and those who believed in the Crescent.

I hasten to add this criticism didn't apply to Red, for he had the gift of writing serious things in an amiable way without clichés and without rancor. Maybe he acquired it here at Notre Dame, but my guess is that he had it in him, because his writing was essentially a reflection of his character. He mastered the art of criticism without hurting people—or leaving so much as a drop of poison in his wake. Maybe this is because he suffered himself along the way.

Finally, it pleases me, Father Hesburgh, to think that Notre Dame is remembering him in this way, for I know he loved this university, and if occasionally even a few students look through his writings, and remember that "living is the trick," that would please Smith—such a common name for so uncommon a man.

When he died, nobody of his generation in our profession was celebrated with more respect from his colleagues—which he prized the most—except perhaps Walter Lippmann, so I'll close with a remark Lippmann made to his own university colleagues many years ago.

"We have come back here, along with those we love," he said, "to see one another again. And being together, we shall remember that we are part of a great company; we shall remember that we are not mere individuals isolated in a tempest, but that we are members of a community—that what we have to do, we shall do together, with friends beside us. And their friendliness will quiet our anxieties, and ours will quiet theirs."

I thank you, Father Hesburgh and the university, for giving me the opportunity to say a few words in honor of so fine a human being.

BLACK STUDENT-ATHLETES: TAKING RESPONSIBILITY[1]

Harry Edwards[2]

A year ago, the editor of this volume observed:

> At a time when the popularity of college sports is at an all-time high, many Americans have been shocked and disillusioned by revelations of altered grade transcripts, false course credits, forgery, violation of recruitment rules, undercover payments to athletes by alumni, hypocrisy in the maintenance of academic standards, and even physical abuse of athletes in intercollegiate competition. Still other revelations of large sums of money earned by schools from televised games, pressures from alumni to produce winning teams, and multi-million dollar salaries offered star collegiate athletes by professional clubs all added to the problem. (*Representative American Speeches, 1982-1983*, p 138)

In an effort to correct some of the abuses cited above, members of the National Collegiate Athletic Association, in January 1983, approved a rule, known as "Proposition 48," which raised academic requirements for freshman players at institutions in the NCAA's top competitive bracket, Division I. Far from solving the problem, the new rule stirred bitter controversy and charges of racial discrimination by some black administrators and leaders.

On October 24, 1983, the College Board, at its national forum and annual business meeting, sponsored a panel discussion on the subject, "Academic Standards and the Student Athlete." The College Board is a national organization that provides direction, coordination, services, and research in facilitating the transition of students from high school to college, and that sponsors a variety of guidance, admissions, and placement examinations throughout the year.

Speaking against Proposition 48 at the symposium was Frederick S. Humphries, president of Tennessee State University, who said that the rule "blames the victims" of exploitation and that the test-score provision would keep many black athletes off the football fields and basketball courts during their first year of college. (*The Chronicle of Higher*

[1]Delivered at a symposium at the College Board National Forum and annual business meetings in a meeting room of the Hyatt Regency Hotel in Dallas, Texas, at approximately 10:45 A.M. on October 24, 1983.
[2]For biographical note, see Appendix.

Education, D. 7, '83, p 27.)

Dr. Harry Edwards, an associate professor of sociology at the University of California at Berkeley, and author of many articles and books on athletics and race, also spoke at the meeting, but in support of the new NCAA regulation. "Sport has . . . been a powerful source of black spiritual sustenance, a forum where black pride, courage, intelligence, and competitiveness have been exhibited and reaffirmed. Indeed, the athletic field is second only to the battlefield in providing demonstrable proof that what blacks have lacked in America is not the competitiveness, the initiative, the will, the fortitude or the intelligence to excel. What we have lacked principally are equitable circumstances and opportunities. Blacks, therefore, must be involved in sport because we are inextricable involved with America."

Dr. Edwards delivered his speech to approximately 200 College Board member representatives, staff, and media reporters in a meeting room at the Hyatt Regency Hotel in Dallas, Texas, between 10:45 A.M. and 12:15 P.M. on October 24, 1983.

Harry Edwards's speech: For as long as organized sports participation has been associated with American education, the traditionally somewhat comic, not altogether unappealing "dumb jock" image of the student-athlete has endured. Though over the years, there have been some notable efforts by journalists, academicians, and sports activists to expose the desperately serious realities masked by this caricature, only recently has American society been jolted into recognizing the extensive and tragic implications of widespread educational mediocrity and failure among student-athletes, and—no less importantly—that "dumb jocks" are not born; they are being systematically created.

The fact of negative academic outcomes, then, does not in and of itself significantly distinguish the careers of black student-athletes from those of their nonblack peers in sports to which blacks have access in numbers—most particularly in basketball and football. Rather, it is the disparate character of black student-athletes' educational experiences that has spawned special concern.

Black student-athletes from the outset have the proverbial "three strikes" against them. They must contend, of course, with the connotations and social reverberations of the traditional "dumb jock" caricature.

But black student-athletes are burdened also with the insidiously racist implications of the myth of "innate black athletic superiority," and the more blatantly racist stereotype of the "dumb Negro"—condemned by racial heritage to intellectual inferiority. Under circumstances where there exists a pervasive belief in the mutual exclusivity of physical and intellectual capability, and where, furthermore, popular sentiment and even some claimed "scientific evidence" buttress notions of race-linked blacks' proclivities for both athletic prowess and intellectual deficiency, it should come as no surprise that the shameful situation of the black student-athlete has been for so long not only widely tolerated, but expected and institutionally accommodated.

But the exploitation of black student-athletes is not occasioned and perpetuated merely through the unwitting interplay of sports lore and racist stereotypes. The sociological etiology of their circumstances is far more complex.

Sports, over the last forty years, have accrued a reputation in black society for providing extraordinary, if not exemplary, socioeconomic advancement opportunities. This perspective has its origin in black identification with the athletic exploits and fortunes of Jesse Owens, Joe Louis, Jackie Robinson and other pre-and early post-World War II black sports heroes. In the contemporary context, blacks also find ample, if only ostensible, vindication of their overwhelmingly positive perspectives on sports. For instance, though blacks constitute only 12 percent of the U.S. population, in 1983 just over 55 percent of the players in the National Football League were black, while twenty-five of the twenty-eight first-round NFL draft choices in 1981 were black. As for the other two major professional team sports, 74 percent of the players making National Basketball Association rosters and 81 percent of the starters during the 1981-1982 season were black, while blacks comprised 19 percent of America's major league baseball players at the beginning of the 1983 season. The last nine Heisman Trophy awards have gone to black collegiate football players. In 1982 not a single white athlete was named to the first team of a major Division I All-American basketball roster. Similarly, twenty-one of the twenty-four athletes selected for the 1982 NBA All-Star game were black. And since 1958, whites have won the NBA's

MVP title only three times as opposed to twenty times for blacks. And, of course, boxing championships in the heavier weight divisions and "most valuable player" designations in both collegiate and professional basketball have been dominated by black athletes since the 1960s.

Black society's already inordinately positive disposition toward sport has been further reinforced through black athletes' disproportionately high visibility in the mass media relative to alternative high-prestige occupational role models (e.g., doctors, lawyers, engineers, and college professors).

Further, black families' attitudes and expectations relative to sports are deeply influenced by the media and by perspectives on sports held more generally in black society. Research carried out by Professor Melvin Oliver of UCLA discloses, for example, that black families are four times as likely as white families to view their children's involvement in community sports as a "start in athletic activity that may lead to a career in professional sports." Similarly, black parents were shown to be four times as likely as white parents to link their children's involvement in community sports programs with prospects for attaining an athletic scholarship. And not only are black families more predisposed than white families toward a high valuation on their children's sports involvement, but the more economically disadvantaged the black family, the greater its propensity toward a high valuation.

The already heightened black emphasis upon sports achievement that is fostered through myths, stereotypes, family and community attitudes, and the media is further intensified by black youths' early educational and athletic experiences. The exaggerated emphasis upon sports leads to a situation wherein by the time many black student-athletes finish their junior high school sports eligibility and move on to high school, so little has been demanded of them academically that no one any longer even expects anything of them intellectually.

At the high school level, the already unconscionable emphasis upon black student-athletes' athletic development is institutionally abetted by policies which make athletic participation conditional upon minimum standards or, more typically, no standards of academic performance. Thus, as late as the spring of 1983, it was still the case that only a handful—about twenty-five—of the nation's sixteen thousand plus high school districts had set minimum academic standards for sports participation. And of those which had such standards, most required only that the student-athlete maintain a 2.0, or "C" average, or that a student-athlete's grade card show no more than one failing grade in an academic year. The problem with these minimum standards, of course, is that they have a way of becoming maximum goals. Student-athletes typically strive to achieve precisely the standards set—nothing more, nothing less.

As a result of a lack of creditable academic expectations and standards, and the disproportionate emphasis placed upon developing their athletic talents from early childhood, an estimated 25 to 35 percent of high school black athletes qualifying for scholarships on athletic grounds cannot accept those scholarships due to accumulated high school academic deficiencies. Because of these academic deficiencies, the fact that black, unlike white student-athletes, must be truly "blue-chip" to receive a scholarship offer from a major college or university (studies show that blacks are overrepresented among starter and underrepresented in reserve positions among scholarship football and basketball players), and because approximately 90 percent of America's collegiate sports activities offering scholarships for all practical purposes are still "lily-white," black athletes get less than 6 percent of all the athletic scholarships given out in the United States.

At the collegiate level, a systematic rip-off begins with the granting of a four-year "athletic scholarship," technically given one year at a time under existing NCAA rules. This means that though the athlete is committed to the school for four years, the school is committed to the athlete for only one. Strictly speaking, each year the athlete is under the pressure of having to earn the scholarship anew.

Another problem with the four-year scholarship is that, more often than not, it takes the average nonathlete student on a major Division I college campus four-and-a-half years to complete a four-year degree. Even special provision for a fifth year of support for the athlete at the athletic director's or coach's discretion—support which few student-athletes actually receive—does little to alter this situation in the black student-athlete's favor because relatively few black Division I football or basketball players complete their sports eligibility with a year or less of academic work remaining before graduation.

Additionally, because normal college student responsibilities—course selection, registration, allocating personal time and resources, etc.—are so frequently carried out by Athletic Department personnel for student-athletes, many do not even get the "education" achieved on the campus but outside of the classroom. This educational experience would include developing personal responsibility and initiative, learning to deal with large bureaucracies effectively, learning to set personal priorities and properly allocate time and resources.

Not surprisingly, then, studies indicate that as many as 65 to 75 percent of those black student-athletes awarded collegiate athletic scholarships may never graduate from college. Of the 25 to 35 percent who do eventually graduate from the schools they play for, an estimated 60 to 65 percent of them graduate either with physical education degrees or in "Mickey Mouse" jock majors specifically created for athletes and generally held in low repute.

Even those student-athletes who are drafted by the pros soon learn that the actual realities are quite diferent from the rumored rewards that have fueled and motivated their athletic development. Approximately 8 percent of the draft-eligible student-athletes in collegiate basketball, baseball, and football are actually drafted by professional teams each year. Of those athletes drafted, only 2 percent will be offered a professional contract, and just over 60 percent of these are back on the street within two to three years. So, before the average black professional basketball, or football player is twenty-nine years old, his sports career is already over, and these former "big guns" face the challenges of making a living utterly unarmed educationally in our technologically sophisticated society.

In terms of resolving this situation, one frequently advocated "option" must be eliminated at the outset. This is the idea of a mass black exodus from American sport. Such a retreat would be ill-advised even were it achievable—which it is not in our sport-saturated society. Sport is simply too important, too influential, and too deeply embedded in American life for blacks to abstain from sports involvement.

It is also the case that, for all of its drawbacks, sports participation has generated many concrete and intangible benefits for black society. It has provided a portion of the black student-athlete population—myself included—a means of achieving an education and of establishing productive careers in both sport and other occupational areas. Sport has also been a powerful source of black spiritual sustenance, a forum where black pride, courage, intelligence, and competitiveness have been exhibited and reaffirmed. Indeed, the athletic field is second only to the battlefield in providing demonstrable proof that what blacks have lacked in America is not the competitiveness, the initiative, the will, the fortitude, or the intelligence to excel. What we have lacked principally are equitable circumstances and opportunities. Blacks, therefore, must be involved in sport because we are inextricably involved with America.

What is called for is not a black retreat from sport but reflection upon the black situation in sport followed by a collective and coordinated offensive aimed, first, at aiding student-athletes presently vulnerable to academic victimization and athletic exploitation, and second, at taking responsibility for eliminating or neutralizing the social and institutionalized forces responsible for the systematic creation and accommodation of the black "dumb jock."

There are most certainly things that the sports establishment can do in this regard—such as the National Collegiate Association's passage of Rule 48 at its January 1983 convention. But, it is by no means sufficient for the colleges and the universities belonging to the NCAA and similar sports governing bodies to establish regulations, such as Rule 48, that essentially impact upon student-athletes' educational preparation at the high school level. College and university officials must specify what they are going to do to correct the situation on their own campuses—especially since it is only at the collegiate level that a direct educational obligation is assumed, by implied contract, in exchange for student-athlete sports participation. And many college and university officials will have an excellent opportunity to do precisely this at the

January 1984 NCAA convention in Dallas, Texas, where some
167 proposals await delegate action as part of the official agenda.
Among these proposals are many which long have been advocated
as steps toward ameliorating the tragic circumstances existing for
many student-athletes in collegiate sports: an end to freshmen athletic eligibility; institution of a guaranteed four-year athletic
grant-in-aid provision for accredited tutorial services; a strict
monitoring of student-athlete majors, graduation rates, and grade
point averages; provision for improved medical care; and increased
funds to lower student-athletes' living expenses and incidentals.

Black communities, black families, and black student-athletes
themselves also have critically vital responsibilities in efforts to
remedy the disastrous educational consequences of black sports involvement. The undeniable fact is that through its blind belief in
sport as an extraordinary route to social and economic salvation,
black society has unwillingly become an accessory to and a major
perpetrator of the disparate exploitation of the black student-
athlete. We have, in effect, set up our children for academic victimization and athletic exploitation by our encouragement of, if
not insistence upon, the primacy of sports achievement over all
else. We have then sold them to the highest bidder among collegiate athletic recruiters and literally on the average received nothing in return for either our youths or ourselves. It would,
therefore, constitute a fraudulent rationalization and a dangerous
delusion for blacks to lay total responsibility for correcting this situation upon educational institutions and sports governing bodies.

As a people, we have a responsibility to learn about the realities of black sports involvement—its liabilities as well as its opportunities—and to teach our children to deal intelligently and
responsibly with these realities. We can no longer permit many
among our most competitive and gifted youths to sacrifice a wealth
of personal potential on the altar of athletic aspirations, to put
play books ahead of textbooks. We must also recognize that, in
large part, the educational problems of black student-athletes will
be resolved not on the campus, but in the home. Black parents
must work toward establishment and enforcement of creditable
academic standards at all educational levels, and they must instill
black youths—athletes and nonathletes alike—with values stress-

ing the priority of excellence in educational achievement irrespective of official school academic standards. If this tack is take, I am convinced black youth will rise to the occasion in academics no less than they have in athletics.

And, finally, it must be made unequivocally clear that in the last analysis, it is black student-athletes themselves who must shoulder a substantial portion of the responsibility for improving their own circumstances. Education is an activist pursuit and cannot in reality be "given." It must be obtained "the old-fashioned way"—one must earn it! Black student-athletes, therefore, must insist upon educational discipline no less than athletic discipline among themselves, and they must insist upon educational integrity in athletic programs rather than, as is all too often the case, merely seeking the most parsimonious academic route to maintaining athletic eligibility. The bottom line here is that if black student-athletes fail to take an active role in establishing and legitimizing a priority upon academic achievement, nothing done by any other party to this American sports tragedy will matter—if for no other reason than a slave cannot be freed against his will.

PRESS FREEDOMS

IT'S TIME YOU TIGERS ROARED[1]

Daniel Patrick Moynihan[2]

On April 25, 1983, Senator Daniel Patrick Moynihan delivered the keynote breakfast address to the American Newspaper Publishers Association at its ninety-seventh annual convention in the Waldorf-Astoria Hotel in New York City. Traditionally, the association has invited only the most highly distinguished public figures to deliver the keynote speech at its annual meeting, and 1983 was no exception. Senator Moynihan, the senior senator from New York, had previously held Cabinet or sub-Cabinet positions under Presidents Kennedy, Johnson, Nixon, and Ford. He is the only person in American history to serve in four successive administrations. He was ambassador to India from 1973 to 1975 and U.S. permanent representative to the United Nations in 1975–1976. Earlier, he had served on various diplomatic missions involving the Alliance for Progress, NATO, and the General Agreement on Tariffs and Trade. He had also been professor of government at Harvard University and director of the Joint Center for Urban Studies of MIT and Harvard.

Senator Moynihan told an audience of over fifteen hundred publishers and their spouses and guests that they had failed to publicize actions by the Reagan administration and Congress that he believed jeopardized constitutional protections for freedom of speech. The senator stated that "this is a truly menacing atmosphere gathering in Washington," but that news organizations had not reported it and that their owners had not lobbied against it. He charged that the press had been negligent in publicizing such matters as the passage of a law that made it a crime to publish the name of a covert intelligence agent even when the name was taken from public documents; the administration's efforts to stop leaks of sensitive information; and the Senate filibuster to stop a proposal to strip the Supreme Court of power to review state court decisions on prayer in schools.

The senator was warmly applauded at the conclusion of his speech and, in interviews afterward, several publishers expressed their agreement with Moynihan's charges.

Senator Moynihan delivered his address in the Grand Ballroom of the Waldorf-Astoria Hotel at 8:30 A.M. on April 25, 1983.

[1]Delivered to the 97th annual convention of the American Newspaper Publishers Association in the ballroom of the Waldorf-Astoria Hotel in New York City at 8:30 A.M. on April 25, 1983.

[2]For biographical note, see Appendix.

133

Senator Moynihan's speech: My grandfather once said of a man of whom he did not wholly approve that he had "the soul of a butler." I would like to think there are none such here. Certainly Judge Medina thought so. "Fight like tigers," he told you here in 1976. But when it comes to defending principles of press freedom, more than great heart is required. Vigilance is required: a matter our ancestors understood perhaps better than we.

Let me speak to some particulars.

First, I would wish to report on the international front. The efforts of the free nations and the free press of those nations to slow the efforts at UNESCO to establish—I use Leonard Sussman's term—"as a universal standard governmental control of the news media" have begun to have effect.

The decisive event here was the meeting at Tailloires, in France, in May 1981, of a group of leading journalists, editors, and publishers which adopted a declaration stating in no uncertain terms that:

There can be no international code of journalistic ethics: the plurality of views makes this impossible.

It also asserted that:

Journalists seek no special protection nor any special status and oppose any proposals that would control journalists in the name of protecting them.

And, speaking directly to UNESCO, the declaration said:

We reject the view of press theoreticians and those national or international officials who claim that while people in some countries are ready for a free press, those in other countries are insufficiently developed to enjoy that freedom.

Thus armed, I went to the Senate floor with an amendment to the Department of State authorization bill asserting the sense of the Congress that the president should withhold from UNESCO that portion of our contribution that would pay for:

Projects or organizational entities the effect of which is to license journalists or their publications to censor or otherwise restrict the free flow of information within or between countries, or to impose mandatory codes of journalistic practice or ethics.

The Senate passed the measure unanimously, and the House strengthened it to bar the transfer of *any* money at all to UNESCO should any part of the so-called new international information order be implemented. The president signed the measure into law on August 24, 1982.

Now, finally, the U.S. position was clear: We would oppose any legitimization of state control of the media and we would not pay for it.

The law (P.L. 97-241) required a report from the State Department, which we received this February. It is sensible, cautious, but positive. UNESCO, it states, "is not, *at this time,* moving further in that direction.

Even so, may I suggest that it took us something like ten years to respond to an event that should have aroused us in ten weeks. It was in 1972 that the Soviet Union first came forward with its proposals for a new international information order. By then, the democratic values of the UNESCO charter had been under a steadily mounting attack, and UNESCO had been politicized with the totalitarians in near complete control. But it is difficult to disagree with Tom Bethell's judgment that the American press did not report this sea change. And so it came to pass that when the press itself began to be attacked, there was for the longest time little if any notice of that either, much less a prompt response.

Just so here at home.

It is something of a routine to decry the insensitivity of successive adminstrations to issues of freedom of information and freedom of the press. Yet one senses that such insensitivity is growing, much as government grows. It is not irony, I fear, but a general direction of history that we observe in the performance of the present administration. It has increased the size of government to unprecedented levels—this coming year federal outlays will be 25.1 percent of GNP—and it has simultaneously increased pressures on the press.

Consider the Agent Identities Protection Act of 1982. I am vice chairman of the Select Committee on Intelligence. I would wish it understood that the time came when we had to legislate on this subject. Not because of anybody or any journal present in this room, but for different reasons altogether. We *had* to legislate.

Even so, we did not have to violate the Constitution. But when we did legislate, that is exactly what we did do.

One section of the bill makes it a crime to identify a covert agent even if the identity was discovered from publicly available information and even if the person disclosing the information had not the least desire to harm the national interest. Section 601(c) of the National Security Act now provides for the imposition of a criminal sanction on a person who discloses the agent's identity:

On the course of a pattern of activities intended to identify and expose covert agents and with *reason to believe* that such activities would impair or impede the foreign intelligence activities of the United States . . .

By a vote of fifty-five to thirty-nine, the Senate substituted this language for similar language adopted by the Judiciary Committee, which included the crucial distinction that such disclosure had to be done with:

intent to impair or impede the foreign intelligence activities of the United States by the fact of such identification and exposure.

The final vote on June 10, 1982 was eight-one to four. Four senators voted no, one was paired against. Five senators in all.

Thus, at the urging of the administration, "reason to believe" was made a crime—a standard which is at home in the civil law of negligence, but hardly a basis for sending an editor to jail.

Philip L. Kurland of the University of Chicago Law School had called this law the "clearest violation of the First Amendment attempted by Congress in this era." I agree, and repeatedly so stated in the course of our debate on the floor of the Senate.

Henceforth, a newspaper must proceed at the peril of prosecution if it publishes the name of a covert agent in a news story intended to inform the public and not to harm U.S. intelligence operations. The risk that proceeds from the uncertainty of the statutory language is the very essence of a "chilling effect." Has any newspaper publisher challenged it in court? I believe not. I trust this reflects only a sound litigative judgment to let the government make the first move—a step we hope never to be taken. But I do implore you *not* to avoid this risk by imposing self-censorship where none is warranted.

More disturbing yet was the legislation advanced in the summer of 1982 by the senior senator of North Carolina to deny voluntary prayer in public schools and public buildings.

Clearly, if the Supreme Court can be denied jurisdiction in one aspect of the First Amendment, it can be denied jurisdiction in any aspect. The First Amendment guarantees that Congress shall make no law "respecting the establishment of religion . . . or abridging the freedom of speech, or of the press. . . . "

Now what is disturbing is that Congress, arguably, *has that power.* This is contained in the so-called Exceptions Clause in Article III, Section 2, of the Constitution:

. . . The Supreme Court shall have appellate jurisdiction, both as to law and fact, with such exceptions, and under such regulations as the Congress shall make.

No less an authority than Justice Owen J. Roberts, speaking to a luncheon of the Association of the Bar of the City of New York on December 11, 1948 (after, that is, his retirement), so stated:

I see nothing. I do not see any reason why Congress cannot, if it elects to do so, take away entirely the appelate jurisdiction of the Supreme Court of the United States over state Supreme Court decisions.

Indeed, disinclined as he was to "tinkering with the Constitution," he proposed to amend it. He thought it was:

Just good housekeeping, just insurance and just good common sense to put into the Constitution explicitly what you and I all think has been there by tradition for a long time and which ought not be subject to change.

But we didn't amend the Constitution. And when the court-stripping bill came to the floor, we did not have the votes to defeat it—the Helms measure. And so on August 16 last year, four of us, lead by Senators Weicker and Packwood, commenced to filibuster. On September 21, a motion to invoke cloture was rejected fifty to thirty-nine. On September 21, a motion to invoke cloture was rejected fifty-three to forty-seven. On September 22, a motion to invoke cloture was rejected fifty-four to forty-six. They were gaining on us. Sixty votes, of course, were needed. But then, on the next motion, their majority dropped by one vote to fifty-three.

An election was coming—five weeks away—the season was advancing, and so the proponents gave up. The bill was recommitted. But note, it was never defeated. There was always a majority for it. This despite the fact that it would have profoundly shaken the balance of powers of the American system of government, and in the face of a courageous statement by the attorney general that:

Congress may not, however, consistent with the Constitution, make "exceptions" to Supreme Court jurisdiction which would intrude upon the core functions of the Supreme Court as an independent and equal branch in our system of separation of powers.

It was a close call. And again may I ask, how well was it reported? How *much* was it reported? In my judgment, very little. In the aftermath, Bill Petersen of the *Washington Post* wrote a good analysis:

The debate was not one of Republicans versus Democrats or Liberals versus Conservatives so much as the moderate center standing up for the Constitution against "the radical right."

But I repeat, How much was it reported?

Let me make a small request. This week while you are in session I am going to introduce the amendment Justice Roberts proposed. If I get any support in the Congress, may I hope for some from you?

And finally to more recent events. On March 11, 1983, the president issued a directive which requires all government employees with access to classified information of any sort to sign standardized nondisclosure agreements subject to judicial enforcement as a precondition to their access, and which authorizes polygraph tests of such employees with respect to suspected leaks. In testimony before joint hearings of the House Judiciary Subcommittee on Civil and Constitutional Rights and the Post Office and Civil Service Subcommittee on Civil Service, Mr. Floyd Abrams, the distinguished authority on press freedom sought, as he put it, to put the directive in historical context. He said:

It is not difficult to generalize about these policies. They are unique in recent history. They are coherent, consistent, and (unlike those of some recent administrations) not a bit schizophrenic. They are also consistently at odds with the notion that widespread dissemination to the public of information from diverse sources is in the public interest. It is almost as if information were in the nature of a potentially disabling contagious disease which must be feared, controlled, and ultimately quarantined.

A singular feature of this directive is that it requires prepublication clearance of articles and books written by policy-making officials *after* they leave government, if they had access to "sensitive compartmented information"—which is intelligence information to which access is limited to protect sources and methods. Suffice it to say that there are presently about 200,000 people in Washington with such clearances—people who can and do contribute much to public debate after leaving office. Abrams observes:

Some of the most important speech that occurs in our society would be subjected to governmental scrutiny and that, if the government in power decided that something could not be written or said, to judicial review.

He reminds us that in 1980, the last year for which we have statistics, the government placed secrecy classifications on 16 million pieces of information. The effect of the new presidential directive could well be to strike at the heart of the ability of the public to be informed about their government.

True, it may spare us some memoirs of presidential aides. But is this sufficient recompense for the silence, or reticence, of the great body of men and women who move in and out of public service in a mode that is, in fact, unique to the American democracy?

Last Thursday we also learned that the March 11 directive was based on an interagency study which proposed prison terms for offenders. Now this could readily lead us to the point where at any given moment half the Cabinet is in jail. Mind, there have been times in the recent past where we almost reached that point without the aid of any special legislation. Even so, one wonders if the republic is really ready for such an experiment.

With something such in mind, on March 22, I wrote the president enclosing a more or less routine press clipping of the day citing "senior Reagan administration" officials and suchlike letting us in on details of "low altitude flights by United States spy planes" flying about Central America. I wrote that I assumed there would be "a thorough internal executive branch investigation of this matter" and asked if the Intelligence Committee might be favored with a copy of the findings. I have yet to hear back on the results.

Nor will I. The president won't reply to me. Nor, probably, should he.

He will respond to you. But I don't think he has heard from you, nor has Congress. This is truly a menacing atmosphere gathering in Washington. And it is not at all confined to the executive branch. Freedom of the press, freedom of information is under attack.

It is time you tigers roared.

THE COSTS OF FREEDOM OF THE PRESS[1]

CAROLYN STEWART DYER[2]

The *Washington Post* spent an estimated $500,000 to $750,000 defending itself against a libel suit by an executive of Mobil Oil. The plaintiff spent an estimated $1 million. Carol Burnett spent about $2 million before her libel suit against the *National Enquirer* came to trial. A freelance columnist accumulated bills amounting to $25,000 just on the appeal of a procedural question in a libel suit initiated by Ralph Nader. It is estimated that pursuing a relatively uncomplicated case through a short trial—perhaps a week—costs about $25,000.

These are just a few of the facts cited by Dr. Carolyn Stewart Dyer in a lecture titled "The Costs of Freedom of the Press" presented to the Humanities Society at the University of Iowa on March 16, 1983. Dr. Dyer, who is an assistant professor in the School of Journalism and Mass Communication at the University of Iowa, announced to her audience that she was going to talk about the meaning of freedom of the press and how the costs of litigation affect the meaning. "The basic questions," she said, "are, What does freedom of the press mean? What is its function in society? How does one determine what it means?" In addition to a Ph.D. degree in mass communications, years of teaching experience, and extensive scholarly publications, Dr. Dyer's qualifications included having worked as a correspondent and reporter for both newspapers and television.

---

[1]Delivered to the Humanities Society of the University of Iowa in the faculty lounge of the English-Philosophy Building at the University of Iowa, Iowa City, at 8:00 P.M. on March 16, 1983.
[2]For biographical note, see Appendix.

Dr. Dyer delivered her lecture, which was one in a series of four sponsored by the Humanities Society, to an audience of approximately fifty faculty members, students, and interested people from the community in the faculty lounge of the English-Philosophy Building at the University of Iowa, Iowa City, Iowa, at 8:00 P.M. on March 16, 1983.

Carolyn Stewart Dyer's speech: I selected this title for my lecture to permit me to decide what to talk about, as my research involves several issues that could fit the title. I have studied the costs of establishing newspapers on the frontier and the question whether it was really possible for anybody to start one to express his views as other historians claim. I have been interested in the emotional costs of the way the media cover rape on the victims. But I am going to talk about the meaning of freedom of the press and how the costs of litigation affect the meaning.

The basic questions are, What does freedom of the press mean? What is its function in society? How does one determine what it means?

Freedom of the press is guaranteed in the First Amendment to the Constitution, which provides that Congress shall make no law abridging freedom of speech or of the press. Therefore, freedom of the press, in a major way, means what the courts, the U.S. Supreme Court in particular, has said it means in the context of particular cases and controversies. But it means more legally, philosophically, politically, and socially.

A *de facto* meaning of freedom of the press may be inferred from the day-to-day performance of the media by assessing their ability and willingness to exercise freedom in their pages and broadcasts and their propensity to go to court to seek clearer definitions or expansions of its meaning.

Freedom of the press may be evaluated by measuring the relative ease with which people who have something to say have access to the media forum in which to say it. And freedom of the press may be estimated by observing the diversity of information and opinion available to the public to hear, see, and read.

I will argue that all of these elements of freedom of the press, or freedom of expression more broadly characterized, are dependent on economic factors. Specifically, those who have money, can get money, or who are willing to take economic risks to engage in litigation are the individuals and institutions that determine the subjects on which new or more finely tuned First Amendment law is made. They often determine the nature and substance of the law as well, as in many cases the questions are narrow and the alternative conclusions are limited.

Conversely, those media that do not have money, that believe or know they cannot get money, or that choose to spend their money in other ways generally perform in a manner designed to reduce or eliminate the risk of becoming involved in litigation. They usually do this by avoiding the full exercise of their free press rights and by declining to embark into unmapped areas of First Amendment law. When they become involved in litigation, they often attempt to negotiate out-of-court settlements that do nothing to clarify the law.

Both behaviors—the self-selection of many, if not most, First Amendment litigants and the abstention from the exercise and testing of First Amendment rights—have consequences for those who have something to say and those wanting or needing to know diverse information and ideas.

At the risk of insulting the intelligence of some of you, I want to outline the general parameters of freedom of the press at the present time, according to the U.S. Supreme Court, as background for the evidence I will present to support my argument.

Freedom of the press, at its most fundamental level, involves the right to publish without prior approval of the government—with some exceptions.

Freedom of the press provides the right to circulate publications without first acquiring a license to do so from the government.

Freedom of the press involves the right to communicate truthfully about and to criticize government, public officeholders, and persons and institutions voluntarily in the public eye.

Freedom of the press, so far, guarantees rather narrow rights to gather, select, and edit information for publication without accountability to the government or individuals allegedly harmed by the information. Despite repeated attempts by the media to have the First Amendment interpreted to include a right to gather news, the U.S. Supreme Court has recognized only a narrow right to attend criminal trials and report on them and a very limited, highly qualified, and, in practice, nearly useless right of journalists to protect the identity of their confidential sources and the unpublished and unbroadcast information they gather for journalistic purposes.

Freedom of the press, finally, requires that when the media are subject to government action, special care be taken to minimize restrictions on First Amendment rights.

Legally, freedom of the press does *not* provide the right to publish and circulate obscene material.

It does not include a right to publish information harmful to national security if that information poses an immediate, highly probable, very serious danger to the government—however all these qualifications are defined at a particular time.

Freedom of the press does not protect the media in willfully or recklessly disseminating false information that exposes a person to harm.

It is in regard to the exceptions, the qualifications, and the limitations that most First Amendment litigation arises and where there is greatest need for litigation to further define and clarify the boundaries and exceptions, to delineate what is and is not protected by the First Amendment. I should acknowledge that some people argue quite convincingly that the press has more freedom without court action; that in nearly any case, even a decision favorable to the press diminishes freedom by more precisely delimiting the boundaries. I think, however, in the real world that litigation is necessary.

I come now to the basic questions I want to address here: What are the costs of freedom of the press? What is the cost of First Amendment litigation? What are the costs of exercising uninhibited freedom of the press? What are the costs to the general public and to people with ideas to communicate an economically determined meaning of freedom of the press?

The evidence with which to fashion answers to these questions is varied. There are, of course, the written opinions of courts in deciding First Amendment cases. There are—more figuratively than literally—account books detailing the expenditures of specific parties on First Amendment litigation and on mechanisms to avoid and protect against litigation. There are the individual and institutional experiences of those who have been parties to litigation and those who have taken measures to avoid it. The content of the media may be studied and compared to the legally defined outline of freedom of the press to determine how narrowly or broadly the media define their freedom in functional terms.

I have used all these devices and sources to complete a series of four case studies on the costs of freedom of the press, and I have foraged through others' writings for the rare tidbits of evidence pertinent to the questions. In general, I have focused my attention on the fringes or extremities—which are not the best labels— where behavior and consequences are most dramatic and the distinctions and qualifications most clearly understood. Specifically, my research includes a study of about fifty legal problems of an underground newspaper, *Milwaukee Kaleidoscope,* during its four years of publication in the late 1960s and early 1970s. I have studied the personal and legal experiences of the editor of another underground newspaper, *Madison Kaleidoscope,* in Wisconsin, and the reaction of the established Wisconsin media to a case in which the editor refused to answer a number of grand jury questions about his sources for a statement published in the paper taking credit for the bombing of a building on the University of Wisconsin campus which took one man's life. He was found guilty of contempt of court and spent longer in jail than any other journalist. With John Soloski, my colleague in the School of Journalism, I have studied the *Progressive* magazine case in which that left-of-center publication asserted a right to publish an article about the so-called H-bomb secret in violation of the Atomic Energy Act of 1954. And Soloski and I have studied a series of related cases initiated by the Gannett media conglomerate in which the company sought access to courtrooms, to other meetings of public importance, and to the records of governmental agencies and institutions working in partnership with the government.

There are several means by which the media become parties to litigation.

Most threatening and offensive to the Constitution are instances in which the media become overt targets of government action to prevent or censor publication before it occurs. The Pentagon Papers and *Progressive* cases fall into this category.

The media can be objects of litigation or defendants in cases initiated by the government and individuals or institutions for violation of criminal laws or rights of individuals to protect their reputations or privacy. In this category are cases involving obscenity, disclosure of secret government information, threats to overthrow the government, and the civil law of libel and invasion of privacy.

More subtly, and more difficult to prove, the media can be targets of law enforcement agents and individuals who attempt to harass the media and mortally wound them through repeated prosecutions and litigation that drain their coffers dry. The underground press, perhaps the *Progressive* and other political journals, have had these experiences.

The media and their employees can be subjects of government efforts to get information from them, usually through subpoenas to present evidence and testimony to grand juries. More recently, this area of the law, referred to as reporter's privilege, has expanded, with journalists being the subjects of subpoenas from criminal defendants and civil litigants to get their testimony and evidence.

Finally, the media can be voluntary litigants by going to court to assert legal or constitutional rights, such as access to places and information controlled by the government.

The evidence to support my argument comes from examples in my case studies and the work of others. For the sake of the argument, I ask you to accept two premises which are, in fact, quite debatable.

1. The government should not interfere directly or indirectly in the media's process of gathering, selecting, and disseminating information and ideas.

2. News, other information, and opinions are perishable commodities; thus a government-enforced delay in publication of even an hour is too long.

I will talk about each element of my argument separately, considering the cost of litigation to media that have engaged in it, the costs relative to the resources of the media and their relative ability to get money to support their litigation, the costs in time and energy to pursue litigation, the extent to which other media in general support the particular media involved in litigation.

What does litigation cost? It depends. It depends on the amount of attorney time involved in consultation, legal research, investigation, drafting of documents, and appearances in hearings and court proceedings. It also depends, to some extent, on how long it takes a case to be concluded. It depends on the length and number of copies of documents to produce and reproduce, miscellaneous expenses such as phone bills, and travel and court fees.

There has been little research on these costs of litigation—the costs of any kind of litigation. The news media have recently begun focusing attention on another cost, the astronomical awards juries have granted in libel cases, such as the $26.5 million a jury awarded a former Miss Wyoming who claimed to be defamed by a fictional piece in *Penthouse*. That award was reduced to $14 million and has been appealed. [The federal Court of Appeals in Denver reversed the verdict in the case, depriving the plaintiff of the reduced award.—*author*] But the media have not generally attended to the costs of the litigation itself, the costs regardless of the outcome of cases. These costs are, in my opinion, more significant because they occur more frequently and are concerns to most of the media.

There are rough estimates available for the costs of several recent libel cases. The *Washington Post* spent an estimated $500,000 to $750,000 defending itself against a libel suit by an executive of Mobil Oil. The plaintiff spent an estimated $1 million or more with the case at trial and an appeal is likely if not already filed. [This case is being appealed.—*author*]

Carol Burnett spent about $2 million *before* her trial in a libel suit against the *National Enquirer*. [The U.S. Supreme Court refused to review the case. The original jury award of $1.3 million to Burnett was reduced to $750,000 by the trial judge and reduced again to $150,000 by a California Court of Appeals.—*author*]

A freelance, conservative columnist had accumulated bills of $25,000 just through the appeal of a procedural question in a libel suit initiated by Ralph Nader.

In general, it is often estimated that pursuing a relatively uncomplicated case through a short trial—perhaps a week—costs about $25,000.

There are some figures available for prior restraint cases, too.

The *New York Times* spent $150,000 for outside legal counsel and the *Washington Post* spent about $70,000 on its attorney during the three weeks the Pentagon papers cases took, and both had other associated expenses. The *Times* spent another $50,000 preparing a defense for the reporter involved in the Pentagon Papers project in anticipation of a prosecution for violation of the Espionage Act, which never materialized.

In a 1976 case in which the Nebraska Press Association and a coalition of media sought to have a judge's order prohibiting publication of certain evidence and testimony presented in an open court hearing ruled unconstitutional, the parties spent about $125,000 in about nine months.

The *Progressive* case, which lasted seven months, cost about $240,000, a figure that does not include the contributed services of ACLU attorneys and representatives of another law firm who worked without charge.

In its series of about fifty legal tangles, incuding two appeals to the Wisconsin Supreme Court and one to the U.S. Supreme Court, *Milwaukee Kaleidoscope* accumulated about $400 in fines, $5,200 in bail and bond—at the rate of about $375 per arrest—and used an estimated $150,000 in contributed legal services in four years. In a brief filed in one of its federal court cases, the newspaper argued that if it had to pay a fine of $2,000 for an obscenity conviction, the paper would be destroyed; the same if it missed an issue.

Gannett spent an estimated $30,000 on its case seeking a ruling by the U.S. Supreme Court that the news media have a right to attend pretrial hearings, and the Richmond, Virginia, newspapers spent about $100,000 to get a ruling by the Supreme Court recognizing a right of the press and public to attend criminal trials.

These costs seem substantial, but their magnitude is more clearly understood relative to the economic resources of the media involved.

For the New York Times Company, its legal expenses for the Pentagon Papers case were a small proportion of its $290 million in revenue in 1971. This point is more evident in comparison to the $250,000 spent preparing the stories on the Pentagon Papers for publication.

Gannett spent about one ten-thousandth of its receipts in 1979 to pursue all its newsroom, or press freedom, cases, expenses in most instances voluntarily incurred by the company.

The collective resources of a large segment of the Nebraska and a few out-of-state news media were undoubtedly substantial, but the $125,000 for its case was paid with numerous contributions generally ranging from $25 to $3,000.

While the Gannett corporation had income of about $1 billion in 1979, the typically small dailies in the chain are operated under economic constraints that make them seem to be a day or two away from bankruptcy. The estimated $30,000 Gannett spent getting its court-access case to the Supreme Court would pay the annual salaries and benefits of perhaps two young reporters in the typical general news section of a Gannett daily which has only about five reporters.

The H-bomb case expenses of $240,000 amount to about one-third of the magazine's annual budget in 1979. And about 20 percent of the budget was a deficit made up by subscriber contributions.

Milwaukee Kaleidoscope had only one profitable year, taking in just over $50,000, most of it from record company advertising, and having a surplus of only $1,000 in 1969. The paper clearly could not have paid for its legal assistance worth about $150,000 with its own resources. Ultimately litigation expenses and a shortage of funds to publish the paper ended the life of *Kaleidoscope*. The *Progressive* faced possible extinction after more than seventy years of publication as a consequence of its litigation expenses.

There are other costs of litigation not usually considered. They are the expenditures of human energy, time, and the will to continue publication.

The editors and publisher of the *Progressive* spent about two-and-one-half months working nearly full time on matters associated with the case, including consultations with attorneys, appearances in court, investigation, giving interviews to other news media, and traveling for speaking engagements ultimately aimed at raising money for the case. Although the case lasted seven months with some periods of relatively little activity, the editor of the *Progressive* said the experience was as if a year had been taken out of his life. He speaks most warmly not of the financial contributions the magazine received, but of the contribution of a copy editor by a New Jersey newspaper. The copy editor worked through a backlog of manuscripts the staff had not had time to work on because of the case.

Its numerous legal battles took a heavy toll on the time, energy, and will of the *Milwaukee Kaleidoscope* staff. For example, on two occasions, staff members had to retrieve copies of the paper from newsstands, once to alter them and another time to destroy them so vendors would not be charged with the sale of obscene material and then refuse to carry the paper in the future. The staff spent many nights waiting for bail bondsmen to release staff members from jail for disorderly conduct, spurious traffic offenses, and other questionable violations of the law. It became routine for the newspaper to go to federal court to seek the right to sell it in suburbs, at fairs, and festivals and in parks without a license. At one point, the paper published a statement that some day it was going to sue everyone, all at once, and get it over with, and it asked for nominations. The paper had an average of one case pending a month, the cases lasting an average of five months with as many as ten cases pending at one time. It won every case it appealed, though the individuals involved had been convicted at trial or denied a right to sell the paper in every instance. In the end, the editor and publisher declared backruptcy and announced that he was too tired to raise more money to fight legal battles and to support the paper. He concluded that the most important thing the paper had done in its four-year history was simply to manage to publish in the face of official conduct designed to prohibit its publication. It won its last case in the U.S. Supreme Court nearly a year after publication ceased.

Although these are only a couple of examples, interviews with other media litigants evoke similar recitations relevant to the facts of their cases—the sapping of their time and energy for legal matters preventing proper attention to their reason for existing, to publish or broadcast.

If a news medium does not have resources of its own to engage in litigation, it has two general options once it's involved—drop out or attempt to raise it. Dropping out often means the media have to permit the censorship demanded or refrain from publishing, concede at least in principle their legal wrongs, and often to cease attempting to exercise broad First Amendment rights. The experiences of the underground newspapers—*Kaleidoscope* and many others—and the *Progressive,* and studies others have done on editorial reaction of the media to First Amendment cases, indicate that success in raising moral support and money for First Amendment litigation has been unpredictable. Success has seemed to depend on the extent to which other media have perceived the potential impact of a legal situation on their publication—or recognized their own self-interest—the media's acceptance of the legal strategy and arguments of the institutions involved, and, most importantly, the extent to which the media approve the political position, sense of responsibility, or propriety of the medium in litigation. In short, journals at the extremes of the political spectrum, the underground press, and the media disseminating allegedly obscene or at least sexually explicit material have had the most difficulty raising money. The ombudsman at the *Washington Post* during the *Progressive* case described the situation as the need for the litigants, such as the *Progressive,* to gain the approval of the "First Amendment Club," by which he meant the *Post,* the *New York Times,* and other large, well-to-do, and presumably influential, media. Without their support, which the *Progressive* generally lacked until late in the development of its case, funds were very difficult to raise. *Playboy* magazine was the only publication to contribute money to its defense fund. A few news organizations eventually signed amicus briefs in support of the magazine. The editor of the *Progressive* described the situation and reaction as if the influential media were asking "what this little magazine was doing jeopardizing OUR First Amendment rights."

The editor jailed for contempt for refusing to answer questions about the sources of a statement attributed to the individuals who bombed the building was treated in news and editorials in Wisconsin newspapers as if he were implicated in the bombing itself. A typical headline read, "Editor Jailed in Bombing." He did not know who did the bombing or where the statement claiming credit came from. He refused to answer the grand jury questions on First Amendment principle, principle that was not appreciated by the established media and wasn't understood by many in the underground press who used press freedom without knowing anything about it. The established media were nearly unanimous in opposing his claim of a reporter's privilege to protect his sources, even though he argued for and won a qualified privilege for all journalists in Wisconsin.

The end result is that for economic reasons, those media with money and those generally approved of by the established influential media—the First Amendment Club at the local, state, or national level—are the ones that determine which cases will be pursued through the court system to final decisions with their elaborations of the meaning of freedom of the press. These media, then, are capable of determining which issues will be raised, and less completely able to decide which will be rejected. With some exceptions, the influential media, such as the *New York Times,* the *Washington Post,* CBS, and others tend to pursue issues that protect the status quo or raise questions of detail within the existing framework of freedom of the press and the political system.

In the Pentagon Papers case, for example, the *New York Times* did not argue that there should never be prior restraint on publication; rather, it argued that prior restraint was appropriate in some instances, just not that one. Without intending to disparage the *New York Time*'s motives in the Pentagon Papers case, I would argue that it was not asking for much—the right to publish a secret historical document which did not really warrant secrecy and which produced no development of the law. In contrast, the *Progressive's* objective was to expose a fundamental error on which nuclear weapons and national defense policy was based, the argument that only a few knew the secret of a workable H-bomb and this technological information could be kept secret in the interest of national defense. Nat Hentoff, in the *Village Voice,* wrote that the opposition to the *Progressive* on the part of the First Amendment Club resulted in part from a thirty-year conspiracy of silence by these influential media on the subject of nuclear weapons. The result was an absence of intelligent discussion of nuclear policy among the people and delegation of all the decision-making to the scientists and defense establishment. The relatively rapid development of support for a nuclear freeze in the past year

or so obscures the radical position taken by the *Progressive* only
four years ago and the vigor with which it was attacked at the
time.

The Pentagon Papers and *Progressive* cases, however, had
vastly different effects on the media pursuing them. While the
New York Times continued, probably without missing a percentage point return on investment, the *Progressive* has wavered close
to extinction as it continues to attempt to pay off the debts from
the case and to raise money to continue publishing, in particular,
its contributions to the debate on nuclear policy. The ability of
each to use the press freedom they have is determined, in part, by
their economic circumstances.

· In contrast to the influential, established media that directly
and indirectly make major contributions to defining the parameters of the legal meaning of freedom of the press and use their freedom on a relatively regular basis, and the politically more activist
and radical media that stretch the boundaries of freedom more often, or at least more dramatically, are the run-of-the-mill daily
and weekly newspapers, radio and TV stations that contribute little to the effort to refine the meaning of press freedom and only
rarely have occasion to use the freedom won by others. Put more
bluntly, the *River City News* probably doesn't need freedom of the
press, because it doesn't use it very often, in large part because it
is expensive to engage in the probing, analytical journalism that
requires freedom, and because they do not want to risk costly litigation by doing so.

In summary, then, economic factors affecting all three groups
of media as I have described them define freedom of the press. The
ordinary local media don't use it or define it because it's too costly.
The media at the fringes of radical politics and social propriety
use all the freedom they can get, but risk litigation, the cost of
which can destroy them and diminish the breadth of debate on
public affairs. And the First Amendment Club members which
use freedom modestly and do engage in litigation to extend it define the parameters within which the law is developed, and those
parameters do not extend as far as they might. The consequence
is an impoverished debate on public affairs.

FINDING MEANING IN LIFE AND DEATH

TRIBUTE TO JOHN F. KENNEDY[1]

THOMAS J. SCANLON[2]

> Summoning artists to participate
> In the august occasions of the state
> Seems something artists ought to celebrate.
> It makes the prophet in us all presage
> The Glory of a next Augustean age.

Actor Cliff Robertson read these words, written by the poet Robert Frost for John F. Kennedy's 1961 presidential inauguration, as part of a free concert at the Kennedy Center for the Performing Arts in Washington, D.C., on November 22, 1983, to commemorate the twentieth anniversary of the president's assassination. The commemoration was an appropriate reminder of the tradition of White House concerts, which Kennedy had begun, and of his determination to create a national cultural center in the capital of the world's richest nation.

The quiet, eloquent observance was the culmination of more than a week of special ceremonies, newspaper and magazine features, and television programs marking the assassination. On November 22, in cities and towns across the country, citizens paused to pay tribute to the fallen president.

In Washington, the day began with a special mass at Holy Trinity Church attended by the Kennedy family. In his eulogy at the mass, the late president's brother, Senator Edward M. Kennedy, said,

> We have known great men and women in our time, in other countries and our own. Yet there was a spark in him so special that even his brief years and early passing could not put it out. He made us proud to be Americans, and the glow of his life will always light the world. For him on this day twenty years ago, the journey came to an end. But for us here and others everywhere, there are "promises to keep" and "miles to go before we sleep."

During the day, more than thirty thousand people streamed past Kennedy's grave, a crowd estimated to be the largest ever to visit Arling-

---

[1]Delivered as part of a concert in memory of President John F. Kennedy at the Kennedy Center for the Performing Arts in Washington, D.C., beginning at 5:30 P.M., November 22, 1983.

[2]For biographical note, see Appendix.

ton National Cemetery in a single day. (Charles Fishman, *Washington Post*, N. 23, '83, p 1)

Among the 2,800 in the audience for the concert in the Kennedy Center were Senator Edward M. Kennedy, Caroline Kennedy, Jean Kennedy Smith, Ethel Kennedy, Sargent Shriver, Joan Kennedy, former defense secretary Robert McNamara, and former senator John Tunney.

Chairman Roger L. Stevens of the center opened the ceremonies with an introduction in which he reminded the audience of President Kennedy's interest in the arts. The first musical offering was an aria from *Adriana Lecouvreur* sung by soprano Grace Bumbry.

At this point, Thomas J. Scanlon, a former Peace Corps member, addressed the assembled concert-goers. He began:

> I have been asked to pay tribute to President John F. Kennedy tonight, and I feel honored. I held no position in his administration. I did not know him personally. I am here only as one of the thousands whose lifes were profoundly influenced by him. . . . I hope that I speak not only for myself here but for all of us whose lives and careers were inspired by John F. Kennedy.

Following Scanlon's eulogy, the concert continued with performances by Isaac Stern, Leonard Rose, Eugene Istomin, and Mistislav Rostropovich, and concluded with choral excerpts from Leonard Bernstein's "Mass."

In his eulogy, Scanlon chose to concentrate on only one of Kennedy's "many achievements that will secure [his] place in history," the Peace Corps, "because it tells us so much about him."

Thomas J. Scanlon's speech: I have been asked to pay tribute to President John F. Kennedy tonight, and I feel honored. I held no position in his administration. I did not know him personally. I am here only as one of the thousands whose lives were profoundly influenced by him.

When John Kennedy took the oath of office, I was a graduate student in philosophy. Six months later, I entered the Peace Corps. Today, I am still involved with the problems I worked on then. The Peace Corps experience led me to a new life work.

I hope that I speak not only for myself here but for all of us whose lives and careers were inspired by John F. Kennedy.

In the past few weeks, television has enabled all of us to remember President Kennedy again in life—how alive he made us feel and how proud to be Americans. In fact, the greatest sacrifice for me in being in the Peace Corps was to be outside our country during much of that magical period.

Yet we volunteers were never really very far from events in the United States. I was stationed in Chile in a small village 6,000 miles south of here. One day I drove my jeep as far as I could toward the coast, walked a few miles to a local mission, and continued on horseback for three hours to a remote Indian neighborhood. I was feeling very proud of myself. Certainly no other American had ever been there. Perhaps they had never even heard of the United States. After a customary cup of tea with my Indian host, he said to me, "Did you know that yesterday was President Kennedy's birthday?"

There are many achievements that will secure John Kennedy's place in history. But the Peace Corps is the one that I choose as my text because it tells us so much about him.

The Peace Corps reflects John Kennedy's vision of America. He brought out a sense of idealism and participation that runs like a deep stream in all of us. Through the Peace Corps he challenged us to go to the remotest parts of the world, to live without privileges of any sort, to learn a new language, and to put our skills and energies to work as a symbol of our country's concern for others.

Ten thousands of us responded to that challenge in the first three months. Today there are over 89,000 Americans who have returned to the United States after serving two years as Peace Corps volunteers in eighty-eight countries.

The impact of these volunteers—and the 5,200 who are serving today—is incalculable. Perhaps it was summed up best by a little girl in Africa who wrote adoringly to her volunteer teacher—in not so perfect English, "You are a blot on my life which I will never erase."

The Peace Corps exemplifies the quality President Kennedy admired most—courage, in this case the willingness to take a risk. There was considerable opposition to the Peace Corps when President Kennedy first announced it. Some called it a children's crusade and a publicity stunt.

The Kennedy administration pressed forward. But one of Sargent Shriver's aides did ask him, fairly early, "Aren't we really going out on a limb with the Peace Corps? We still don't know whether the idea will work or whether the volunteers will be accepted."

"Out on a limb, nothing!" Shriver replied, "We're out there walking on the leaves."

The Peace Corps symbolizes John Kennedy's commitment to world peace. The Peace Corps itself was a peace initiative. In teaching hundreds of languages to volunteers, the Peace Corps learned that in many languages the word for "stranger" is the same as the word for "enemy." The Peace Corps has shown that the more we know about each other, the less likely it is that we will consider one another as enemies. As John Kennedy said to the Irish Parliament in the summer of 1963, "Across the gulfs and barriers which divide us, we must remember that there are no permanent enemies."

Today the question of peace involves no less than our survival as a planet. In the tragic operas or dramas which we witness here at the Kennedy Center, simple misunderstandings lead the action unavoidably toward its tragic end. This is the essence of tragic art. In the real world of international politics, one such misunderstanding could bring the ultimate tragedy which would end all music and all art.

John Kennedy was possessed by this realization. His eloquence and conviction were prophetic. Popular consciousness of the dangers of nuclear war is only now beginning to catch up with him.

Finally, the Peace Corps highlights John Kennedy's compassion for the billions around the world who live in an abject poverty and misery. People ask why John Kennedy is so beloved in the developing world? The answer to that question is clear. John Kennedy truly cared about that half of humanity which lacks the basic necessities. He made promises to them and he delivered. He convinced the Congress to approve levels of development assistance and Food for Peace which have never been equaled since.

Then, of course, there was Peace Corps itself. The people in developing countries saw us as the direct expression of John Kennedy's interest in them. "Children of Kennedy" we were called in many parts of Latin America; "wakima Kennedy" or "followers of Kennedy" in Africa.

Twenty years ago this evening, there were 5,937 volunteers serving in forty-six countries. Each of them remembers vividly the outpouring of grief which his death occasioned. In Nepal, some villagers walked for five days to where the volunteers were to bring them the sad news. In Iran, a local co-worker told a volunteer, "Our president is dead." In Bangkok, people dressed in mourning garb. Schools everywhere searched for flags to fly at half mast. A volunteer wrote from Brazil:

If then this awful thing could reach out to the farthest corner of the world and have the effect on all people that I believe it did—then there is a real brotherhood among men—only one family of man.

History must judge John Kennedy not only by what he was able to accomplish in a thousand days but also by what he inspired all of us to volunteer—in the broadest sense—to do for our country.

So might I suggest that there is a most fitting tribute which all of us can pay to John Kennedy here this evening. We can pay him this tribute in our own lives; in our concern for a just and compassionate society here at home; in our willingness to assist the masses of poor throughout the world; and, most important, in assuring our nation's commitment to take the first steps toward peace. We can be prepared, in his memory and in his honor, to go out and "walk on the leaves."

LOVE AND DEATH[1]

F. FORRESTER CHURCH[2]

At the Unitarian Church of All Souls on the upper east side of Manhattan, the congregation had often heard the minister speak about the fragile nature of human life. However, in the sermon delivered on the morning of Sunday, January 23, 1984, words like life and death took on a special meaning.

"As many of you know, my father is seriously ill," said the minister, the Reverend Dr. F. Forrester Church, the eldest son of former Senator

[1]Delivered to the Unitarian Church of All Souls, New York, New York, at 11:00 A.M. on Sunday, January 23, 1984.
[2]For biographical note, see Appendix.

Frank Church of Idaho. "In light of this, I know you will forgive me for
changing the sermon topic and even for saying some things which you
may have heard me say before. This morning, I need to grapple once
again, in new ways and old, with love and death."

In a moving fifteen minute homily, Dr. Church spoke of his father,
dying at the age of fifty-eight, a champion of liberal causes, who had
served twenty-four years in the United States Senate and who in 1976
had run unsuccessfully for the Democratic nomination for president. Dr.
Church, who is thirty-five years old, devoted his sermon not to his father's
long political career but to a rich life spent in defiance of death. "My parents have lived on borrowed time," Dr. Church told about 300 worship-
ers. "Fully aware of life's fragility, they have not been afraid to risk and
give of themselves fully. Life for them is not a given, but a gift. . . .
Death is the ultimate mystery. But there is a way to counter this fear. We
can live in such a way that our lives will prove to be worth dying for."

Before the service, Dr. Church stood on the steps of the church building at 80th Street and Lexington Avenue and greeted his congregants
with handshakes, kisses on the cheeks, and warm embraces, and answered
queries about his father's health. The seventy-five minute religious service had none of the gloom one might expect under the circumstances.
The music included a spirited "Coronation March" by William Walton
and "Sing God a Simple Song" by Leonard Bernstein. Dr. Church wore
a red and black velvet gown and apologized with good humor for the long
list of announcements of coming activities.

In the printed program, the topic of the sermon was listed as "Martin
Luther King Jr.'s Legacy," but it was not until the end of the sermon that
Dr. Church spoke of the civil rights leader. The printed program also list-
ed "The Battle Hymn of the Republic" to follow the sermon, but Dr.
Church requested that another hymn be substituted, "Rank by Rank
Again We Stand." The congregation rose and sang and found special
meaning in the final verse:

> Ours the years' memorial store,
> Honored days and names we reckon,
> Days of comrades gone before,
> Lives that speak and deeds that beckon.
> One in name, in honor one,
> Guard we will the crown they won;
> What they dreamed be ours to do,
> Hope their hopes, and seal them true.

F. Forrester Church's speech: Of all my duties, of all the things
I am called upon to do as your minister, none has proved of greater
value to me than the call to be with you at times of loss. I would
almost go so far as to say that I did not become a minister until
I performed my first funeral. When asked at a recent gathering

of colleagues what gives most meaning to my work, I replied that, above all else, it is the constant reminder of death. Death awakens me to life's preciousness and also its fragility.

How often this happens. My desk and mind may be littered with a hundred petty tasks and grievances, things to begrudge life about, trifling justifications for self-pity or recrimination. Then death or the threat of dying comes calling at my door. All of a sudden, like a bracing wind, it clears my being of all pettiness. It awakens me to the precariousness of life and the wonder of love. It brings me a renewed perspective upon life's real joy and real pain.

What a blessing this is, not death but life, fully felt, demanding all of my human resources. This is death's hard gift to my life. It not only justifies my work, but makes me whole again.

In large measure, this is what religion is all about. Put simply, religion is our human response to the dual reality of being alive and having to die. All religious beliefs and the actions stemming from them reflect an attempt, human and therefore imperfect, to make sense of life and death by finding meaning in both.

Regardless of faith or creed, in this we are all companions. You know what the word companion means. It goes back to the Latin roots, "con," meaning with, and "pan," meaning bread. A companion is one with whom we break bread. In a spiritual, rather than material sense, the ultimate bread we mortals break together is the bread of life and death. This bread is precious. It is salty and bitter and good.

In a way, death is life's heaven. That we know we are going to die not only places an acknowledged limit upon our lives, it also gives a special intensity, a special poignancy and moment to the time we are given to live and to love. The very fact of death gives meaning to our love, for the more we love the more we risk to lose. Love's power comes in part from the courage that is required in giving ourselves to that which is not ours to keep: our spouses, children, parents, dear and cherished friends, even life itself. And love's power also comes from the faith that is required to sustain that courage, the faith that life, howsoever limited and mysterious, contains within its margins, often at their very edges, a meaning that is redemptive, a meaning that redeems from death life's pain.

Today, all of this has a very personal meaning for me. As many of you know, my father is seriously ill. In light of this, I know you will forgive me for changing the sermon topic and even for saying some things which you may have heard me say before. This morning, I need to grapple once again, in new ways and old, with love and death.

When I was two months old, my father was diagnosed as having terminal cancer. For over a year he had been having severe back pains, which he attributed to stress. He was newly married. He had just finished his first year at Harvard Law School, where he worked hard enough and did well enough to win early appointment to the *Law Review*. Ever since returning from China, where he served as an army intelligence officer during the Second World War, he had been in a great hurry to finish his schooling and establish a career. Back pain seemed to come with the territory.

You may remember the winter of 1948. It was a severe winter, with several great blizzards back-to-back. My mother is a very strong-willed woman. After one winter in Boston, she was not about to suffer another, especially with a baby on the way. And so it was that my father sacrificed his newly won position on the *Law Review* and my parents packed themselves off to the more gentle and familiar climes of Palo Alto, California, where my father enrolled for his second year of law school at Stanford.

I was born in September. Throughout the fall my father's back pains grew worse, leading him to consult a series of specialists at the Stanford Medical Center. The diagnosis was cancer. They immediately operated but the cancer had spread, and he was given no more than six months to live.

Had my father remained in the cast, he probably would have died that winter. As it happened, the Stanford Medical Center was sponsoring a radical, new experimental program in radiation therapy for terminal cancer patients. Every morning he was radiated with a megadose of cobalt. He attended all his classes, studied through the afternoon, played with his infant son, had dinner, and then got violently ill, fighting nausea until, exhausted, he fell asleep. This continued every day. At the end of six months, he weighed 125 pounds, but he was alive and the cancer was gone.

Just last spring, a friend gave me a book written by a woman who has been living with cancer since the early 1970s. Her name is Natalie Davis Spingarn and her book is entitled *Hanging in There: Living Well on Borrowed Time.*

In this book the author quotes from a letter written to her by my mother. "Bethline Church wrote to me recently that I am quite right in feeling that the cancer twilight zone is a world that other people haven't lived in." Describing Senator Frank Church's fight with cancer thirty years ago, and their feeling that he then had only six months to live, she said that forever after he had been a different person. It had been somehow easier for him to do the things that needed to be done, and let the things that did not matter go. We are all different people during, and after, an experience with life-threatening illness.

I was reminded by this, and again during the past few days, of how much my parents have taught me. Most of it has been taught by example and not by words. They never sat me down to inculcate the lessons that both of them had learned when my father was so very ill. They simply incorporated those lessons into the way they live their lives. Ever since my father's illness and recovery, my parents have lived on borrowed time. Fully aware of life's fragility, they have not been afraid to risk and give of themselves fully. Life for them is not a given, but a gift. It is a gift with a price attached. That price is death.

I am sure that they are still afraid of death. Few of us are not. Death is the ultimate mystery. But there is a way to counter this fear. We can live in such a way that our lives will prove to be worth dying for. It lies in our courage to love. Our courage to risk. Our courage to lose. Many people have said it in many different ways. The opposite of love is not hate. It is fear.

Think of the many ways in which this principle manifests itself. For instance, we do not hate the Russians. We fear them. We speak of windows of vulnerability. We arm ourselves to the teeth, rather than risking some accommodation that might lead to mutual cooperation and greater real security. It will take great courage to reduce our nuclear stockpiles, courage by both parties, because they fear us as much as we fear them. When Jesus said that we should love our enemies, he was challenging us to risk our very lives for the sake of a higher truth. Such risk is redemptive simply because it changes our lives. Each of us will one day die. The question is, betweeen now and then, how shall we choose to live?

Let me offer a second example. All of us are aware that beneath the shadows of our very houses there live hungry and homeless people. It is frightening even to contemplate. When one passes a "shopping bag person" on the street, one is tempted to avert one's eyes, to walk on by and not let it register.

At our church we have a soup kitchen and also a hospitality and shelter program for homeless women. Everyone who has served in these programs has dared to risk an encounter with people whom before they had feared more than pitied. Such encounters are redemptive for all concerned. These people have begun to overcome their fear of us. We have begun to overcome our fear of them. In lowering our defenses in order to meet these people where they are, we have learned to live a little more fully the meaning of the second great commandment: "Thou shalt love thy neighbor as thyself."

Beyond this, there are so many instances in our daily lives when our fears stand in the way of our potential to love. How many ways we find to armor and protect ourselves. We sense the risk, of course. That is the main reason we act in the ways we do. Every time we open ourselves up, every time we share ourselves with another, every time we commit ourselves to a cause or to a task that awaits our doing, we risk so very much. We risk disappointment. We risk failure. We risk being rebuffed or being embarrassed or being inadequate. And beyond these things, we risk the enormous pain of loss.

For instance, however much we try, we cannot fully protect our loved ones from fatal illness or accidental death. However much we love them, we cannot insulate them from failure and disappointment. However much we would wish to, there are times when we are powerless to heal or save.

Every time we give ourself in love, the burden of our vulnerability grows. When those we love die, a part of us dies with them. When those we love are sick, in body or in spirit, we, too, feel the pain.

All of this is worth it. Especially the pain. If we try to protect ourselves from suffering, we shall manage only to subdue the very thing that makes our lives worth living. Though we can, by a refusal to love, protect ourselves from the risk of losing what or whom we love, the irony is, by refusing to love we will have nothing left that is really worth protecting.

We, of course, are ready with a thousand excuses. There is always a perfectly sound or prudent reason to refuse to come out of hiding, to budget our strength, to cover our flanks, to pretend that if we are careful enough we will not be hurt or look foolish or have to do something that we do not want to do.

I am not talking here only about love between two people. I am also talking about the love of ideals and the love of institutions that embody those ideals. Whenever we ally ourselves, we run risks, sometimes enormous risks. At the very least, such allegiances demand our time and our money and our energy. They call on us to come out of hiding. They call on us to risk our hearts by giving of our love.

This morning we celebrate the birthday of a modern prophet and martyr, Martin Luther King, Jr. His was a gospel of love, love answering hate, love overcoming fear and even death. He preached the kinship of all people, and witnessed to his faith by countering violence with nonviolence. Not unlike my father, he did not spend his life, he invested it in things that would ennoble and outlast him. His witness is a powerful beacon of hope that still illumines the public landscape in these dark and difficult times. Certainly, Martin Luther King, Jr. lived in such a way that his life proved to be worth dying for. Especially when it came to love, he knew that the only things which are truly ours are those things we are prepared to give away.

This, too, is the lesson that my parents taught me. I keep forgetting it, of course. It is one of those lessons that one has to learn over and over again. It is one of those lessons that we learn by doing and forget by not doing. It is the lesson of love. Love thy enemy. Love thy neighbor as thyself. Cast out thy fear with love. And then—this I know—it will be somehow easier for us to do the things that need to be done, and to let the things that do not matter go.

THE QUALITY OF LIFE IN AMERICA

AN EPIDEMIC OF VIOLENCE[1]

C. Everett Koop[2]

The surgeon general of the United States, Dr. C. Everett Koop, rising to the defense of the television networks on the subject of violent programs, said in a major speech that the real question for social researchers was not whether violence in television programs can cause violent behavior among viewers, but "why on Earth does anybody watch that stuff?" After studying the problem for many years, Dr. Koop said he had reached the conclusion that broadcasters and mental health researchers were equally sensitive to the social problems caused by some television shows.

Dr. Koop made his remarks in the keynote speech to a day-long conference sponsored by the National Coalition on Television Violence held in Washington, D.C., on October 6, 1983. His speech was a strong dissent from the messages carried to the meeting by most speakers about the effects of television violence on children and society. He argued that instead of more studies on the linkage of television and violence, there should be research into why people experience fear in American society, why they are insecure, and why they withdraw from the real world.

The special conference, entitled "Violence on Television: A National Health Issue," was made possible by a grant from the American Medical Association. The National Coalition on Television Violence (NCTV) is an organization devoted to effecting a major decrease in the levels of television violence. It endorses action to reach this goal, including public education, the monitoring of television programming, research, and pressure upon those responsible for the broadcast of television violence. The objectives of the conference were to raise public awareness of violence in television and its impact on behavior; to provide a forum for ideas on how to reduce adverse effects of violent programming; and to promote greater awareness of the NCTV. The day-long meeting attracted approximately a hundred people including media representatives, researchers, activists, and religious leaders.

Dr. Koop's presentation was preceded first by opening remarks from Dr. Thomas Radecki, chairman of the NCTV, and then by two research

---

[1]Keynote address to a one-day conference sponsored by the National Coalition on Television Violence delivered at 12:30 P.M. in the Marvin Center ballroom of Geoge Washington University in Washington, D.C., on October 6, 1983.

[2]For biographical note, see Appendix.

panel presentations. Surgeon General Koop delivered his address at 12:30
P.M. in the Marvin Center ballroom of George Washington University in
Washington, D.C.

The National Coalition on Television Violence believed the conference succeeded in meeting its objectives, noting in a newsletter that media
coverage had been good and that attending groups had been familiarized
with the issue so as to be receptive to further action.

The surgeon general had spoken on the effect of violence on health
before. (See his speech, "Violence and Public Health," in *Representative
American Speeches, 1982–1983*, p. 207.) An articulate spokesman, Koop
is aided by his appearance and demeanor:

> With his beard and armor-piercing gaze, Dr. C. Everett Koop re-
> sembled an Old Testament prophet who has discovered his neighbor
> is making graven images. Actually, he is not fierce, but is determined
> to be heard, which is good because that is his job. He is Surgeon
> General of the United States. (*Birmingham Post Herald*, N. 15, '82)

Surgeon General Koop's speech: I'm pleased to be your keynote
speaker today. As you well know, this topic of violence on television is as much a part of the Office of Surgeon General as the flag
and the uniform. And violence is every bit a public health issue
for me and my successors in this century, as smallpox, tuberculo-
sis, and syphilis were for my predecessors in the last two centuries.

And it is understandable, especially when we apply the term
"epidemic." And I think it is fair to do that. Violence in American
public and private life has indeed assumed the proportions of an
epidemic. Assaults, child and spouse abuse, homicides and suicides
among young adults, these indicators of violence in our population
are still climbing. They are occurring at a rate "beyond what is
normally expected," to use the phrase used by epidemiologists to
define the term "epidemic." The occurrence of a case or an illness
beyond what we might expect, based upon past experience, is an
epidemic.

One of the best examples of that would be the great flu epidemic of the winter of 1980–1981. We might have expected something on the order of seventeen thousand deaths from pneumonia
and influenza during that twelve-week winter period. Instead,
there was total of fifty thousand deaths, nearly triple the expectation.

Of course, people don't "expect" any of these things. We don't
look forward to their occurring. And while some people may be

unfamiliar with the symptoms of certain diseases, I don't think
that's the case with violence. I would guess that we all know what
violence looks like.

And we don't like what we see. Whenever and wherever it occurs, it shocks and frightens us. And when it occurs more often—
that is, more frequently than we might expect, based on our past
experience—we conclude that we are in the midst of an epidemic
of violence. And we are.

Violence comes in guises. But let me speak of just one: the rate
of murder among young adult white males, age fifteen to twenty-
four. This rate, the homicide rate, was down around 3.7 deaths
per hundred thousand population back in 1950. Translated into
terms of the real world, that means an estimated 366 young white
men were murdered in 1950. Over the next fifteen years, the
homicide rate crept up, but very slightly. The homicide rate
among young white men in 1965 had risen to 4.9 deaths per hundred thousand population, or a total of about 740 deaths. That
was twice the 1950 figure, but then that age group itself had
grown one and a half times.

An epidemic? We didn't think so at the time. The annual inci-
dence of homicides among white males age fifteen to twenty-four
was still well under one thousand, and the rate per hundred thousand population was creeping up but very slowly, still nothing to
be seriously alarmed about. It was not pleasant, it was not comfortable, but it was not totally unanticipated either.

Today, the situation is quite different. We've gone well beyond that thousand-death threshold. In 1980—the year for which
we have the latest data—the homicide rate for this group of young
men was 15.5 per hundred thousand population. That means the
"body count" had jumped to 2,800 murdered young men.

Compared to the year 1965, that population group of young
white males grew by 17 percent. But over the same fifteen-year
period, 1965 to 1980, the total of homicide victims in that group
increased by 400 percent. In other words, murder is now claiming
four times as many young white men age fifteen to twenty-four
as it claimed only fifteen years ago.

I think that's a startling figure. It is proof enough that we are
not witnessing a phenomenon that "can be expected." It is obvi-

ously well beyond *any* reasonable expectation. It is nothing less than an epidemic of murder, an epidemic raging among young men. But that's not the full picture. The sharp rise in the homicide rate is mirrored elsewhere in society as well: The suicide rate today is triple what it was in 1950 among young men, both black and white, and young white women. The death rate for motor vehicle accidents has climbed to triple the homicide rate.

But all violence does not end only in death. Child abuse is a form of violence that usually does not end in physical death, but it may produce emotional and psychological death in the child. The number of reported cases of child abuse has more than doubled over the past half-dozen years, from 416,000 cases in 1976 to 851,000 cases in 1981. The National Center for Child Abuse and Neglect, however, estimates there may be another million cases of child abuse and neglect not reported and not seen, known only to the family members involved and maybe a friend or neighbor. If the center is right, that would mean close to 2 million instances of child abuse and neglect occurring each year in our society. That is certainly beyond anything we might "reasonably expect." Some of these statistics are open to question because our systems of reporting violent episodes are not what they should be. Assistant Attorney General Lois Herrington mentioned this problem in the opening pages of the report by the President's Task Force on Victims of Crime:

Every 23 minutes, someone is murdered, every six minutes a woman is raped. While you read this statement, two people will be robbed in this country and two more will be shot, stabbed, or seriously beaten. Yet, [she says,] to truly grasp the enormity of the problem, those figures must be doubled, because more than 50 percent of violent crime goes unreported.

I think it still may be safe to say that the majority of Americans—so far, at least—have never been the victims of violence. But nearly everyone has *witnessed* violence take place or has seen its terrible results in the aftermath. Maybe we know people who no longer have the full function of one or several limbs—an elbow broken or a knee injured, an eye lost, a face disfigured, a jaw broken and now in recurrent pain, the loss of full hearing.

The real world of violence is a nightmare, one from which a victim may never fully awake. How different all that is from the fantasy violence on television. On the little screen, one huge man will physically assault another and run away. The second man, the victim, will reappear with a small bandage on his forehead and continue in hot pursuit of his attacker. But in real life, it's very, very different.

Were a typical TV assault to occur in real life, the real victim would be hospitalized, be bandaged and immobilized, maybe have a cast on one hand and wrist, if not on both, have impaired eye-sight from multiple contusions, maybe suffer from an impaired sense of balance, and be in no shape at all to pursue his attacker for at least the rest of the year, if ever.

I guess I'm much more conscious of this difference because I spent so many years in surgery in Philadelphia. Every day I saw the human toll of violence: highway violence, violence in the home, violence at the work place, personal, individual, irreparable catas-trophes. And you just never get used to it and hardened by it. I don't believe that at all. Every new victim you see is a direct chal-lenge to your own sense of humanity. You can't allow yourself to turn away.

I think that is at the root of the government's concern with vio-lence. I'd like to think so anyway. The government really should have no option but to be concerned, once it sees what the problem is. And the public health service first got a look at this problem over a dozen years ago.

You recall that it was Surgeon General Jesse Steinfeld who first took a look at the problem of television violence back in 1969. Then the National Institute of Mental Health turned out its first report in 1972 on violence on television. And ever since then, the U.S. Public Health Service and its surgeons general have re-mained close to this issue.

In think Dr. Steinfeld and his colleagues were on the right track. I think his successors were, too. And I am ready to keep the fires of interest alive during my tenure as well. It would be derelict for me or any of my successors to say, "It's over. There is no prob-lem anymore."

Certainly, the research leads us to quite a different conclusion. And here I am speaking of the research sponsored by N.I.M.H. [National Institute for Mental Health]. We've come quite a distance since 1972. I believe we've produced a good body of research on the subject. I know there are still a great many questions that need to be answered. For example, we ought to take a much closer look at all our methodologies to see if we are truly applying the ones that will yield the most helpful results to persons both in public health and in television.

I will stress that point because I am not at all happy at the adversarial tone that permeates all our discussions between the mental health community and the networks. The reasons for the existence of such an unprofessional tone are understandable, but that still doesn't give me any peace.

I've been concerned about this for some time and I suspect that one reason for difficulty in a package of misconceptions that each side carries with it at all times. Let me list a few of these.

Misconception number one: The N.I.M.H. studies zero in on the possibility of television having a serious, adverse effect on behavior, especially the behavior of children, and that the chief behavior of concern is violent behavior, violence against others, violence against one's self. *But it does not follow* that such studies can become the basis for further regulation of the industry.

Regulation of TV content is a legitimate concern for everyone in media. But it is very far off the mark here. The research can be useful—and I believe it already has been useful—to both the TV industry and public health practitioners everywhere. But it is truly useless as an argument for regulation. I think that is a misconception and fear that ought to be aired out here and then put to rest.

Misconception number two: The TV industry is exactly that, an industry functioning within the American marketplace economy. As such, each network and each station has certain responsibilities that are fundamental to any business or industry. Of course, we hope every private for-profit enterprise can be both prifitable and socially useful. And I would have to say that all our media—regardless of the anxieties we may have about their conduct now and then—all our media have done very well in maintaining this touchy balance between profitability and social utility. Still, most of them do.

Misconception number three: We may have our differences over how to define the term "violence," but sometimes there is unanimity. Some shows will have a segment that teeters along the edge of what can be tolerated and public health people leap to some murky judgments about the broadcaster's motivation. The real issue, however, is this: Why on Earth does anybody watch that stuff?

We are upset when one or another network broadcasts violent programming and, in doing so, gathers a larger audience share. Why a network would broadcast that program is quite clear: precisely to get that larger audience share. We may be uncomfortable about it, but we would have to admit that the decision makes sense from the viewpoint of the health of the network.

Why the audience switches to that channel to watch is not as clear. But we can't answer the second question if we continue to be frustrated over the first.

We may be very unhappy over the fact that millions of people—including thousands of impressionable children—will voluntarily watch something that we believe to be violent and socially harmful. Our job, it seems to me, is to research further into the motivations of the audience, rather than to continue pounding away at the broadcaster.

I think after all these years, the broadcasters and mental health researchers are equally sensitive to the social problems caused by some popular shows. But refusing henceforth to broadcast those shows could be ruinous for a network. That's true. But why should that be? We need to find out.

Refusing to broadcast such shows would probably trigger a loud complaint from the viewing public. I think that would happen. But why should that be? We need to find out.

Refusing to broadcast them would probably cause large groups of viewers to shift from the "good" channel to another that is "not so good." I think that's true. But why should it be? We need to find out.

I believe we ought to be at that stage now when we no longer have to trade research studies like cannon volleys between Parklawn Drive in Rockville, Maryland, and Sixth Avenue, New York City. I happen to think that the N.I.M.H. work is good. I also happen to think the network research is *not* as good. Honest people can differ about that. But at this stage, it is almost beside the point.

But that is not the end of our studies. Our work in television violence should serve to entice us further along the horizon of understanding. It would be appropriate for the many professions represented here today—the medical, mental health, social science, political science, and public interest professions in particular—to direct their resources toward finding answers to other, new, and far more disturbing questions.

Why do people experience fear in our society? We have enough anecdotal information to convince us that genuine fear of the environment is present among large numbers of the elderly, among children, among women, and among racial and ethnic minorities. Journalists, social service workers, and others who study contemporary life all feel this to be true. Why is this so?

Despite an extensive 200-year-old body of American law to protect the weak and the innocent, Americans who *are* weak and innocent do not feel secure. They frequently identify themselves as *victims* in our society. This is a deeply disturbing aspect of contemporary life. We know very little about its origins and even less about a response.

We also are seeing more and more people withdraw from the real world to find sanctuary. That's very worrisome. Our society has not been built on a premise of fear and isolation among its members. On the contrary, we rely on the *participation* of all our peoples, not on their *withdrawal*.

The political and social health of this nation is endangered when any citizen feels unjustly threatened and withdraws in fear. But that's happening with greater frequency among vulnerable groups in our society. We need to know much, much more about this and how it is affecting the nature of American life.

One of the complaints registered against television is its stereotyped portrayal of victims; they *do* tend to be children, women, minorities, or old people. In this way, TV not only mirrors real life but tends to reinforce the victim's perception of life as a terrible ordeal.

This is especially saddening to someone like myself, who has traveled a great deal not only around this country but overseas also. If you had been along with me on these trips over the past thirty-five to forty years, you too would have sensed the great well-springs of generosity that still exist among the American people. "We give." That's more than a slogan. It's an ethical imperative of the American people.

And we have our heroes. Some appear with great suddenness, like Leonard Skutnik, who dove into the icy Potomac two winters ago and pulled a drowning person to safety. Others help their neighbors in less dramatic, but no less meaningful, ways. And we cherish them for their example.

And, in a country like ours, where government at every level still delivers so many health and social services, we nevertheless have the most active and successful examples of private charity.

Yet, we also sense that many more people, untouched by the generosity around them, are growing more detached, disengaged, and disconnected. They are mute bystanders to events. For them, an evening with the TV set is the best protection they can get from the environment outside. We have been reminded of this phenomenon in our society many times, unfortunately more often than we have seen the gifts of the Lenny Skutniks of this world.

This detachment is relative to the violent world, in that it even has a name, a name that recalls a victim, a circumstance, a crime, and the failure of a neighborhood that was detached and did not want to get involved: it's called the "Kitty Genovese syndrome."

You may remember that incident. On a cold night in March of 1964, Miss Catherine Genovese—"Kitty"—came home late from her job as manager of a neighborhood bar in Hollis, Long Island. She was attacked 100 feet from her apartment house in Kew Gardens. She screamed for help, but no one came. During the next thirty-five minutes, twenty-nine year-old Winton Moseley repeatedly stabbed Kitty Genovese to death.

Thirty-eight of Miss Genovese's neighbors admitted to hearing her scream, "Oh, my God, he stabbed me! Please help me! Please help me! I'm dying!" Some even *saw* the murder taking place. But no one came to her aid. And no one called the police until her screams stopped and she was dead—*thirty-five minutes* after her first loud scream for help.

Kitty Genovese has been dead for twenty years, but the circumstances of her death have not been forgotten. I doubt if they ever will be. First, it was a frightening reminder of how fragile is our existence together. And secondly, every year brings its own crop of new and equally frightening events.

Just this past year a young woman was brutally raped in New Bedford, Massachusetts, while other men stood and watched. And in St. Louis a young girl was raped in a public fountain while ordinary people walked by uncaring, except for a little boy who raced away on a bicycle to get a policeman.

I'm sure there is no one in this room who would want to have been among the bystanders in Kew Gardens in 1964 or in New Bedford or St. Louis in 1983 to witness those acts of criminal violence. Those events still send cold chills through our hearts.

But very few of us can say with all candor and sincerity that, had we been there, we would have intervened. Maybe we would have—then again, maybe not.

The fact is, *we just don't know*. And when we have to say, "I honestly don't know what I'd do," then it is time that we direct more of our resources to address that very dilemma, the dilemma of the detached bystander in the presence of violence. I'm saddened to have to say that it's an especially appropriate subject for social science research in this country.

That's a far more significant issue than whether one or another television show promotes violence. I believe we must confront the hard fact that if all the television stations in this country were shut down tomorrow:

Millions of Americans would still be frightened of the life around them.

Hundreds of thousands would be victimized and not cared for in the most compassionate and effective manner.

And many millions would continue to stand aloof from the pain of their neighbors, hoping not to "become involved."

That's a very serious situation and we need the courage to go to work on it.

This coming winter of 1984 will mark the twentieth anniversary of the death of Kitty Genovese. In her memory, the Center for Responsive Psychology at Brooklyn College plans to hold a symposium on what we've learned in the past twenty years about bystander behavior and victim behavior, and what kinds of things we still need to know.

There is still a great deal of information we need to learn from both the people who witness acts of violence—the bystanders— and the *victims* of violence themselves. How do *they* perceive the event? How does it register in their consciousness? How does it affect their lives?

What made the men of New Bedford feel safe enough to commit rape in a crowded pool hall? We don't know. But it is imperative that we try to find out.

In the Public Health Service, we are taking these questions quite seriously. We've set up a "Violence Epidemiology Branch" in our Centers for Disease for Control in Atlanta. It's a multidisciplinary unit, with personnel from the fields of psychiatry, medical anthropology, criminology, public policy development, and statistics.

The professionals in this important branch are pooling their insights and experiences in the search for patterns of circumstances—patterns of action and reaction—from which we might draw some conclusions about the etiology of violence and what society might do about it.

If this kind of effort generates good information in the next few years—and if the same thing happens elsewhere among public health researchers—then maybe we can help people exercise their better, more humane, and more compassionate instincts, rather than let them fall victim to the violent, antisocial instincts of a neighbor, a friend, or a parent.

It is in our society's highest interests that we all be truthfully supportive and reassuring, that we understand how we all need each other, that we can be good both *for* and *to* each other, and that each of us be responsible for making these notions a reality.

At this stage, we have the rhetoric, but we don't know how to guarantee that the rhetoric will come alive and happen.

When we do—when we see that people feel good again about being responsible for one another—then the issue of violence on television will be academic. Conferences such as this one will not be needed. The violence that may remain will have far less of an effect that it now has.

Let me close by saying I do not entirely despair of the television industry. It's an extraordinary medium and, for many millions of Americans, it is their best connection to the rest of society and the world. And many times in the course of a broadcast day, American TV will reveal its good humor, gentleness, and human caring. We don't want to lose that either.

Again, let me thank you for your kind invitation to be here today. And please accept my best wishes for a candid and successful conference.

BROKEN FAMILIES AND HOMELESS CHILDREN[1]

Bruce Ritter[2]

In his 1984 State of the Union message, President Ronald Reagan mentioned five unsung "heroes of the '80s." Each was a relatively unknown person who, in the opinion of the president, had made a significant contribution to the country. One of the five singled out for recognition was Father Bruce Ritter, a Franciscan Roman Catholic priest who founded and serves as president of Covenant House, a young people's aid and rehabilitation organization in the Times Square area of New York City. The organization, which has branches in Toronto and Houston, each year provides shelter, food, and counseling for more that fifteen thousand young runaways, drug users, abused children, and youngsters exploited by pornographers and pimps.

Father Ritter, who has a doctorate in medieval history and who had been a college teacher for several years, decided to take a more active role in caring for desperate and frightened children when he was challenged by students at Manhattan College, where he served as chaplain.

> My teaching career came to a rather abrupt end one Sunday as I was preaching to the college kids on campus. My sermon that day was on "Zeal and Commitment"—the need for my students to be more involved in the life and work of the church. At the end of my sermon, the president of the student body stood up in church and said, "Bruce, we think you should practice what you preach and show us a little of that zeal and commitment you just talked about."

[1] Delivered to the Senate Caucus on the Family in the Mansfield Caucus Room (S-207) of the Capitol Building, Washington, D.C., at noon on January 26, 1984.
[2] For biographical note, see Appendix.

The outcome of that suggestion was that Father Ritter asked for and was given a new assignment to live and work among the poor in the East Village of New York City.

On January 26, 1984, Father Ritter addressed the second meeting of the Senate Caucus on the Family. The caucus, organized the previous June by Senators Jeremiah Denton and Dennis DeConcini, sought to focus attention on the needs of children and families. Its purpose was to study issues and government policies affecting families, to gather information and make recommendations, and to promote legislation to strengthen families. The organizers of the caucus were concerned by the "nation's alarming rate of family disintegration," teen-age suicide, and juvenile delinquency. (Bryan Nutting, *Congressional Quarterly,* Je. 18, '83, p 1236)

Father Ritter spoke to the caucus at a luncheon meeting in the Mansfield Caucus Room (S-207) of the Capitol Building at noon on January 26, 1984. His immediate audience consisted of five senators, approximately thirty staff members, and about ten press representatives. The reporters were allowed to interview Father Ritter and the senators after the presentation.

In his introduction of Father Ritter, caucus co-chairman Senator Jeremiah Denton of Alabama said:

> We are very fortunate to have with us today an individual whom President Reagan last night termed one of the "unsung heroes" of our times. Father Bruce Ritter is indeed a hero. He has made as his life's ministry the aiding of children under the age of twenty-one who come from the most desperately troubled sectors of our society. They are homeless and runaway children, primarily victims of the "sex industry" around the Times Square area of New York. While we here in the Senate talk about abstract ideas and theories that we write into laws for others to implement, Father Bruce rolls up his sleeves and himself helps desperately needy children.

Although the immediate audience was small, publication of the speech in the *Congressional Record* and stories in the *New York Daily News* and other newspapers brought Ritter's speech to the attention of a larger reading audience. Senator Denton said that the priest had spoken "convincingly and eloquently about the problem of broken families and homeless children" and that he could think of no individual better qualified to speak about the crisis. Congressman Robert Michel characterized Father Ritter's remarks to the caucus as inspiring and sobering.

Father Ritter's speech: Ladies and gentlemen of the Senate, my name is Father Bruce Ritter, a Franciscan priest from New York. I am delighted and privileged to have this opportunity to speak to you this morning about my concerns and those of my friends.

Concerns based on more than fifteen years caring for some of the most desolate children in our society.

I am president of Convenant House, a child-care agency I founded almost fifteen years ago to care for street children. If I may take the liberty of speaking for a few moments about how our work began, I think you may find our early history somewhat entertaining, but it will also certainly provide you the context from within which you can understand the sort of problems, indeed the fearful suffering, faced by these children.

Within my order I was trained as an academician. I have an earned doctorate in late medieval history of dogma, and I taught that rather arcane subject for about ten years. I spent the last five years of the teaching part of my priesthood in New York City at Manhattan College, where I also became chaplain to the student body.

My teaching career came to a rather abrupt end one Sunday as I was preaching to the college kids on campus. My sermon that day was on "Zeal and Commitment," the need for my students to be more involved in the life and work of the church. At the end of my sermon, the president of the student body stood up in church and said, "Bruce, we think you should practice what you preach and show us a little of that zeal and commitment you just talked about."

Well, as a result of that rather coercive invitation, I asked for a new assignment: to live and work among the poor in the East Village of New York City; that's a very large slum on the lower east side of Manhattan. It's an area of New York completely taken over by the hard drug scene. I moved off campus into a junkie's apartment near the East River and almost immediately became involved with the problems of some of the hundreds of houseless kids that lived on the streets and in the abandoned buildings in that neighborhood.

One night at two o'clock in the morning in the middle of a blizzard these six kids knocked on my door: four boys and two girls, all under sixteen—runaways from all over the country. They asked if they could sleep on the floor of my apartment. The next morning it was still quite cold and snowing and the kids obviously did not want to leave. One boy, however, did go outside for just a few minutes and brought back four more kids. "This is the rest of us," he said, "the rest of our family." He said, "They were afraid to come last night, they wanted us to check you out first. And I told them that you did not come on to us last night, so that it was probably okay."

These ten children had been living in one of the abandoned buildings on the block with a group of junkies who were exploiting them sexually—were pimping them; that's how the junkies were supporting their habit. And when the kids refused, the junkies simply burned out the apartment the kids were living in and threw them out in the snow. A week before that, these kids had been forced to make a porn film in order to get some food. Hating what was happening to them, horror-stricken at the direction their lives were taking, these ten children fled the junkies and came down the street to my place.

That was the beginning of Covenant House. I could not find a single child-care agency that would accept these children, so I kept them. The problem was that the next day two more kids came in. And the next day two more. And then literally dozens and dozens of other homeless, runaway kids began knocking on our door, so many that eventually my friends and I founded Covenant House. We specialize in caring for runaway kids and homeless teenagers. We operate crisis centers in many cities now; this year we'll care of over fifteen thousand children and young people. Every month more than a thousand kids come into residence in our programs.

Let me break that number down for you just a little bit: two-thirds of these kids are boys. Twenty-five percent are fifteen years old and younger, 25 percent sixteen and seventeen; the other half eighteen, nineteen, and twenty. Eighty to 90 percent come from their home cities—runaway kids never run very far. Most of these kids come from abusing, one-parent, alcoholic families. There are few mysteries about why these kids run away. Most of them have suffered some form of exploitation on the street.

They are good kids. You would be wrong if you thought they were not good kids. Most of them are simply trying to survive. When you are thirteen, or fourteen, or fifteen, or for that matter, sixteen, seventeen, or eighteen, and you have no place to live, you are cold and hungry and scared, and you've got nothing to sell except yourself—you sell yourself. A tragically high number of these kids become the merchandise in a massive, well-financed, well-developed American sex industry. They have become the commodities, the merchandise in our sex-for-sale society, where it has become okay to pay for sex and be paid for it. It is no exaggeration to say that there are hundreds of thousands of teen-agers in this country involved in commercial sex for sale. I can't tell you how tragic their lives are.

In the beginning, these kids do not really understand what is happening to them. I mean, in the beginning a girl will say to me, "Bruce, he ain't no pimp, he is my boyfriend, and he needs me." And in the beginning a boy will say to me, "Bruce, I ain't gay, I ain't no hustler, I'm just trying to make a few bucks." In the beginning. But after a hundred johns, it becomes increasingly difficult then, quite simply impossible, to separate what you are from what you do. You become what you do and you no longer even care. The girls seem to show it first in their faces. The boys can hide it longer. But the boys die sooner, the girls can survive longer. You see, it is simply more acceptable for a girl to work the street than a boy.

In our brief history as a child care agency, more than fifty thousand kids have come to us. Most of them have suffered some form of exploitation. We are simply overwhelmed with the problems of the thousands upon thousands of homeless and often exploited children that will come to us this year.

Our child-care records at Covenant House read like hip versions of William Blake's "Songs of Innocence and Experience," with one great difference. Unlike Blake's little waifs, most of our kids were never allowed any innocence to lose, instead they have had to earn innocence through pain, pain at their homes and greater pain on the street.

I know my kids don't look innocent when you first see them. Their life on the street is saturated in the raw need to survive, a need that leads many into crime, many into every sort of prostitution, formal and informal. Yet by and large they are innocent. They are victims of social decay and family disintegration, caught up in a nightmarish struggle for survival before they have had a chance to grow into physical and moral maturity. Their incredible courage in that struggle, and their desperate groping for purpose and meaning in life are the very essence of real innocence.

Today, however, I will not dwell on the specific needs of street kids; their pain is only a symptom of a much deeper disorder in our society, the disintegration of families and of the environments in which they once prospered. As much as I am honored by your invitation to speak today, I am more deeply gratified that there exists a group of distinguished public servants willing to confront that disorder head-on. It is a task which will lead you not just into the most complex questions of social policy, but into a reconsideration of the role of fundamental moral values in a pluralistic, democratic society. And it is a challenge that faces not only you who are in government, but all of us who have made the care of children our life's work. The traditional American family is an awesomely strong and resilient institution, but it has probably never been closer to collapse than it is now.

For example, from 1970 to 1980, the number of married couples with children under eighteen declined, while the number of single-parent households doubled. The divorce rate has tripled since 1960. Of the children who come to Covenant House, less than a quarter have been raised in two-parent homes. In counseling our kids and working with their parents, we see day after day the overwhelming emotional and economic burdens that single parenthood imposes, all the more overwhelming because so many single parents assume that role while they are still little better than children themselves.

Instability in family life is both evidenced and exacerbated by the mushrooming mobility of American society. Fully 45 percent of Americans changed their residence between 1975 and 1980. The children who come to Covenant House once again illustrate the extreme effects of this new trend: almost two-thirds have moved at least once during the past year, and about 25 percent have moved four or more times. Family life for many Americans has become an erratic, rootless journey from one faceless neighborhood to another. Is it so surprising that many of their children eventually take to the road as well? Slowly, progressively alienated from neighborhood, from family, from any stable contact of relationships and values, many Americans and their children become slaves of our treasured mobility.

When we look under the surface of family life in this country, some ugly, frightening facts emerge. From 1977 to 1980 alone, the number of reports of child abuse and neglect rose by over 50 percent to 785,000. Is that simply better reporting? All of us know it's not. At Covenant House half of our kids have been the victims of repeated physical abuse. Nationally we have reason to believe that 25 percent of girls and 10 percent of boys will have suffered some form of sexual abuse by age eighteen. Fully a quarter of our girls admit that they have been raped. It is an ominous fact that the girls at Covenant House most likely to become teen-age mothers are those who have suffered abuse.

The increase of single parenthood, the declining loyalty of Americans to their neighborhood, and the devastating phenomenon of child abuse, these are developments which seem to be the result of individual decision rather than social policy. But if we turn for a moment to examine other powerful forces at work, both economic and cultural, a more complex image emerges. On the economic front, for example, families have not fared well during the past decade. The average income of families in constant dollars declined 6 percent from 1972 to 1981. Yet the federal tax burden on those families has increased—once again in real terms—by over a third. By contrast, single and married taxpayers with no children have suffered only a tiny real increase in their tax burden during that same period. It is an incredible fact that in 1984 a single parent with two children can expect to pay higher taxes on the same income than a married couple with no children. Ten years ago that same single parent would have paid only two-thirds as much.

Painful as it is, the economic plight of families, and particularly families at risk of disintegration, is worth pursuing further. A recently completed Columbia University study of children who come to our New York program found that about half came from families receiving public assistance. That isn't very surprising in light of recent statistics showing that over 20 percent of all children under eighteen live in families with income below the poverty line. According to the scholarship of our own Senator Daniel

Moynihan, indeed, one-third of all children born in 1979 can expect to live in single-parent homes on public assistance prior to
their eighteenth birthday.

Public assistance, however, becomes less and less useful to
families in need. In real dollars, the typical AFDC [Assistance for
Families with Dependent Children] grant was cut in half during
the 1970s. When no more than half of all divorced women can expect to receive full child support from their former husbands, it
is clear that many will be forced to turn to a public assistance system that cannot meet their and their children's basic needs.

Raising a child, I am told, is an expensive business. U.S. Department of Agriculture estimates place the cost at about $2,000
a year per child on even the barest bones budget, just for essentials.
What is more, the cost of raising a child increases constantly as
he grows, so that the costs for a sixteen-year-old are one-third
higher in real dollars than for a six-year old. When most American families are not experiencing continuous real increases in income, the economic pressures of that increased cost can be severe.
For families on public assistance, the rise in child-rearing costs as
children grow older is devastating. If we recognize how economic
difficulty can cause severe strain and breakup of marriages, how
can we ignore its effects on a parent–child relationship?

All of us feel safe discussing economic trends and strains because of the large amount of "objective," quantifiable data avail-
ble. But we don't need statistics to identify a source of family
trauma in this country far more profound than changes in their
income: the deterioration, the virtual collapse, of a social and moral climate which supports and nourishes family life.

Ours has become a deeply materialistic, even hedonistic culture, a society of consumers. One of the great minds in deferral
tax policy, Henry Simons, has said that children are a "form of
consumption" for their parents. That is, he believed the birth of
a child into a family should be treated for tax purposes no differ-
ently from the purchase of a new boat or car or any other luxury.
Distinguished advertising firms carefully manipulate children to
develop their consumer mentality, then cynically turn around to
use children in seductive, sexually suggestive ad campaigns to sell
products to adults. Surrounded by a culture which regards chil-

dren more as objects than as developing human beings, it is hardly a shock that many parents treat them as objects, too.

At its most extreme, this dehumanization of children can lead to cultural perversions that are deeply humiliating to those who love the best in America. Six years ago it took merely a walk through Times Square, with child pornography on open display, to see how deep that perversion runs. Now the world of child prostitution and pornography has moved underground, but the exploitation of children as sexual objects and partners remains a brutal part of our moral landscape. That terrain gives little shelter to values that support and sustain healthy family life.

So let's be fair to American families. If it is true that we as a people are less faithful, less tender to our families than ever before, it is also true that factors out of our control have served to hasten family disintegration. And though we can indulge in endless speculation about the causes of that decay, we must accept the fact that the family will always remain a stubbornly mysterious institution, a compound of love, commitment, weakness, and practicality.

Whatever its origin, the effect of family disintegration on kids is agonizing to review. For young men the suicide rate increased by almost 50 percent from 1970 to 1979. In some other post-industrial societies, the rate of young suicides is even higher than ours. At Covenant House, one-third of the girls and one-sixth of the boys have previously attempted suicide. Half of our residents seriously consider suicide as their only way off the street. According to a recent study, as many as 82 percent of our residents suffer from extreme depression or another significant psychiatric disability.

For a short-term crisis program like ours, the plight of those children presents an overwhelming burden. We can only claim to succeed with a third, either through family reconciliation, appropriate referral to a longer-term program, or establishment in independent living. Of course, we could do some things better, but we will always fail with most of them. The time for repairing endangered families and rescuing their children is not after they have fallen apart.

Broken families and homeless children present a searing challenge. It is, in my view, the deepest ethical and moral challenge of our generation. Whether we respond to it will depend not simply on your resolve as members of Congress, but on the willingness of the entire private sector to commit itself to the care and protection of family life.

Private sector employers must undertake a wide variety of initiatives on behalf of their employees' families. Provision for child care for working mothers at or near the work site could make it possible for hundreds of thousands to get off public assistance and into the working force. It didn't escape my notice that the Senate has recently done precisely that for its employees, and that now the House is scrambling to catch up. Flexible scheduling of work hours and, where possible, structuring work that can be done in the home, could allow many other parents to work without shortchanging their children's need for nurture.

We in social services must accept heavy responsibility for developing effective, imaginative responses to what seems a hopelessly complex problem. We have to begin with the recognition that family reconciliation, not youth emancipation, must be our primary hope. But very often, where families are irretrievably broken, we must focus on ways of reintegrating homeless children into their own communities, settings which give them continuity of environment and values. And finally we must lead the way in designing ways to provide the emotional support, remedial education, and job training they desperately need. That includes beginning model business enterprises employing homeless youths to show the private sector how to tap their potential. Nevertheless, with unemployment and illiteracy among youth at desperately high levels, our task is indeed a heavy one.

In prevention of family breakup, the prospects are brighter. Churches and community groups should be able, with proper financial support, to provide training in parenting to young mothers of children at risk. Ongoing support for families is always stronger if it comes from church and neighborhood rather than from government. It is a national scandal how relatively little many of our local religious and community organizations do to reach out to families in need. As long as we persist in thinking that only government can solve problems of poverty and social disintegration, the prospect of any breakthroughs in those areas will remain bleak.

But that is not to say government is free from responsibility for immediate, thoughful action on behalf of families. Direct government intervention into family life is only rarely successful and always expensive, but government can create a climate that nourishes family cohesion. I claim to be no expert in national affairs, but I think you ought to consider a few ideas for action on the federal level—action aimed at strengthening families all across the economic spectrum.

First, I challenge you to consider carefully the current structure of federal taxation as it applies to families. I mentioned earlier the disproportionate burden of taxation borne by families with children, and that may be a subject for careful review. Short of wholesale tax reform, however, a few relatively minor adjustments in the federal tax laws could make a substantial difference in helping the private charitable sector do its work in reaching out to families and children in trouble. Some ideas for such adjustments are:

First, establishment for a tax credit, in addition to currently allowed deductibiity, for all charitable contributions aimed at specific kinds of problems faced by youth and families; for example, contributions to organizations established to provide remedial education, job training, crisis and long-term shelters for street youth, search networks for missing children, parenting programs, and day-care centers. Tax credits to businesses employing disadvantaged youth could be expanded, as could new tax credits for employers who establish child-care programs for their employees. Provision of accelerated depreciation and tax credits for investments in property used by programs benefiting children and families could attract substantial private capital. If we are to have tax shelters in this profit-oriented society, why not direct them toward investments that will directly help families at risk?

Second, I urge you to give careful consideration to at least minor adjustments in federal public assistance programs. In particular, you should consider establishing income supplements for AFDC families with older children, for whom child-rearing costs are higher. Those supplements could be made conditional on the youths' regular attendance in school or in job-training, thus encouraging poor families both to stay together and to keep their children in school. Special income supplements could also be made available to single parents who enroll in parenting, remedial education, and vocational education programs, all as incentives to move toward independence, and to cover increased costs of child care and transportation, resulting from participation in those programs. In addition, AFDC rules might be adjusted to allow for "team parenting" by mothers on public assistance; that is, cooperative living and child-rearing to two single parents to allow one or both to leave on staggered schedules for school or work, without drastic loss of public assistance. These are investments that I believe would quickly repay their cost by encouraging those on welfare to raise children who can break out of the welfare cycle.

Finally, I urge you to continue to battle against the exploitation of children who have landed on the street. This year the Senate took a great step in passing S. 1469 cosponsored by many in this room, to expand federal prohibitions against the use of children in pornography. As some of you may know, that is legislation we at Convenant House fought for actively—both among you and through our participation as "friend of the court" in the Ferber decision last year. But now it is critical to provide support for law enforcement efforts across the country to fight the daily battle against child prostitution and pornography—and to provide support, as well, for police efforts to find missing children. Unless law enforcement officials have the mandate and the support to protect vulnerable children, we know only too well that beautifully written laws can become a dead letter.

I throw out these ideas timidly, knowing that you face heavy demands from many worthy comers. Our perspective at Convenant House is admittedly a limited one: We see the desperately wounded and the dying among our children. You here have the ability to take the broader view, to examine the crisis of the family from every angle, and to seek solutions in every quarter. You have the credibility and the clout to lead our country toward a responsible, generous concern for families. Hundreds of thousands of letters from Covenant House supporters have convinced me that the American public eagerly, almost angrily, awaits a serious national policy on behalf of family health and unity. If you take the lead, they will follow.

Before beginning to formulate that policy, however, all of us in and out of government need to accept one great, if unpleasant, fact. The nature of "family" in our society has changed. Now millions of children are raised by single parents, millions of mothers now work, and millions of "latchkey" children must get along without constant parental supervision. There is nothing wrong with our traditional ideals of family life, but those ideals must not be allowed to stigmatize the single parents and working mothers who work desperately to care for their children. The fact that you in this caucus have, in your Statement of Purpose, recognized the difficulties facing all types of families—and set out to find ways of helping to ease them—is a measure of the leadership you have begun to provide on this most complex of national problems.

In one of her great novels George Eliot paused a few lines to explain why, in a time crowded with war, crime, and disease, she devoted herself to stories about the narrow world of women and families. That world, she explained, was the "vessel" which carries "the treasure of human affections," the means by which mankind's noblest instincts survive from one generation to the next. Surely all of us here find ourselves often preoccupied with the great questions of war and peace, prosperity and want, freedom and slavery. But if we take for granted too long that best part of our nation's life, its families, we may live to see what is noblest within us perish, and what is kind within us fade.

LAW ENFORCEMENT PROBLEMS

ANNUAL MESSAGE ON THE ADMINISTRATION OF JUSTICE[1]

WARREN E. BURGER[2]

In his fifteen years on the United States Supreme Court, Chief Justice Warren E. Burger has stepped down from the lofty environs of the court each year to address the American Bar Association's House of Delegates at its annual midyear meeting. The speech, which he calls his annual State of the Judiciary address, gives the chief justice, in his words, a chance to "hit the bar over the head every once in a while" on topics ranging from lawyer competence and overburdened courts to prison reform. (For earlier addresses to the American Bar Association, see *Representative American Speeches, 1980–1981*, pp 40–60, and *Representative American Speeches, 1981–1982*, pp 78–88.)

According to David Margolick (*New York Times*, F. 14, '84, p 9), Burger's addresses to the American Bar Association often have a schoolmasterish tone, particularly because they always follow the Pledge of Allegiance and "The Star Spangled Banner." In spite of the tongue-lashing nature of some of his remarks, his reception can only be described as regal. Margolick explains, "From the moment he arrives, he is honored, flattered, and pampered mightily."

Burger's address to the 1,400 lawyers and guests at the annual midyear convention in Las Vegas on February 12, 1984, contained some of the harshest comments he had ever made on the ethics of the bar. The chief justice suggested that lawyers were "hire guns" and "procurers" rather than "healers"; that they contributed to court congestion, overcharged clients, tolerated dishonesty in their midst, and marked up their services as if they were selling "mustard, cosmetics, laxatives, or used cars." Burger also attacked "absurd lawsuits" that only promote fat fees for attorneys.

The lawyers' reaction to Burger's attack was mixed. Somewhat surprisingly, the delegates gave him a standing ovation at the conclusion of the speech, and ABA President Wallace D. Riley observed that it was a "twinging of the conscience. . . . I don't think he was too tough on us." (James H. Rubin, AP, Baton Rouge *State-Times*, F. 13, '84, p 24) Some

---

[1]Delivered at the midyear meeting of the American Bar Association, Grand Ballroom of the Las Vegas Hilton Hotel at noon on Sunday, February 12, 1984.

[2]For biographical note, see Appendix.

prominent members, however, disagreed with the chief justice. Former ABA president David Brink (see *Representative American Speeches, 1981–1982*, pp. 54–61) commented, "I wouldn't say the profession is in quite as dire shape as he has said." (*New York Times*, F. 13, '84, p.11) Robert Davis, head of the National Organization of Bar Counsel, said he was "disappointed in the failure of the chief justice to recognize the significant and hard won progress made" in improving disciplinary procedures of lawyers in recent years.

In editorial comment following the speech, the *Christian Science Monitor* (F. 14, '84, p. 17) called Burger "a straight-talking no-nonsense jurist," and observed:

> There are now over 650,000 lawyers in the U. S.—two-thirds of all the legal advocates in the world. And the litigation explosion seems to be keeping pace. Mr. Burger's voice of reason and restraint is sorely needed.

Curtis J. Sitomer noted later:

> Sometimes it is cheaper and more efficient to resolve disputes without a lawyer. Fees for a simple litigation often exceed $100 a day. While no one suggests lawyers aren't necessary, calls for reform have been heard at several levels. Voices of concern range from the ranks of the prominent—Chief Justice Warren Burger and Harvard President Derek Bok, for example—to the grass roots level. . . . Aims and constituencies differ somewhat, but there is agreement on two points: Lawyers, together with excess litigation, need to be reined in, and the costs of resolving disputes need to be curbed. (*Christian Science Monitor*, Ap. 12, '84, p. 27)

Chief Justice Burger delivered his speech at noon on Sunday, February 12, 1984, in the Grand Ballroom of the Las Vegas Hilton Hotel. The speech received wide coverage in newspapers, news magazines, and legal periodicals and on radio and television.

Chief Justice Burger's speech: The response of this association in our time to the needs of the courts and the American people is in considerable contrast to the response of this association to a speech given seventy-eight years ago by Roscoe Pound, a young man from Nebraska, who later become one of the great deans of the Harvard Law School. At the meeting of this association in 1906, he addressed "The Causes of Popular Dissatisfaction with the Administration of Justice." At that time, this association was hardly representative of the legal profession in America. It had only 2,600 members as compared with over 300,000 today. It was an establishment-oriented organization quite satisfied with the status quo. The leaders of the association rejected Pound's criticisms to the point that the association initially refused to publish his speech. And it was not published until sometime later. Now we know it as a classic—so much so that eight years ago, our association joined the Conference of Chief Justices of the States and the Judicial Conference of the United States to sponsor one of the more significant legal meetings in recent times. By design, that conference, which came to be known as the Pound Conference, was held in St. Paul, Minnesota, and was convened in the very room of the state House of Representatives and at the very lectern where Pound made his 1906 speech.

The response of the association to that 1976 reexamination of Pound's criticism was immediate, and you are familiar with the various programs it generated. One very important program was aimed at developing alternative methods for resolving disputes which now inundate all the courts of this country. Another was directed at delays in litigation and abuse of the discovery process, and I will return to those subjects in a few minutes. Today, the American Bar Association is the most powerful and effective instrument for the improvement of justice in our country, and this is shown by the development of such institutions as the National Judicial College, the Institute for Court Management, the National Center for State Courts, the National Institute for Trial Advocacy, and the monumental study on Standards of Criminal Justice, to name only a few.

We are living in a period of dramatic, spectacular, and rapid change. This is especially true in the world of science, for we are told—incredible as it seems—that in some fields of science there has been more development since World War II than in the previous 500 years. Not only is the world of science undergoing momentous changes, but as we learn every day, indeed twice a day, on the morning and evening news, this is also true in the political world and in business and industry.

These changes have an impact on all of us, as well as on the participants and the victims, and many of these changes—scientific, economic, and political—have an impact on the administration of justice. Change, of course, is the law of life, but the pace of change we now witness is staggering.

Some startling changes have taken place in our profession in the last two decades. One very desirable change was introduced by the profession itself—the growth in the use of paralegals to reduce the costs of service to clients. Another change is the growth of large law firms and the large increase in branch offices of law firms. We are told that the number of American lawyers approaches, if it has not already exceeded, 650,000! It has been reported that about two-thirds of all the lawyers in the world are in the United States, and of those, one-third have come into practice in the past five years.

We are also told that in the past ten years, the legal profession has experienced a sharp decline in public confidence as measured by opinion polls.

Is there a connection between this sharp decline in public confidence in lawyers and the doubling of the number of lawyers in the last twenty-odd years?

Does this decline in the standing of lawyers relate in some way to the high cost of legal services and the slow pace of justice?

Does it come from a growing public opinion that our profession is lax in dealing with the incompetent lawyer or the errant and dishonest lawyer?

Is the public perception of lawyers influenced sometimes, and to some extent, by absurd lawsuits which we have not yet found a way to restrain—a father suing the school board to raise little Johnny's grade in English from C to B? Or the football fan who sues to revise a referee's ruling on a forward pass or a fumble?

If, as some assert, there are too many lawyers, that should mean greater competition, and we Americans have always thought competition brings the highest quality of goods and services at the lowest cost. In our free society, we believe in competition, but is competition in a profession the same as competition in the marketplace? Given the article of faith that competition reduces costs, should we not inquire as to the reasons why—after this enormous growth in the number of lawyers—there is a widespread hue and cry, which increases steadily, about lawyers' fees and litigation costs?

The criticism of our profession is not casual or irresponsible. Many of our own leaders have addressed it. Just last year, a dis-

tinguished lawyer and educator, Derek Bok, formerly Harvard's
law dean and now its president, made some strong observations
on the subject. He said this:

The blunt, inexcusable fact is that this nation, which prides itself on efficiency and justice, has developed a legal system that is the most expensive
in the world. . . .

Many of the activities and studies of our association acknowledge
our own appraisal that all is not well, that our legal system is not
as efficient as it should be.

Lawyers have never been loved, before or since Shakespeare
had his revolutionary character propose to "kill all the lawyers."
Perhaps this is because, in part, our most visible colleagues, the
litigators, can hardly please all of the observers. Even the winning
client often disapproves when he considers the stress of litigation,
the net results of the courtroom battle, and pays his legal fees and
costs. Added to that, the behavior of some of the more visible advocates is not such as to reflect credit on our profession.

Increasingly in the past few years, critics have warned that
lawyers must be careful not to price themselves out of the market.
We know what happens when that occurs in any field of activity:
The consumers of the services or goods find other sources of supply. We saw that when the quality and price of the automobiles
made in this country were found unacceptable. The consequences
were very painful for our economy, and for our pride.

We lawyers have always been fond of quoting the French and
English legal philosophers to make a point, and, today, I will call
on Edmund Burke, one of the great eighteenth century legal
thinkers most admired by lawyers. He said this:

People are qualified for civil liberty in exact proportion to their disposition to put moral chains on their appetites.

Other philosophers have echoed this, saying that the preservation
of a civilized society depends upon the willingness of its members
to forego some of their freedoms. If this is true of society generally,
it is even more so in a profession like law or medicine. That is
what sets the professions apart from the marketplace of barter and
trade.

In the past, the professional standards and traditions of the bar served to restrain members of the profession from practices and customs common and acceptable in the rough-and-tumble of the marketplace. Historically, honorable lawyers complied with traditions of the bar and refrained from doing all that the laws or the Constitution allowed them to do. Specifically, they did not advertise, they did not solicit, they kept careful separate accounts of clients' property, they considered our profession as one dedicated to public service. We still pay homage to the idea that lawyers are "officers of the courts"—or is that just lip service?

Along with the decline of public esteem of our profession, we have witnessed the decline in the public confidence in the media. Some responsible journalists attribute this decline to an insistence of some of their clan in exercising their First Amendment rights to the outer limits or beyond. Some journalists acknowledge that this is an abuse of their First Amendment rights. Others disagree.

Does our profession's low public standing derive, in part at least, from the insistence of some lawyers on exercising their First Amendment rights to the utmost? In current polls, lawyers and journalists rank roughly near the "bottom of the barrel." Perhaps neither likes the company they find themselves in!

One recent development may shed some light on the public perception of our profession. When the Supreme Court declared that the First Amendment allows advertising by lawyers, it placed lawyers in much the same posture, with respect to advertising, as all other occupations. But to those who still regard the practice of law as a profession of service—with high public obligations, rather than a trade in the marketplace—the professional standards against advertising are still widely observed. One study made by the association estimates that as many as 10 to 13 percent of the lawyers engage in some form of advertising. But some of this small segment treat this freedom as a release from all professional restraints and use it as a license. We see some lawyers using the same modes of advertising as other commodities, from mustard, cosmetics, and laxatives, to used cars. A hypothetical case will make my point.

Imagine a day when thousands of eyes are focused on a football game. An ad comes on the TV, perhaps during the halftime.

The scene is much like the contest the viewers have just been observing—a spectacular 90-yard touchdown run in which the star
eludes all tacklers. The scene then changes. A fine-looking fellow
comes on the screen in business clothes, and it turns out he is a
popular football star. He says something like this: If you have a
legal problem or case—and if you want to score—go to my friends,
Quirk, Gammon & Snapp. At this point, one by one, three, well-
dressed fellows come on stage, perhaps against the background of
the *United States Code Annotated* or the *United States Reports*.
The speaker goes on:

If you really want to make a touchdown against your opponents, go to
Quirk, Gammon & Snapp. For an appointment call (800) 777-1111.
They are the best! There will be no charge for the first conference on your
problems. They have a special rate on uncontested divorces during the
holidays. Don't wait.

There are some variations of this unseemly practice, such as
house-to-house distribution of coupons giving a $15- or $25-credit
on the first conference with a lawyer identified in the coupon.

This is happening in a profession that once condemned cham-
perty and maintenance and drove ambulance chasers out of the
profession.

Having said this, however, we must be careful to recognize
that not all the developments in higher lawyer visibility and advertising are undesirable or unprofessional. Some of them, for example store-front, street-level offices of so-called legal clinics that
publish dignified announcements of their availability, have helped
bring low-cost legal services to lower-income people long denied
access to legal assistance.

Ten years ago, I suggested that up to one-third or one-half of
the lawyers coming into our courts were not really qualified to
render fully adequate representation, and that this contributed to
the large cost and the delays in the courts. We know that a poorly
trained, poorly prepared lawyer often takes a week to try a one-
or two-day case. My purpose was to stimulate debate, and some
of you, very appropriately, challenged my statements. Later on,
in the debate that followed, the president of our association said
that my figure was too high, and that the correct figure was not
more than 25 percent. Our distinguished colleague Griffin Bell,

then attorney general of the United States, made an estimate of 30 percent. I responded to this in 1979 on an occasion such as we have today. I accepted the estimates of the president of our association and the attorney general. Then I asked for a show of hands of the audience as to how many thought a figure of 25 to 30 percent of courtroom incompetents was tolerable. Not a single hand was raise. Of course it was not tolerable.

When surveys and studies were made by the association and other responsible bodies, it developed that even my estimate of below-standard courtroom performance was too low!

Our association and its component state and local associations and committees moved swiftly. And the law schools, including Harvard's $2 1/2 million project on trial advocacy, developed broad-scale programs on trial advocacy and related subjects. In the past decade, a majority of our law schools have followed the lead of the early pioneer schools in focusing attention on the elements of trial advocacy, the techniques of negotiation and of arbitration.

In 1976 the Judicial Conference of the United States launched a study of the quality of advocacy in federal courts, and in 1979 the so-called Devitt Committee Report recommended experiments with special standards for admission to the federal courts. The judicial conference then established an implementation program which is now proceeding in thirteen pilot federal districts under the chairmanship of Judge Lawrence King of Florida.

I recall these developments to you because they show that the leadership of this association has never failed in modern times to respond to the needs of our profession and the interests of the public.

In a country as large as ours, with our system of federalism, regulation of the bar cannot be centered entirely in one place as it is in England and some other common-law countries. Fourteen years ago, Justice Tom Clark chaired the association's committee on disciplinary enforcement by the bar. That committee's report said this:

After three years of studying lawyer discipline throughout the country, this Committee must report the existence of a scandalous situation that requires the immediate attention of the profession. With few exceptions, the prevailing attitude of lawyers toward disciplinary enforcement ranges from apathy to outright hostility. Disciplinary action is practically nonexistent in many jurisdictions; practices and procedures are antiquated; many disciplinary agencies have little power to take effective steps against malefactors.

That report stimulated action by some state bar associations, but any fair-minded examination of the whole picture today will reveal that what we have done falls short of what is needed. There are an increasing number of good state programs on discipline, financed by annual assessments on practitioners. The public interest first, and the long-range interest of our profession, require a comprehensive reexamination of the mechanisms we now have to deal with dishonest and unethical practices. The alternative is that state legislatures may move independently if our profession does not act. The 1970 Clark Report on lawyer discipline must be brought up to date because more vigorous programs are imperative if we are to have the confidence of the public.

I now turn to another matter internal to the profession and in the courts, and of significance and importance to the public. We remember that in the 1930s, by rules, new procedures for pretrial discovery were introduced in the federal system, but they did not come into full bloom for some years. The association's committees have long been concerned about the growing problem of discovery abuses which are damaging not only in terms of costs to clients, but to the perception of the profession. In 1983 these discovery rules were amended in response to the rising demand to curb widespread abuses of discovery. These amended rules give trial judges important pretrial management and oversight responsibilities, and direct the judges to impose sanctions directly on attorneys who abuse the court's processes.

Recently, I invited a group of twenty-four representative members of our profession to Washington to focus attention on these amended discovery rules. This task force included practicing lawyers, judges, and law teachers. Two of the practicing lawyers were formerly federal judges. At the conclusion of these sessions, I invited them to give me their views. One distinguished member of the group wrote that we may have a "break down in the professional standards of the entire profession." He went on to focus on the abuses of discovery by lawyers saying, "We have allowed discovery to take on a life of its own."

Another member expressed the view that some lawyers have exploited pretrial discovery with at least an excess of adversary zeal and, at worst, something approaching its use as a tool of extortion. Another, with long experience as a practitioner, lamented the practice which he described as "filing a complaint based almost on rumors and then embarking on months of extensive pretrial discovery to find out if his client had a case." One of the responses provided an apt summary of the whole problem:

Some basic institutional reform in the legal profession is what is needed—lawyers have got to stop using the court system as a means of enriching themselves at the expense of their clients. And the courts have got to stop allowing the lawyers to do it.

These are hard—even harsh—appraisals, but they come from responsible, thoughtful lawyers and judges.

What this means is that, under the 1983 rule changes, judges must not remain aloof from what is going on in a case simply because the parties have not presented themselves in the four walls of the courtroom to begin a trial. The 1983 amendments require that judges take a more active role in overseeing pretrial proceedings. Judges in some state courts and in federal courts have exercised their discretionary authority to impose sanctions both on attorneys and their clients for filing frivolous cases for abuse of discovery processes. In one state case, a trial judge held that the plaintiff's case was based on totally frivolous allegations and ordered the payment of nearly $2 million in fees and expenses. Another judge imposed heavy costs against both the plaintiff and the attorney based on the state's new civil code of procedures that authorized trial judges to impose sanctions on parties and attorneys who litigate in bad faith. In the federal courts, the amended rules now authorize sanctions on lawyers for abuse of the privilege. A few, carefully considered, well-placed $5,000 or $10,000 penalties will help focus attention on the consequence of abuses by lawyers.

Another important development is under study. We are exploring the possible strengthening of Rule 68 of the Civil Rules to allow either party to offer a settlement. If the offer is refused and the case goes to trial and results in a judgment less favorable to the "refusing party" than the offer it rejected, that party would, in the discretion of the court, be subject to payment of all costs the opposing party incurred after rejection of the offer, including attorneys' fees. Cost shifting, subject to court approval, has long been a part of the administration of justice in other common-law countries, and we must study their experiences.

I suspect some of my judicial colleagues will respond that heavily overburdened judges—and they are overworked—should not be further burdened. But the day has long since passed when we can simply "let the lawyers run it." Although pretrial proceedings are not open as a trial is open, litigation becomes a matter of the court's responsibility as soon as judicial power is invoked. The dangers in leaving everything to the lawyers outweigh the logic of the situation. Some of our ablest judges have developed ways to keep in touch with the cases during the pretrial stage to make sure that that process is not being abused. This is the essence of sound judicial administration.

At the March meeting of the Judicial Conference of the United States, I will request the conference to consider a program in each federal circuit and district to deal with this problem, particularly to promote wider understanding and use of the 1983 amendments to the Civil Rules. After one recent conference on the new rules, the very next court day, one judge levied costs on a litigant for the burden imposed on the other litigant by duplicative motions. I urge the association, the state bar, and local bar leaders to cooperate with these programs. The discovery task force that I referred to earlier will provide a helpful blueprint which can be adapted to the needs of each district. Now if it seems to you that I am unduly hard on lawyers today, let me close this subject by acknowledging that, at times, we judges and law enforcement officers make up the system of justice. Together, we are responsible for insuring the rule of law. To retain the respect of the people, we must deserve their respect.

We know, of course, that the association has long been aware of some of the problems I have been discussing and programs are under way to deal with some of them. But are they enough? What we need is a comprehensive and coordinated reexamination of all of these areas.

The story of justice, like the story of freedom, is a story that never ends. What seems unrealistic, visionary, and unreachable today must be the target, even if we cannot reach it soon or even in our time. If we ever begin to think we have achieved our goals, that will mean our sights were set too low or that we had lost concern for our profession or the public interest.

This association has long advocated the great ideals that distinguish our profession from the actors in the marketplace. We Americans are a competitive people and that spirit has brought us to near greatness. But that competitive spirit gives rise to conflicts and tensions. Our distant forebears moved slowly from trial by battle and other barbaric means of resolving conflicts and disputes, and we must move away from total reliance on the adversary contest for resolving all disputes. For some disputes, trials will be the only means, but for many, trials by the adversary contest must in time go the way of the ancient trial by battle and blood. Our system is too costly, too painful, too destructive, too inefficient for a truly civilized people. To rely on the adversary process as the principal means of resolving conflicting claims is a mistake that must be corrected. No other nation allows the adversary system to dominate relationships to the extent we do. We lawyers are creatures—even slaves—of precedent which is habit. We tend to do things in a certain way "because we have always done it that way." But when we must constantly witness spectacular expansions of court dockets, requiring more and more judges, something is wrong. When we see costs of justice rising, when we see our standing in public esteem falling, something is wrong.

If we ask the question, "Who is responsible?" the answer must be, "We are. I am. You are."

The entire legal profession—lawyers, judges, law teachers—have become so mesmerized with the stimulation of the courtroom contest that we tend to forget that we ought to be healers—healers of conflicts. Doctors, in spite of astronomical medical costs, still retain a high degree of public confidence because they are perceived as healers. Should lawyers not be healers? Healers, not warriors? Healers, not procurers? Healers, not hired guns?

There are other problems that deserve our attention, but those I have discussed today seem to me the most urgent, and at the same time, they have long-range implications.

In closing, Mr. President, I propose to you and our fellow members of the association, that we create a study group of representative leaders of our profession to examine these problems and report to the association. It might well be useful to include leaders from other disciplines as we take a careful look at ourselves.

Nearly fifty years ago, one of my most distinguished predecessors, Chief Justice Hughes, said this to our profession:

In the midst of a task so great as this, there may come a time of discouraging reflection upon the immense needs of the administration of justice and the extreme difficulty of finding ways by which [we] can solve the problems. . . . [W]e cannot afford to take a defeatist attitude. . . . The most important lesson of the past is to strive and never be disheartened because of the immensity of the task. The ultimate goal may seem to recede as we advance, but we must press on.

This association has repeatedly shown that it is the most powerful, the most influential force in this country for improving the system of justice, and I am confident the association will always act in the public interest.

Mr. President, in that spirit, I pledge my full cooperation should you elect to act on these problems to help us prepare for the years ahead.

LEGAL AND ILLEGAL IMMIGRATION: THE IMPACT, THE CHOICES[1]

CHARLES R. STOFFEL[2]

No one knows how many illegal aliens are in the United States, but most authorities agree that the number is large and increasing. While the United States historically has welcomed immigrants and takes pride in its description as the melting pot of the world, the problem of illegal immigration was a matter of concern to large numbers of Americans in 1983–1984. They worried that illegal aliens are taking jobs from Americans who desperately needed employment, were burdening taxpayers by

[1]Delivered to the California Roundtable at the San Francisco Airport Hilton Hotel, San Francisco, California, at 9:30 A.M. on May 4, 1983.
[2]For biographical note, see Appendix.

their increased use of social services, and that this country simply could not take care of all of the world's dispossessed.

In the spring of 1984, several congressmen introduced bills to cope with the problem, the best known being the Simpson-Mazzoli bill, which would penalize employers who knowingly hired illegal aliens and offered legal status to many illegal aliens already in the country. In the days leading up to the debate on "the most important piece of immigration legislation to come before Congress in over twenty years," Representative Bill Lowery inserted in the *Congressional Record* a speech by Charles R. Stoffel of the Federation for American Immigration Reform, a national nonprofit organization concerned with immigration problems.

In his well-documented address, Stoffel pointed out that,

> One of the lowest estimates of the number of illegal workers in the United States is 6 million. If only half of them are in jobs that would otherwise be held by U.S. workers, eliminating this displacement could bring unemployment down by one-third.

As a nation, he said, we have to ask three basic questions:

> First, how many people will we admit to this country for permanent residency? Two, who will get the slots? Who, of the 600 million people around the world who want to migrate, most of them to the United States, will be allowed entrance to our country? And, three, how are we going to enforce the rules of our immigration policy?

Stoffel delivered the speech at 9:30 A.M. on May 4, 1983, at the bi-monthly meeting of the California Roundtable held in the San Francisco Airport Hilton Hotel. His audience consisted of approximately seventy-five prominent California corporate executive officers and deputies.

Charles R. Stoffel's speech: Our nation has a proud history of responding compassionately, and humanely, to the world's oppressed people. We are, after all, a nation of immigrants. Most Americans would agree that we should continue to honor our tradition of help. But it must not blind us to the fact our nation's resources are limited, and that our economy cannot long sustain the pressures of a continuing flood of immigrants.

FAIR [Federation for American Immigration Reform] was founded in 1979 to tackle the intricacies of the immigration issue. Today, it is still the only national nonprofit organization in the country that is educating the American people to the problems uncontrolled immigration pose to our future. FAIR believes that unlimited immigration is contrary to the national interest, that illegal immigration can and should be ended, and that all legal immigration should be placed within a single, stable ceiling that is consistent with our country's history of compassion and generosity for less fortunate people.

Immigration has always benefited America. But legal immigration at today's massive levels and illegal immigration that is completely out of control have numerous negative results. These negative effects can be seen in pressures on social welfare and health care systems unable to cope with this growing population, in job competition between illegal immigrants and American minority and youth job seekers, and in ethnic conflicts. Conceivably, a majority of Americans might in the end come to the conclusion that all immigrants hurt the country, and this could be the greatest tragedy of all.

I think that this growing awareness has come about in part because of the realization that our resources are not limitless. If we have learned anything from the long gas lines and water shortages here in the West in the past few years, it is that we are beginning to run short—that our melting pot, like any pot, indeed has a bottom.

Every nation has as one of its sovereign rights the right to control the flow of people into its country. Of the 165 nations on this planet, 164 do so rigidly. Only the United States has a lax immigration policy. If you or I were to go to Mexico or Canada, it would be next to impossible under their laws for us to cross the border, get a job, or become productive members of their societies. What we have to ask as a nation are three basic questions:

First, how many people will we admit to this country for permanent residency?

Two, who will get the slots? Who, of the 600 million people around the world who want to migrate, most of them to the United States, will be allowed entrance to our country?

And, three, how are we going to enforce the rules of our immigration policy?

I think this public debate, the answering, if you will, of these three questions, is going to involve two stages. The first, and the one that Washington is grappling with now, is an attempt to form a consensus on the fact that we must limit immigration into this country.

The second stage, the one that will come after this agreement, is what that limit should be. What is the number of people that should be allowed into our country every single year as immigrants? Will it be 400,000, 800,000, or over a million, as we're getting today from both legal and illegal immigration?

What are the impacts of current and prospective patterns of immigration in the U.S. labor market and economic system? There are those who have driven across that "empty space" of America and say that we have room to accommodate many, many, more people. What they don't understand is the need for this empty space in America to support our crowded urban population and the hungry world population which depends in ever increasing amounts on our grain. The economic competition felt by poor, minority, and lesser skilled Americans when the volume of illegal immigration is high is another major problem. The main victim of illegal immigration is the unskilled domestic American worker.

Dr. John Reid is a graduate professor in sociology at Howard University. In December 1981, a study he did on the economic advancement of "Black America in the 1980s" was released. Dr. Reid writes:

Blacks are affected more than any other U.S. group by the massive increase in immigration since the mid-1970s. The surge of legal and illegal immigrants and refugees, no longer white Europeans, but primarily Hispanics and Asians, ironically presents new competition for black Americans, just as they have finally begun to edge up the socio-economic ladder . . . it us clear that right now the masses of new immigrants are taking jobs away from disadvantaged blacks, particularly black teenagers. Furthermore, it cannot be argued that U.S. blacks and whites shun the kinds of jobs that illegal immigrants typically fill.

Then Dr. Reid presents evidence from the Department of Labor that a third of all workers employed in this country, 34 million people, hold jobs in exactly the kinds of low-skilled industrial, service, and agricultural jobs in which illegal aliens typically find employment, and that 10.5 million workers are employed at or below the minimum wage.

Though there are necessarily two parties in this offering and accepting of employment, only undocumented foreign nationals are legally culpable. Worse yet, this legal inequity increases the dependence of undocumented aliens on their employers, making them even more vulnerable to exploitation.

In other words, as the law now reads, it is illegal for an illegal alien to take a job; it is illegal to harbor an illegal alien; but it is not illegal to hire one. It must be understood that undocumented wokers do not make less than the minimum wage. Recent governmental surveys have shown that the average illegal alien makes between $4 and $5 per hour. To the extent that they take good jobs at good pay with the protection of the law, they are competing illegitimately and unfairly for the jobs that many Americans want and need.

Former secretary of labor, Ray Marshall, has observed, "I am convinced that we are sowing the seeds of a serious future civil rights struggle. We would be better off if we could confront it now."

For years we have heard that undocumented workers are a cost-free benefit to the United States. The argument rests on the belief that low-skilled American workers at worst are lazy, and at best choosy, about the jobs which they will do, and that they will no longer take jobs which they consider to be demeaning. Therefore, there exists a number of jobs that, if they are to be done at all, must be done by illegal immigrants.

This widespread myth is not supported by any data. Nor is the data that Americans won't take hard, dirty jobs supported by surveys of thousands of Americans. An Ohio State University study of young Americans performed for the Labor Department found that a majority of young people would take low-paying jobs in fast-food restaurants, cleaning establishments, and supermarkets as well as washing dishes—exactly the types of occupations most associated with undocumented workers. A substantial number of the young people in the survey said they would work at wages even below the minimum wage.

At *Los Angeles Times* survey published on April 7, 1981, found that, "The widely accepted notion that some jobs are so menial only illegal aliens will take them is untrue . . . among unemployed people interviewed seventy-five percent said they would apply for jobs paying between $3.35 an hour, the legal minimum wage, and $4.50 an hour."

Former secretary of labor, Ray Marshall, stated in the *Los Angeles Times* on December 2, 1979:

It is false to say American workers cannot be found for all of the jobs filled by undocumented workers. The truth is that there are millions of American workers in all of these low-paying occupations already. The job market in which they (the illegal aliens) compete is highly competitive, with a surplus of people vying for a shortage of jobs, no matter how undesirable the jobs may be.

One of the lowest estimates of the number of illegal workers in the United States is 6 million. If only half of them are in jobs that would otherwise be held by U.S. workers, eliminating this displacement could bring unemployment down by one-third.

Recently, in Hempstead, Long Island, a new hotel opened up and 4,500 people stood in line to apply for 280 jobs as bellboys, busboys, and dishwashers—exactly the same types of jobs usually associated with illegal aliens and that many would like us to think no one else is willing to do.

The real tragedy of this displacement is that its burden falls on the most vulnerable people in our society, minority teen-agers, women who head families, and older workers. Their high rates of unemployment are public record. They will continue to suffer if high levels of illegal immigration continue.

Secretary Marshall has stated, "We may need foreign workers, but they should only be allowed to work here legally, under the protection of our laws."

In the past decade a number of very impressive groups have studied the problem. In the sessions of Congress in 1971–1972, the House Judiciary Committee took a detained look. The Domestic Policy Council reported to President Ford in December of 1976 on the subject. President Carter set up an Interagency Task Force in 1977. There was a Presidential Bipartisan Select Commission chaired by Father Theodore Hesburgh of Notre Dame that issued its report in 1981. President Reagan set up a commission to restudy that report and make its recommendations.

Every single one had concluded that we cannot regain control of our borders unless we make it first illegal to hire illegal immigrants. So long as people have a certainty of being able to get jobs when they get here, they will continue to come, and you cannot blame them. If you're in Mexico making 30 cents an hour and you can cross that border and be assured of getting a job that pays between $4 and $5.60 an hour, and the worst thing that can happen to you is to get caught and sent home, you're going to come.

Changing the law in that regard will remove this magnet of jobs and thereby make it possible to control the flow of illegal immigrants into this country. In a recent interview with *U.S. News,* Jorge Bustamante, Mexican population expert, stated, "Eighty-one percent of the people that come from Mexico go to the United States for jobs." While sanctions alone will not stop illegal immigration, nothing else without it makes sense.

Let us now take a look at the status of illegal immigration as regards social services. Recent court decisions expanding the rights of illegal aliens in the United States have given at least some illegal aliens the right to claim at least some public benefits hitherto reserved for United States citizens and legal immigrants only. Today, illegal immigrants are not only willing to seek welfare and other social services, they are applying for and receiving hundreds of millions of dollars worth of services at the same time these programs are being cut back for disadvantaged Americans.

The available evidence suggests that publicly financed health services (especially emergency, obstetric, and pediatric care) are widely employed. Of all births in Los Angeles County public hospitals in 1981, 67.5 percent were to illegal aliens. And this was all at a cost of more that $100 million to the taxpayers of Los Angeles County. In Denver, Colorado, in 1981, 81 percent of the births were to illegal aliens. And this creates an entirely new problem, because now we have children who are American citizens and their parents are here illegally.

The cost of educating the children of illegal immigrants, and nobody says we should not do this if they're here, in Los Angeles County alone, is more that $200 million a year. In a recent meeting I had with the Board of Education, I was told that the Los Angeles County School System adds 25,000 children of illegal immigrants a year, or the equivalent of twenty new schools.

Unemployment insurance is used to varying degrees. The worst example I have heard is in Illinois, where a recent study showed that in 1982, 45 percent of new applications for unemployment benefits were from illegal aliens. And Social Security retirement benefits currently are used very little primarily because undocumented workers tend to be very young.

At the same time, they do pay taxes to support such services, though in the case of the low-paid workers who apparently predominate among illegal immigrants, such taxes are, of course, very low.

There's another side to this; on September 10, 1982, the *Los Angeles Times* reported on a study issued by the private nonprofit population research group, The Environmental Fund. After a computer analysis of Census Bureau and United Nations data, they found that:

Illegal aliens cost the federal government in payments to displaced U.S. workers in unemployment insurance and food stamps alone, $8 billion to $18 billion a year.

And, this at a time when we are confronting a $200 billion deficit!

To summarize the state of knowledge regarding social service costs, immigrants both legal and illegal cannot be blamed for the rapid increase in governmental expenditures, but their impact is by no means trivial.

Where are we in regard to enforcement of existing laws? In 1980 we had 6 to 9 million illegal immigrants in the United States, and our borders were, for all practical purposes, unguarded. We have fewer people guarding our 1,750-mile border with Mexico than guarding the 103 acres of the United States Capitol; and they do it all with a budget less than that of the Baltimore Police Department. Is it any wonder why so many consider enforcement of American immigration law by the Immigration and Naturalization Service to be poor? Under present circumstances, the chances are very low of even detecting, much less apprehending, most illegal immigrants.

As an example, several weeks ago in San Ysidro, two border patrol agents came upon 350 Mexican nationals crossing the border at one time. They were able to stop forty of them, and the rest got through.

A couple of weeks ago, I was in San Ysidro myself, and I went out with the border patrol. I spent the night and we went out on

Kearney Mesa, looked through the scopes and watched as people crossed the Ensenada Highway into the United States, got into automobiles, and were picked up. That night we stopped a car and found six teen-agers in one trunk, forty-eight in the back of a U-Haul trailer. That night, which was described as being slow, on a stretch of border $8\frac{1}{2}$ miles long, 572 illegal aliens were caught. The tide has become a wave. And, as long as we continue to ignore that problem, and as long as Mexico continues in its current economic crisis, that tide will not slow.

Part of the problem is that the increase in illegal immigration has not been accompanied by a significant increase in the resources available to the INS. It alone is not an effective or sufficient strategy for controlling illegal immigration.

Unfortunately, the world of the 1980s is a less stable place, both in political and in economic terms. Domestic or international conflicts may produce real or only Pyrrhic victors, but they always seem to produce refugees. Increasing strife, coupled with populations that are today more than twice as large as those of 1950, portends burgeoning numbers of refugees seeking asylum in the coming decades. Modern communication has brought into our homes the suffering of refugees on the high seas or in hastily erected encampments, suffering of which most of us would have been unaware in the past.

Whe emigration occurs, we must remember that the poorest of the poor, the sick and the old, do not migrate. They lack the requisite resources. Those who do come to the U.S. are those who are advancing within their societies; those who have attained the necessary knowledge of America and how to get here; those who have accumulated or been able to borrow the funds necessary to pay for their airline tickets or their smugglers; those that the sending countries can least afford to lose because their contributions to the future of their nations stand to be the greatest.

To go back to that interview in *U.S. News* with Jorge Bustamante, he stated flatly:

The people that are coming to America to look for jobs are those that Mexico has invested the most in, in terms of education and job training.

The people that they need to build their economy and make their country as strong as it can be.

I firmly believe that we need to be committed to our southern neighbors, to helping them out of their current economic crisis, and to creating jobs there. It's our moral responsibility and it's in the best interest of the United States. Let's take a look if we can just very briefly at some numbers. The labor population in Mexico has grown from 20 to 40 million people in the last twenty years. They're experiencing 40 percent unemployment or underemployment. And by the year 2000, there will be 70 million people in the labor pool in Mexico. That's 30 million more in the next seventeen years. And unless we are willing to be a safety valve for that many people, we have got to encourage them to make the difficult decisions they have thus far put off within their economic and social structure. How do we know there are going to be that many people in the labor market? Because they're already born. But, it is not just Mexico.

Increasingly, we have to look at the Caribbean basin—Mexico, Central America, and the island nations. If we look at that region, in 1950 there was a population of 51 million people. In 1981 there were 117 million. By the year 2025, just thirty-seven years from now, that population will more than double to 298 milion peole. They are going to demand jobs and housing and all that they need. The problem we're facing throughout Central America is one that has been coming on for years, one we have known has been coming and one we need to help these countries correct. One of overpopulation, lack of resources, and lack of jobs.

But, we must also understand that the problem of the illegal immigrant is not just a U.S. /Mexican problem. In 1981, 800,000 more people flew into the international airports of this country than left. And nobody knows where they are! That's more in one year than the population of Washington, D.C., San Diego, or San Francisco. And that does not count the estimated 500,000 from Mexico. The numbers are staggering: in Los Angeles County alone, it is estimated that there are 900,000 illegal immigrants; the population of Santa Ana, in Orange County, is estimated at 25 percent illegal; San Jose, in northern California, more than 30 percent illegal; at these levels, we are importing a new generation of poverty into this country every year.

Kevin F. McCarthy of the Rand Corporation, a Santa Monica-based Think Tank, was quoted in the *Torrance Daily Breeze* on January 20, 1983, as saying in an El Segundo speech, "It is no exaggeration to say that California is really the Ellis Island of the 1980s."

To sum up the major points, I feel very strongly it's essential to stop illegal immigration into this country for four central reasons:

Number one, illegal immigrants are in increasing amounts using social services in this country at a time when those same social services are being cut back for disadvantaged Americans.

Two, there is increasing evidence that illegal immigrants take jobs that Americans are willing to take and that Americans desperately need in a time of high unemployment.

Three, illegal immigrants, most of whom come to this country as undocumented workers, are the people sending countries can least afford to lose because they're those that stand to make the greatest contributions to improving their own societies.

And lastly, America currently takes in one half of all people who emigrate from anywhere to anywhere else in the world and America simply cannot be the home of the world's dispossessed.

However, we must insist that new policies not stop immigration. But, we must recognize that immigration, in the broadest sense, is a solution to human problems which, though it seems to have worked for this country at a very different demographic and ecological time, increasingly is a solution only for the very few. In fact, it delays the devising of solutions for the great masses of humanity whose lives will be spent not in escape, but in learning how to manage to live where they are.

We must balance the idea that the size of the U.S. population must be controlled with the desire that the American nationality never be perceived as fixed in its ethnic or cultural components. We must never allow our policies to be derived from, nor encourage, racial or ethnic discord or ideological intolerance. Our public policy, however, must change as the world changes. Abraham Lincoln said it well, "As our case is new, so must we think and act anew. We must disenthrall ourselves."

APPENDIX

BIOGRAPHICAL NOTES

BELL, TERREL HOWARD (1921–   ). Born, Lava Hot Springs, Idaho; B.A., Southern Idaho College of Education, 1946; M.S., University of Idaho, 1953; Ed. D. (Ford fellow, 1954–55), University of Utah, 1961; high school teacher, Eden, Idaho, 1946–47; superintendent of schools, Rockland (Idaho) Valley Schools, 1947–54, Star Valley School District, Afton, Wyoming, 1955–57, Wiber Country (Utah) School District, 1957–62; professor of school administration, Utah State University, 1962–63; superintendent of public instruction, state of Utah, 1963–70; associate commissioner for regional office coordination, U.S. Office of Education, 1971, commissioner for education, 1974–76; superintendent, Granite School System, Utah, 1971–74; commissioner of education, state of Utah, 1976–81; secretary, U.S. Department of Education, 1981–   ; chairman, Utah Textbook Commission, Utah Course of Study Commission; served with U.S. Marine Corps Reserve, 1942–46; author, *The Prodigal Pedagogue*, 1956, *Effective Teaching: How to Recognize and Reward Competence*, 1962, *A Philosophy of Education for the Space Age*, 1963, *Your Child's Intellect—A Guide to Home-Based Preschool Education*, 1972, *A Performance Accountability System for School Administration*, 1974, *Active Parent Concern*, 1976.

BORMANN, ERNEST G. (1925–   ). Born, Mitchell, South Dakota; B. A., *magna cum laude*, University of South Dakota, 1949; M.A., University of Iowa, 1951, Ph.D., 1953; instructor, University of South Dakota, 1949–50; assistant and associate professor, Eastern Illinois University, 1953–56; associate professor, Florida State University, 1956–59; assistant and associate professor, 1959–65, professor, 1965–   , director of graduate studies in speech communication, 1971–78, University of Minnesota; Outstanding Individual in Speech Communication award, Speech Association of Minnesota, 1983; Charles H. Woolbert award for research, Speech Communication Association, 1983; technical corporal, Engineer Combat Battalion, United States Army, 1943–46; author, *Theory and Research in the Communicative Arts*, 1965, *Discussion and Group Methods: Theory and Practice*, 1969 and 1975, *Interpersonal Communication in the Modern Organization* (with William S. Howell, Ralph G. Nichols, and George L. Shapiro), 1969, 1981, *Forerunners of Black Power: The Rhetoric of Abolition*, 1971, *Presentational Speaking for Business and the Professions* (with William S. Howell), 1971, *Effective Small Group Communication* (with Nancy C. Barmann), 1972, 1976, 1980, *Speech*

Communication: An Interpersonal Approach (with Nanch C. Barmann), 1972, 1977, 1981, *Communication Theory,* 1980; member, Phi Beta Kappa.

BURGER, WARREN E(ARL) (1907–   ). Born, St. Paul, Minnesota; student, University of Minnesota, 1925–27; LL.B., *magna cum laude,* St. Paul College of Law (now William Mitchell College of Law); Doctor of Laws, 1931; honorary degrees, LL.D., William Mitchell College of Law, 1966, and New York Law School, 1976; admitted to Minnesota bar, 1931; faculty, William Mitchell College of Law, 1931–53; partner, Faricy, Burger, Moore & Costello (and predecessor firms), 1935–53; assistant attorney general in charge of Civil Division, U.S. Department of Justice, 1953–56; judge of U.S. Court of Appeals, District of Columbia, 1956–69; Chief Justice of the United States, 1969–   ; lecturer, American and European law schools; faculty, Appellate Judges Seminar, New York University Law School, 1958–   ; member and legal adviser to U.S. delegation to International Labor Organization, Geneva, 1954; contributor to law journals and other publications. (See also *Current Biography,* November 1969.)

BUSH, GEORGE HERBERT WALKER (1924–   ). Born, Milton, Massachusetts; B.A., Yale University, 1948; honorary degrees, Adelphi University, Austin College, Northern Michigan University, Franklin Pierce College, Allegheny College, Beaver College; co-founder, director, Zapata Petroleum Corporation, 1953–59; president, Zapata Off Shore Company, 1956–64, chairman of the board, 1964–66; member of 90th–91st U.S. Congresses, 7th district of Texas; U.S. ambassador to the United Nations, 1971–72; chairman, Republican National Committee, 1973–74; chief, U.S. Liaison Office, Peking, People's Republic of China, 1974–75; director of Central Intelligence Agency, 1976–77; vice president of the United States, 1981–   ; director, 1st International Bank, Ltd., London, 1st International Bank, Houston, Eli Lilly Corporation, Texasgulf, Purolator; chairman, Heart Fund; trustee, Trinity University, Baylor College of Medicine, Phillips Academy, chairman, Republican Party of Harris County, 1963–64; delegate to Republican National Convention, 1964, 1970; served as lieutenant (j.g.), pilot, U.S. Naval Reserve, World War II; decorated, D.F.C., air medals. (See also *Current Biography,* September 1983.)

CHURCH, FRANK FORRESTER IV (1948–   ). Born, Boise, Idaho; B.A., with dinstinction, Stanford University, 1970; M. Div., *magna cum laude,* Harvard University, 1974, Ph.D., 1978; minister, Unitarian Church of All Souls, New York City, 1978–   ; author, more than twenty books and articles on New Testament studies, the history of early Christianity, the history of liberal religion, and contemporary theological and ethical topics.

DYER, CAROLYN STEWART (1943–). Born, Gardiner, Maine; B.A., Beloit College, 1965; M.A.; University of Wisconsin–Madison, 1973, Ph. D., 1978; completed Training Institute in Quantitative History, Newberry Library, Chicago, 1979; newswoman, WJPG-AM, Green Bay, Wisconsin, 1965–66; reporter, Green Bay (Wisconsin) *Press Gazette,* 1966–70; capital correspondent, Madison news bureau, Green Bay (Wisconsin) *Post-Crescent,* 1970–71; lecturer, visiting assistant professor, University of Wisconsin, Madison, summers, 1973–75; assistant professor, Colorado State University, 1974–78, University of Iowa, 1978– ; president, Journalism Council, Inc. of Association for Education in Journalism and Mass Communication, 1979–81, vice president, 1981–82; author, articles in journalism and communications publications.

EDWARDS, HARRY (1942–). Born, East St. Louis, Illinois; B.A., California State University, San Jose, 1964; M.A., Cornell University, 1966, Ph.D., 1972; lecturer, University of Santa Clara, 1967, California State University, San Jose, 1966–68; assistant professor, University of California, Berkeley, 1970–77, associate professor, 1977– ; honorary doctorate, Columbia College, 1981; visiting distinguished scholar, Oregon State University, 1980, University of Illinois, 1982, Norwegian College of Physical Education and Sport, Oslo, 1983, Indiana State University, 1984, University of Charleston, 1984; lectures on sports, race, and education delivered at more than 500 colleges and universities; author, *The Revolt of the Black Athlete,* 1969, *Black Students,* 1970, *Sociology of Sport,* 1973, *The Struggle That Must Be* (1980), many articles and editorials.

FEINSTEIN, DIANNE (1933–). Born, San Francisco, California; B.S., Stanford University, 1955; intern in public affairs, Coro Foundation, 1955–56; assistant to California Industrial Welfare Commission, 1956–57; member and vice chairman, California Women's Board of Terms and Parole, 1962–66; chairman, San Francisco City and County Advisory Committee for Adult Detention, 1967–69; supervisor, City and County of San Francisco, 1969–78; mayor, San Francisco, 1978– ; president, San Francisco City and County Board of Supervisors, 1970–72, 1974–76, 1978; member, Mayor's Commission on Crime, 1967–69; chairman, Environment Management Task Force, Association of Bay Governments, 1976–78, executive committee and delegate to general assembly, 1970– ; board of governors, Bay Area Council, 1972– ; member, Bay Conservation and Development Commission, 1973–78; chairman, Board of Regents, Lone Mountain College, 1972–75; recipient, Women of Achievement Award, Business and Professional Women's Club of San Francisco, 1970, Distinguished Woman Award, *San Francisco Examiner,* 1970. (See also *Current Biography,* June 1979.)

GERLACH, LARRY REUBEN (1941–). Born, Lincoln, Nebraska; B.S., University of Nebraska, 1963, M.A., 1965; Ph.D, Rutgers University,

1968; assistant and associate professor, 1968–73, professor, 1977–   , associate dean, College of Humanities, 1982–83; chairman, History Department, University of Utah, 1983–   ; recipient, William Adee Whitehead Award, New Jersey Historical Society, 1973, Award of Merit, American Association for State and Local History, 1977, Society of the Cincinnati in New Jersey Award, 1981; author, thirteen books including *The American Revolution: New York as a Case Study,* 1972, *Prologue to Independence: New Jersey in the Coming of the American Revolution,* 1976, *The Men in Blue: Conversations with Umpires,* 1980, and articles and essays in historical and sports journals.

HOOKS, BENJAMIN LAWSON (1925–   ). Born, Memphis, Tennessee; student Lemoyne College, 1941–43, Howard University, 1943–44; J.D., De Paul University, 1948; LL.D (honorary), Howard University, 1975, Wilberforce University, 1976, Central State University, 1976, admitted to bar, 1948; individual law practice, 1949–65, 1968–72; assistant public defender, Memphis, 1961–64; judge, Division IV, Criminal Court of Shelby Country, 1966–68; ordained to the ministry, Baptist Church, 1956; pastor, Middle Baptist Church, Memphis, 1956–64, Greater New Mt. Moriah Baptist Church, Detroit, 1964–72; co-founder, vice president, director, Mutual Federal Savings and Loan, Memphis, 1955–69; member, Federal Communications Commission, 1972–78; executive director, National Association for the Advancement of Colored People, 1977–   ; producer, host of television program, "Conversations in Black and White"; co-producer, "Forty Percent Speaks"; panelist, "What is Your Faith?"; board of directors, Southern Christian Leadership Conference, Tennessee Council on Human Relations; Memphis and Shelby County Human Relations Committee; served with the U.S. Army in World War II. (See also *Current Biography,* April 1978.)

KENNEDY, DONALD (1931–   ). Born, New York City; B.A. Harvard University, 1952, M.A., Ph.D., 1956; faculty member, Syracuse University, 1956–60; faculty member, Stanford University, 1960–77, professor of biological sciences, 1965–77, chairman of the department, 1965–72; senior consultant, Office of Scientific and Technological Policy, Executive Office of the President, 1976; commisioner, Federal Drug Administration, 1977–79; vice president and provost, Stanford University, 1979–80, president, 1980–   ; board of overseers, Harvard University, 1970–76; fellow, American Academy of Arts and Sciences; member, National Academy of Sciences, American Physiology Society, Society of General Physiologists, American Society of Zoologists, Society of Experimental Biology (U.K.); author (with W. H. Telfer), *The Biology of Organisms;* 1965; editor, *The Living Cell,* 1966, *From Cell to Organism,* 1967; editorial board, *Journal of Experimental Zoology,* 1965–71, *Journal of Comparative Physiology,* 1965–76, *Journal of Neurophysiology,* 1969–75, *Science,* 1973–77.

KENNEDY, EDWARD MOORE (1932-). Born, Boston, Massachusetts; B.A., Harvard University, 1956; student, International Law School, The Hague, The Netherlands, 1958; LL.B., University of Virginia, 1959; honorary degrees, thirteen institutions; admitted, Massachusetts bar, 1959; assistant district attorney, Suffolk County, Massachusetts, 1961-62; U.S. senator, Massachusetts, 1962- ; former assistant majority leader, U.S. Senate; president, Joseph P. Kennedy Jr. Foundation, 1961- ; member, board of trustees, universities, hospitals, libraries, the Boston symphony, John F. Kennedy Center for the Performing Arts, and Robert F. Kennedy Memorial Foundation; named one of ten outstanding young men in United States by Junior Chamber of Commerce, 1967; author, *Decisions for a Decade, In Critical Condition*; Democratic candidate, U.S. president, 1980. (See also *Current Biography*, October 1978.)

KOOP, CHARLES EVERETT (1916-). Born, Brooklyn, New York; B. A., Dartmouth College, 1937; M.D., Cornell University, 1941; Sc.D., University of Pennsylvania, 1947; LL.D., Eastern Baptist College, 1960, M.D. (honorary), University of Liverpool, 1968; L.H.D., Wheaton College, 1973; D.Sc., Gynedd Mercy College, 1978; intern, Pennsylvania Hospital, 1941-42; surgeon in chief, Children's Hospital of Philadelphia, 1948- ; with University of Pennsylvania School of Medicine, 1942- , professor, 1959- ; fellow in surgery, Boston Children's Hospital, 1946; consultant, U.S. Navy, 1964- ; Surgeon General of the U.S., 1982- ; member, board of directors, Medical Assistance Programs, Inc., Daystar Communications, Inc., Eastern Baptist Seminary and College; fellow, American Academy of Pediatrics, member, American Surgeons Association, Society of University Surgeons, British Association of Pediatric Surgeons, International Society of Surgery, Société Française de Chirurgie Infantile, American Medical Association, Deutschen Gesselschaft für Kinderchirurgi, Société Suisse de Chirurgie Infantile, Order Duarte, Sanchez y Mella, Dominican Republic; contributor to surgical, physiological, biomedical, ethical, and pediatric journals. (See also *Current Biography*, September 1983.)

LAUTENBERG, FRANK R. (1924-). Born, Paterson, New Jersey. B.S., Columbia University, 1949; D.H.L., Hebrew Union College, 1977; Ph. D. (honorary), Hebrew University, Jerusalem, 1978; founder, Automatic Data Processing, Inc., 1953-, executive vice president of administration, 1961-69, president, 1969- , chief executive officer, 1975- , chairman of the board. U.S. senator, 1983- ; member, policy holders committee, New England Life Insurance Co.; advisory board, *Present Teuse* magazine; commissioner, Port Authority of New York and New Jersey; associate, School of Business, Columbia University; national president, American Friends of Hebrew University, 1973-74; president, National United Jewish Appeal, 1975-77; member, President's Commission on the Holocaust; founder, Lautenberg Center for General and Tumor Immunology, Hebrew University, Jerusalem, 1971; member, finance council, Democratic National Committee; served with armed forces, World War II; recipient, Torch of Learning Award, American Friends of Hebrew University, 1971, Scopus Award, 1975; president, 1968–69, and director, 1974–   , National Association of Data Processing Services Organizations.

MOYNIHAN, DANIEL P. (1927–   ). Born, Tulsa, Oklahoma; B.A., Tufts University, *cum laude,* 1948, M.A., 1949; Ph.D., Fletcher School of Law and Diplomacy, 1961; LL.D., St. Louis University, and Political Science, 1950–51; M.A. (honorary) Harvard University, 1966; recipient, more than twenty-three other honorary degrees, 1966–72; special assistant to U.S. secretary of labor, 1961–62, executive assistant, 1962–63; assistant secretary of labor, 1963–65; director, Joint Center Urban Studies, Massachusetts Institute of Technology and Harvard University, 1966–69; professor, education and urban politics, senior member, Kennedy School of Government, Harvard University, 1966–73; assistant for urban affairs to president of United States, 1969–70; counselor to President Nixon, member of Cabinet, 1971–73; U.S. ambassador to India, 1973–74; U.S. ambassador to United Nations, 1975–76; United States senator from New York, 1977–   ; U.S. Navy Reserve, 1944–47; member, American Academy of Arts and Sciences, numerous committees, including New York State Democratic Convention, 1958–60, New York state delegation, Democratic National Convention, 1960; vice chairman, Woodrow Wilson International Center for Scholars, 1971–   ; author, *Maximum Feasible Misunderstanding,* 1969; (with Nathan Glazer) *Beyoind the Melting Pot,* 1963. (See also *Current Biography,* February 1968.)

RESTON, JAMES BARRETT (1909–   ). Born, Clydebank, Scotland; B.S., University of Illinois, 1932, LL. D. (honorary), 1962; Litt. D., Colgate University, 1951, Oberlin College, 1955, Rutgers University, 1963; LL. D. (honorary), Dartmouth College, 1959, New York University, 1961, Boston College, 1963, Brandeis University, 1964; D.H.L., Kenyon College, 1962, Columbia University, 1963, University of Michigan, 1965, Colby College, 1975, Yale University, 1977; honorary degrees, University of Maryland, Northeastern University, 1976; staff, *Springfield* (Ohio) *Daily News,* 1932–33; publicity department, Ohio State University, 1933; publicity director, Cincinnati Baseball Club, 1934; Associated Press reporter, New York, 1934–37, London, 1937–39; reporter, *New York Times* London bureau, 1939–41, Washington bureau, 1941–   , chief Washington correspondent, 1953–64, associate editor, 1964–68, executive editor, 1968–69, vice president, 1969–74, columnist, consultant, 1974–   ; director, New York Times Co.; co-publisher, *The Vineyard Gazette,* 1968–   ; recipient, Pulitzer Prize, 1945 and 1957, Overseas Press Club Award, 1949, 1951, and 1955, George M. Polk Memorial Award, 1953, University of Missouri Medal, 1961, J.P. Zenger Award, 1964, Elijah Parrish Lovejoy Award, 1974; decorated by Legion d'Honneur, Order of St. Olav (Norway), Order of Merit (Chile). (See also *Current Biography,* November 1980.)

REYNOLDS W. ANN (1937-). Born, Coffeyville, Kansas; B.S., Kansas State College, Emporia, 1958; M.A., University of Iowa, 1960, Ph.D. 1962; D.Sc. (honorary), Indiana State University, 1980; assistant professor, Ball State University, 1962–65; assistant professor, University of Illinois, College of Medicine, 1965–68, associate professor, 1968–73, research professor, 1973–78; professor of obstetrics, gynecology, and anatomy and provost, Ohio State University, 1979–82; chancellor, California State University, 1982– ; president, Prenatal Research Society, 1978; associate fellow, American College of Obstetricians and Gynecologists, 1977; fellow, California Academy of Sciences, 1983; author or coauthor, more than a hundred scholarly works in the sciences and medicine.

RITTER, BRUCE (1927-). Born, Trenton, New Jersey; admitted, Order of Friars Minor Coventual and studied for priesthood, St. Francis Seminary, Staten Island, New York, 1946–50; B.A., Assumption College (Chester, Pennsylvania), 1952; student, St. Anthony-on-Hudson (Rensselaer, New York), 1953; ordained, 1956; D.Th., Franciscan Pontifical Faculty of Theology, Rome, 1958; teacher, St. Anthony-on-Hudson, 1959–60, St. Hyacinth's Seminary, Granby, Massachusetts, 1961, Canevin High School, Pittsburgh, 1962–63; professor and chaplain, Manhattan College, 1963–68; left teaching to work with poor in East Village, New York City; founder and director of Covenant House, New York City, 1972- , Under 21, New York City, 1977- , Under 21, Toronto, 1982- ; served, U.S. Navy, 1945–46. (See also *Current Biography,* June 1983).

SAGAN, CARL EDWARD (1934-). Born, New York City; B.A., University of Chicago, 1954, B.S., 1955, M.S., 1956, Ph.D, 1960; D.Sc. (honorary), Rensselaer Polytechnic Institute, 1975, Denison University, 1976, Clarkson College, 1977; D.H.L. (honorary), Skidmore College, 1976; research fellow, University of California, Berkeley, 1960–62; visiting assistant professor, Stanford Medical School, 1962–63; Smithsonian Astrophysics Observatory, 1962–68; lecturer and then assistant professor, Harvard University, 1962–68; member of faculty, Cornell University, 1968- , professor 1970- , David Duncan professor of physical sciences, 1976- , director of Laboratory of Planetary Studies, 1968- ; visiting professor and guest lecturer, various colleges and universities; lecturer for the Apollo flight crews of NASA, 1969–72; narrator, BBC/PBL television production, "The Violent Universe," 1969; recipient, Smith Prize, Harvard, 1964, NASA medal for scientific achievement, 1972, Prix Galabert, 1973, John Campbell Award, 1974, Klumpke-Roberts Prize, 1974, Priestley Award, 1975, NASA Award for Public Service, 1977, Pulitzer Prize for *The Dragons of Eden,* 1978; National Science fellow, 1955–60, Sloan Research fellow, 1963–67; author *Atmospheres of Mars and Venus*, 1961, *Planets*, 1966, *Intelligent Life in the Universe*, 1966, *Planetary Exploration*, 1970, *Mars and the Mind of Man*, 1973, *The Cosmic Connection*, 1973, *Other Worlds*, 1975, *The Dragons of Eden*, 1977; editor and author of various articles in scientific and astronomy journals. (See also *Current Biography*, April 1970.)

SANFORD, JAMES TERRY (1917–   ). Born, Laurinburg, North Carolina; B.A., University of North Carolina, 1939, J.D. 1946; assistant director, Institute of Government, University of North Carolina, 1940–41, 1946–48; special agent, Federal Bureau of Investigation, 1941–42; admitted, North Carolina bar, 1946; practiced, Fayetteville, 1948–60; partner, Sanford, Adams, McCullough, and Beard, 1965–   ; governor, North Carolina, 1961–65; president, Duke University, 1969–   ; member, Carnegie Commission on Educational Television, 1964–67; president, Urban America Inc., 1968–69; member, North Carolina Senate, 1953–54; delegate, National Democratic Convention, 1956, 1960, 1964, 1968, 1972; chairman, National Democratic Charter Commission, 1972–74; trustee, Cordell Hull Foundation for International Education, National Humanites Center; board of directors, Children's TV Workshop, 1967–71; served as first lieutenant, U.S. Army, 1942–46. (See also *Current Biography*, November 1961.)

SCANLON, THOMAS J. (1938–   ). Born, Scranton, Pennsylvania; B.A., University of Notre Dame, 1960; M.A., University of Toronto, 1965; M.A., Columbia University, 1965; executive assistant, Agency for International Development, 1965–67; independent consultant, 1967–70; president, Benchmarks, Inc., 1970–   ; director, The Public Welfare Foundation, 1973–   .

STOFFEL, CHARLES RANDALL (1947–   ). Born, Syracuse, New York; B.A., Syracuse University, 1970; student, University of Southern California, 1980–81, University of California, Irvine, 1981–83; public relations counsel to the chief of police, Syracuse, New York, 1970–71; staff assistant, Occupational Safety and Health Administration, U.S. Department of Labor; served, Federal Energy Office in the Executive Office of the President, 1973; partner, Stoffel and Starck, public affairs consultants, 1973–76; director of marketing, American Telephone and Telegraph Recording, Hollywood, California, 1977–79; sales and management officer, Caldwell Banker Residential Real Estate, Los Angeles, 1979–82; president, American Redevelopment, Long Beach, California, 1983–   ; California director, Federation for American Immigration Reform, 1982–84, member of national advisory board, 1984–   ; envoy manager, Los Angeles Olympic Organizing Committee, 1984; member, Regional Commissioners Advisory Council, Los Angeles Public Affairs Officers Association, National Association of Realtors; co-author, *No U Turn: A Portrait of Charles Goodell*, 1970; editor, *Federal Energy Briefing Book*, 1974.

CUMULATIVE SPEAKER INDEX

1980-1984

A cumulative author index to the volumes of *Representative American Speeches* for the years 1937-1938 through 1959-1960 appears in the 1959-1960 volume, for the years 1960-1961 through 1969-1970 in the 1969-1970 volume, and for 1970-1971 through 1979-1980, in the 1979-1980 volume.